THE SAINTS
AND OUR
CHILDREN

"Let all thy works, O Lord, praise thee: and let thy saints bless thee. They shall speak of the glory of thy kingdom: and shall tell of thy power: To make thy might known to the sons of men: and the glory of the magnificence of thy kingdom."
—Psalm 144:10-12

THE SAINTS
AND OUR
CHILDREN

By

Mary Reed Newland

"Now therefore you are no more strangers and foreigners; but you are fellow citizens with the saints, and the domestics of God, built upon the foundation of the apostles and prophets, Jesus Christ himself being the chief corner stone: In whom all the building, being framed together, groweth up into an holy temple in the Lord. In whom you also are built together into an habitation of God in the Spirit."
—Ephesians 2:19-22

TAN BOOKS AND PUBLISHERS, INC.
Rockford, Illinois 61105

Nihil Obstat: John A. Goodwine, J.C.D.
                      Censor Librorum

Imprimatur: ✠ Francis Cardinal Spellman
                      Archbishop of New York
                      New York
                      February 24, 1958

Originally published by P. J. Kenedy & Sons, New York, in 1958.

Library of Congress Catalog Card No.: 94-61998

ISBN: 0-89555-517-4

Printed and bound in the United States of America.

TAN BOOKS AND PUBLISHERS, INC.
P.O. Box 424
Rockford, Illinois 61105
1995

To Bill—
and Monica, Jamie, John, Peter,
Stephen, Philip, Christopher
and their Saints,
and all the Saints in this book,
and all the Saints
who wouldn't fit in this book:
May the ones who are,
help make saints of the ones who aren't!

ACKNOWLEDGMENTS

I WISH to thank the following people for help with this book: Miss Sylvia de Santis of the Monson Free Library of Monson, Massachusetts; Miss Anna Manning of the Boston Public Library, Boston, Massachusetts; Miss Mollie Greeley, Holyoke, Massachusetts; Father Sylvester, O.F.M. Cap., Librarian at the Franciscan College of St. Lawrence, Rome; Father Bruno, O.F.M., Cap.; Brother Stanley Mathews, S.M., of the Marian Library, University of Dayton; and Father Philip Hoelle, S.M., editor of *The Marianist* where the chapter, "The Holy Family," first appeared.

Also, Father Francis N. Wendell, O.P., editor of *The Torch* where five of these chapters first appeared; Father Mark Heath, O.P.; Father Paul Joseph Dignan, C.P.; Father William Kelley, S.D.B.; Father Frank Russo; Father Richard Hoey, pastor of St. Patrick's parish, Monson, Massachusetts; Mother Kathryn Sullivan, R.S.C.J.; Miss Julie Kernan, general editor, and Miss Elizabeth Bartelme, editor, P. J. Kenedy & Sons, New York, and the Kenedys for allowing me to borrow freely from their *Butler's Lives of the Saints*; all the publishers who kindly have granted permission to quote from their books; and, last but not least, all the darlings — family and friends — who prayed endlessly that "mother will finish her book."

M.R.N.

WHY THESE SAINTS?

Sт. Thomas Aquinas was once asked by a married sister what one did to become a saint. He replied, "Will it." He meant, of course, that since it is God's will that we be saints we must join our wills to His, for becoming a saint is not a matter of do-it-yourself. But there is no getting away from the fact that God cannot do it all by *Himself* since we *do* have wills and they *can* stand in the way.

This being so, we must get to work. The will of God, said St. Paul, is your sanctification; and to be a saint, the Church says, one must practice heroic virtue. This sounds like one must at least be off in Indo-China having his head chopped off. But Blessed Claude de la Colombière*says other things can be the means of heroic virtue: ". . . a word escapes which should not have been spoken, or some one utters another that offends us; a servant (*waiter, clerk, counter boy*) is clumsy or slow in waiting on you; a child inconveniences you, a bore stops you, a heedless fellow jostles you, a horse (*taxi, bike, truck*) be-spatters you with mud; you don't like the weather, your work is not proceeding according to plan; a piece of furniture is broken, a dress is stained or torn. I know that this is no occa-sion for practicing very heroic virtue, but I do say that this would be enough to acquire it without fail, if we really wished to." Thank goodness we have saints who can tell us these things. Certainly no one is better qualified.

Why did we choose these saints? Because these are some we have loved in our family and from whom we have learned much. The chapter on Abraham grew out of our need to know the beginning of the Jews, since God whose life flows into us at the baptismal font chose to accomplish this by becoming a Jew. The chapters on St. John Bosco, St. Dominic Savio, St.

---

*Now *Saint* Claude de la Colombière (canonized May 31, 1992).—*Publisher,* 1995.

Maria Goretti, St. Bernadette and St. Thérèse of Lisieux grew from our need to know what part their parents, their families, their teachers, their environments, their times played in forming them, and how they overcame faults and difficulties, grew in virtues and love. How did they do it, we wanted to know. Or, if one cannot say *they* did it, how did they cooperate with God who did it? How much of the making of a saint depends upon the family and how much upon special grace? One thing we discovered is that there is no answer to that last question — unless it answers it to say these people did not *have* to become saints. God did not force them to be saints. The chapter on the Holy Family answers our own question, "How can we possibly imitate *them*? It is hard enough to imitate saints — but God and His Mother and His foster-father? Isn't this impossible?" No, it is not.

The chapters in Part II are different. They are meant to help parents when a saint story is called for, and the teaching and correcting and conversation of Christian parents ought to lean heavily on the saints for help. This is how saint stories are best used: to make a point, to warm a heart, to stir up a hunger. Three saints give advice to parents on the preventing of pride and vainglory in children, on the folly of customs which are a risk to the chastity of children, on how children can be taught to work with Christ to save souls. The bit on St. Catherine of Siena is not in any way a comprehensive sketch of her life, but rather an introduction to a saint who is rarely introduced to children. St. Catherine is like a girl in a fairy tale only better — St. Catherine came true. St. Philip Neri's genius and wit help with the matter of boredom, impatience and pride, while St. Perpetua and her friend St. Felicitas contribute lessons in stories on Purgatory, modesty and love.

The last chapter has twenty stories to help parents impress certain virtues, stories easily learned by parents and readily loved by children. Often, when a correction is over and done with, it will be the story that will remain in the mind and

heart, continuing to press home the lesson in holiness. There
are stories to help with obedience, perseverance, criticism, selfishness, devotion at prayers, answers to prayers, bad tempers
and learning to love. There is one frightful episode, a horror
story. I have included this because it happened. It is as terrify-
ing as any story you could make up, any episode out of history
or off the front page, out of any television thriller. It is horror
with the relation to God made clear which redeems even horror. This is one of the things we must understand and can
learn only from the lives of the saints: that in a fallen world
there will be violence and murder, torture and atrocities, but
Christ has given these a relation to Himself by being their victim first. We must begin to teach our children that this is what
the blow on the cheek at Confirmation means: one will go the
whole way for Him, blood and all if need be.

We are not yet saints but it is an odd kind of humility for a
Christian to say he can't be. That is to betray holy hope. Better
he say he won't be — unless he chooses to be. That is why St.
Thomas said, "Will it." He won't be until the last gasp even then,
for there is always the chance he will fall. But he must try.
How dare he not! This is the point of it all — to be saints; to
grow so in love with God that nothing else matters but that
He has given us Himself to love.

M. R. N.
Feast of the
Immaculate Conception
December 8, 1957

CONTENTS

Why These Saints?   ix

PART I

1. Abraham Our Father   3
2. John Bosco, Saint and Teacher of Saints   15
3. Dominic Savio, Schoolboy Saint   44
4. St. Maria Goretti, Model of Chastity   65
5. St. Bernadette Soubirous, Model of Humility   82
6. Thérèse of Lisieux, Stubborn Saint   107
7. The Holy Family   149

PART II

1. Advice to Parents from St. Thomas More · Blessed
   Claude de la Colombière · Sister Josefa Menéndez   161
     On Preventing Pride and Vainglory in Children   161
     On Parental Duty and How Parents Let Their
       Children Risk Chastity   164
     On How Our Work Is Love, and How We Can Work
       with Christ to Save Souls with Our Love   168
2. Three Saints with Three Stories Each that Children
   Love to Hear and Tell   177
     St. Catherine of Siena: On Loving Your Neighbor
       and Seeing Christ in Everyone — On Giving to the
       Poor and How Our Treasure Is in Heaven — On
       How God Is Everywhere   177
     St. Philip Neri: St. Philip's Suggestion for People
       Who Have Nothing to Do — How He Learned
       Patience — How He Did Not Trust Himself   181
     St. Perpetua and St. Felicitas: About Perpetua's Little

Brother in Purgatory — About Her Modesty as a Martyr in the Arena — About Her Darling Friend St. Felicitas 183

3. Twenty Stories of Saints to Help Parents Impress Particular Virtues 186

Obedience: The Story of St. Francis and the Cabbages 186

Perseverance: A Story from the Desert Fathers to Help One Stay with What Grows Wearisome 187

Criticism: St. Simeon Stylites Helps Children Accept the Differences in Men as well as Their Sameness 187

Selfishness: A Story about St. Macarius the Younger for People Who Take the Largest Piece 189

Prayer: A Story from the Lives of the Brethren of the Order of Preachers to Help Children Say Prayers with Devotion 190

Waiting for Prayers to Be Answered: A Story about St. Vincent de Paul to Show That God Does Answer Prayers 191

Hear No Evil: A Story about Father John Gerard, S.J. and the Clanking Chains 193

Impure Thoughts: About St. Camillus de Lellis and What He Used to Say to His Spiritual Sons 195

Dare to Be Different: A Story about St. Galla of Rome 196

Humble Confession: A Story about Father Damien the Leper 197

Temper Trouble: A Story to Tell about One of the Desert Fathers 198

Humility and Detachment: Some Good Advice from St. Syncletica Who Might Be Called One of the Desert Mothers 199

Pain and Suffering: A Story about St. Patrick and the Prince 200

How God Provides: About St. Paul the Hermit and St. Anthony of the Desert 201

How the Devil Tempts Us: As Told by the Devil to St. Dominic 202

St. Isaac Jogues: A Story to Remember When One Is Tempted to Sin with His Hands 203

About Not Holding a Grudge: From the Story of St.
John Gualbert   206

How Sanctity Does Not Come Easily: About the
Struggle of St. Benedict of San Fradello   207

St. Madeleine Sophie Barat: A Story About Love   210

And Now a Word to Us All from Blessed Oliver
Plunkett, Followed by a Fitting Conclusion from a
Desert Father   210

Bibliography   213

THE SAINTS
AND OUR
CHILDREN

PART I

1

ABRAHAM OUR FATHER

ABRAHAM stands at the beginning of our learning about God and His Church and His saints. It is true that others — Adam, Eve, Abel, Noe — preceded him, but Abraham's role is different from theirs. He is unique. For God calling Abraham out of Ur and telling him to go to a land where He would lead him "marks the opening of sacred history — perhaps indeed of all history. It is the first appearance of historical action by the living God." [1]*Abraham was the "first parent" of the Jews who would produce Christ who would redeem the world. Out of Abraham came the Church, Christ's Mystical Body, in which men are united to Him to live divine life. By this life, men willing, Christ perfects men's wills and makes them saints.

Abraham leads the procession of saints that makes its way through the Old Testament to Christ, then in Him through the New Testament up to our own day. We read their names in our missals and in the lives of the saints, in the headlines and in the parish register. We are supposed to add our names to theirs and imitate them. But most families tend to think — as we originally thought — that no saints lived before the time of the Apostles.

So it is good for us to know that the saints who followed Christ were preceded by a shining host of Old Testament men and women who practiced heroic virtue, who were faithful to God's commands although they did not yet have the example of

---

[1] Jean Danielou, *Advent* (New York: Sheed & Ward, 1951), p. 25.

* Or rather, with Abraham there begins "a new period in the religious history of man's salvation." (Steinmueller/Sullivan: *Catholic Biblical Encyclopedia,* 1956, p. 13).—*Publisher,* 1995.

Christ, the Church, the Sacraments to help them. Unlike the saints of the New Testament they did not recognize the importance of detachment from worldly goods. Yet when they were called upon to do so they left home, country, possessions to follow unquestioningly the will of God. St. Paul speaks of them as those "of whom the world was not worthy." Abraham, chief of these ancients, is a symbol of fidelity, of the faith we must have before we can follow Christ and of the willingness to go where He leads.

In the beginning Abraham's name was Abram and it was not certain if he worshipped the One God always or was once a worshipper of idols like his father.* Some say in his heart he worshipped God in a blind way, not knowing who He was; others say "Abraham was God's convert." However it was, it would not have been surprising if Abram *had* worshipped as his father had. Truths were handed down by word of mouth in the ancient days and generation after generation told them to their children and bequeathed them customs of worship. Over thousands of years segments of Noe's family broke away and wandered off to settle in new places, and they drifted from the revelations of Adam's and Noe's God. They multiplied God by His attributes and His wonders and made many gods of Him, and grew degenerate in their worship of them. Intuition told them there were powers higher than themselves, but they were spoiled by sin and wearied by its punishments and their convictions became guessings which led them far afield. What a wonder was Abram, who was spoken to out of the blue by the Only God and who believed Him and set off into the unknown.

He lived in Ur, the land of the Chaldees, about four thousand years ago, in the fertile valley of the Tigris and Euphrates Rivers which are said in Genesis to have flowed through the garden of Eden. You may show it to your children on a map of modern Iraq across the Euphrates from An Nasiriya and a bit south.

It was here that God first spoke to Abram and bade him

---

*The Bible seems to indicate that Abraham always "worshipped one God of heaven," having forsaken the gods of his ancestors. See *Judith* 5:6-9. (See Steinmueller/Sullivan: *Catholic Biblical Encyclopedia*, 1956, p. 13).—*Publisher,* 1995.

take his family to a new land. So Abram began to move them northward, more than a hundred in all, their belongings packed on the backs of their beasts, driving their sheep and goats before them. They reached the town of Haran where they stayed until Thare, Abram's aged father, died and then God spoke to Abram again, telling him once more to leave his country, his kinsfolk, his father's home behind him and go to a land He would show him. "Then I will make a great people of thee . . . and make thy name renowned, a name of benediction . . ." (Gen. 12:1–3, Knox).[2]

Thus did God the Father begin to unfold His plan for our redemption. Abram was to be the Father of the Jews out of whom would come Christ in whom all the races of the world would find a blessing.[*]

Once again he set out with his wife Sarai, his nephew Lot and all the members of his household and their belongings. They journeyed into the land of Chanaan (Palestine) by the route all nomads took, bearing to the south following the rich pasture lands, staying where they found grass and moving when it grew sparse. The Chanaanites lived in the towns and cities and permitted wandering nomads this freedom. When they came to a place called Sichem (Nablus), God spoke to Abram again, "To thy seed will I give this land" (Gen. 12:7, Douay).

Long before Noe had cursed his grandson Chanaan for laughing at him when he lay naked and asleep after innocently drinking too much wine. "Cursed be Chanaan . . . he shall be the slave and drudge of his brethren." Then Noe blessed his son Sem, "may Chanaan be a slave to him" (Gen. 9:25–26, Knox). Now at long last the children of Sem, the Semites, were about to receive from God the land in which Chanaan's children had settled.

"To thy seed I will give this land." To Abram's children — but Abram had no children! Sarai was barren; it was her disgrace.

---

[2] The quotations from Genesis, unless otherwise specified, are from the *Old Testament* in English, Vol. 1, in the translation of Monsignor Ronald Knox, Copyright 1948, Sheed & Ward, Inc., New York.

[*] More properly speaking, Abram was to be the Father of the *Israelites*, as the Chosen People were called throughout most of the Old Testament times. —*Publisher*, 1995.

She was sixty-five and Abram was seventy-five and her years of childbearing were over. But Abram had not accepted this promise because it appealed to *reason*. He *believed* God, and did what he did because he was told to do it. Why should he question the promise of seed? He built an altar to commemorate the words God spoke to him and moved on. Now in a mountain place he rested, and building another altar, he "called upon His name." All the gods of Abram's childhood had names. They had rites and sacrifices and prayers to be said to them before altars built to them. Abram followed the patterns of remembered pagan rites to worship his strange new One God, but he did not know His name.

Next they went south to the hot dry plains of the Negeb and since famine was upon them they crossed over into the fertile places of Egypt. Wandering tribes, desperate with famine, crossed periodically into Egypt to pasture their herds and flocks. Each year the flooding Nile carried rich black silt across the plains, renewing the top soils so that the grass grew and tempted the wanderers. The Egyptian farmers did not like this invasion by strangers, but men and beasts must eat to live and hunger is a bold herdsman. So Abram herded his family and servants and flocks across the border.

Crossing into Egypt, Abram considered the beauty of his wife and, suspecting how she would move the Egyptians, how they might report of her to Pharao, suggested that she explain herself as his sister. It was half true; she was his half-sister. He knew well enough that if a Pharao coveted the wife of a foreigner he was not above slaying the man to have her. His suspicions were borne out. Sarai was seen and when Pharao heard of her beauty he sent for her and she was put with the women of the palace, apparently to be prepared as a wife to him. Abram her "brother" was well treated for her sake. We can teach our children of the inviolability of marriage through this trial of Abram. For Pharao did not keep Sarai long. God sent a series of calamities to him such as could only mean divine displeasure, whoever your gods, and Pharao, discovering Sarai was already a wife, was angry and straightway gave orders for Abram and Sarai to leave, bag, baggage and all.

They returned to Chanaan with riches of gold and silver, with sheep and oxen, he-asses and she-asses, menservants and maidservants, and an especially fine gift of camels — novelties for a chief like Abram whose home was a wanderer's tent.

Now among the relatives traveling with Abram was Lot, the son of his dead brother, and on their return to Chanaan the herdsmen of Lot began to quarrel with the herdsmen of Abram. So Abram suggested they part. There was room for both in the land and to show his good faith he offered Lot his choice of all the regions about. Abram would go where Lot did not. Lot chose the land around the Jordan, rich and fertile like the plains they had left, and took his family and belongings into the vicinity of Sodom.

When Abram was alone again and in peace, he heard the voice of God telling him to look to the east and the west, the north and the south, for all the land he could see would God give him and his seed forever. God said, "If any man be able to number the dust of the earth, he shall be able to number thy seed also." (Gen. 13:16, Douay) This He said to the man who had no children. Abram was almost a hundred years old, yet he believed it when God said his descendants would outnumber the dust of the earth.

Now during the years before Abram's return to Chanaan, a struggle had disturbed the little kingdoms about the Jordan and, after an independence of only one year, the Mesopotamian war lords attacked them again and overthrew five of the local kingdoms. Among these was Sodom, whose king escaped but who lost as spoils much wealth and many subjects including Lot and his family and possessions. This engagement was lost, moreover, though the local force had outnumbered the enemy and lured them into a wooded valley spotted with tar pits (the same from which Noe and his sons had drawn caulking for the ark in an area probably covered today by the Dead Sea).

An escaped Sodomite sought out Abram and told him of the

fate of his nephew. Abram gathered a force of three hundred and eighteen men, armed them, and set off in pursuit. He followed the enemy to the topmost border of Chanaan and there attacked after nightfall in such a way that he triumphed and carried back with him not only Lot and his family and possessions but wealth and women and common folk as spoils.

Returning, Abram was met by the grateful king of Sodom from whom he would take no favor beyond the food his men must eat, and — more important to us — he was also met by the mysterious and beautiful figure of Melchisedech, the priest of the most high God who brought bread and wine for sacrifice, and blessed Abram and his family.

Melchisedech is a mystery. There is no trace of his origin, his geneology, his end, says St. Paul. His priesthood is a fact recorded without explanation, yet his sacrifice is linked with Abram's in the Canon of the Mass. For years our family hurried by his name not knowing why it was there. If the name of Melchisedech, as well as Abram and Abel, was familiar, no one had made an intelligent connection for us between it and the Mass. Our children should know who all these figures are and why they are there, and knowing this will make the Mass much more intelligible to them. We must show them that Melchisedech is a type of our priests, not descended from a special line such as the Jewish Levite priests, but *one called by God to be a priest.*

He appears in the story of the Jews because God planned it and called him there: a high priest, a king whose name Melchisedech means king of justice; whose kingship over Salem (which means peace) means he is rightly called king of peace; whose city Salem, it is now thought, would one day be called Jerusalem. The order of his priesthood is continued forever, and in the ordaining of every new Catholic priest are the words, "thou art a priest forever, according to the order of Melchisedech."

After Melchisedech had blessed Abram, the Lord again spoke to the latter in a vision and promised him that his reward would be exceedingly great. And Abram asked, a little wistfully, what his reward would be. The only heir he had was Damascus, the son of his slave Eliezer, who had been born in his house. Was Damascus to be his heir? Was it *his* seed God was talking about? But the Lord said no, Abram's heir would spring from his own body.

The next is the loveliest scene so far. The Lord took Abram out into the night and bade him gaze at the stars. "Look up to heaven and number the stars, if thou canst. . . . So shall thy seed be" (Gen. 15:5, Douay). He would have that many descendants! And Abram believed God.

When you live in the country you can see the whole sky and all the stars at night; when you live in the city you can climb up to the roof and see the stars, or go to the park or beside the river to see them. Wherever you go, they are the same stars Abram saw. They could remind our children of God's promise to him. So many children see the stars and think, "Twinkle, twinkle, little star. . . ." To them the stars *could* come to mean God and Abram and his seed Christ. They could mean God's plan for our redemption; how He loves the Jews. When He was showing Abram the stars, He was foretelling the numbers of the Jews and the flesh He would take on Himself. They are *His* people. Let the stars remind us to pray to Abram for the Jews so they will know Christ.*

Then God told Abram to prepare animals for the sealing of this promise. To seal a covenant, as it was called, it was customary for animals to be slain and the carcasses divided and laid in two rows, whereupon the parties making the covenant would walk between the rows. God spoke and dealt with His people in terms they understood. Abram complied with God's instructions and when night came he fell into a deep sleep and heard a voice tell him that the family he would start would dwell in a strange land for four hundred years, be ill-used and in slavery, and finally be freed to return to their own land. This would not happen in Abram's days, however, for he would die in peace in his old age and be buried with his fathers, so he was

---

*Spiritually speaking, it is the followers of Christ who are the present-day "children of Abraham." The Jews are no longer the Chosen People, although they are physically descended from Abraham and are "most dear for the sake of the [Old Testament] fathers." (*Rom.* 11:28).—*Publisher,* 1995.

told. Then in the dark of the night Abram saw a smoking oven and from it a torch of fire passed mysteriously between the divided halves of the animals as God confirmed His promise: "To thy seed I will give this land."

But Abram's wife Sarai continued to be restless. She had not borne him a child in spite of the promise of God, so finally she told Abram to beget a child by her Egyptian maid Agar. We must not be astonished by what seems to us a sinful suggestion, for we have to remember that standards of human conduct in Abram's day had not developed to the high spiritual and moral level taught by Christ. Polygamy, forbidden to the Christian, was then permitted. Monogamy was the ideal but it was not prescribed, and it was a commonly accepted practice for a man to take a second wife if his first wife bore him no sons. It was not wrong, then, for Abram to beget a child by Agar, but it was looked upon with approval, even by Sarai, for it was according to an ancient Chaldean custom.

Abram consented and Agar conceived and began to scorn Sarai. Of what use was it to be rich or the first wife, if one could not bear a child? Agar was puffed with pride, and her scorn stung Sarai, so that at last she complained to her husband. But the maid was hers, Abram reminded Sarai, over whom she had the right to do whatever she pleased; let her do it.

Then Sarai abused Agar so grievously that Agar ran away to the desert, where an angel of the Lord found her sitting by a well. To his questioning she answered that she was fleeing from the anger of her mistress. Through His angel God replied, telling Agar that she was to return and humble herself under her mistress and bring forth her son and God would multiply her seed exceedingly. It would be beyond numbering. And from the son whom she called Ismael, and who was fathered by Abram, have come blood brothers to the seed of Sarai's son Isaac, also fathered by Abram. We call them by different names: Arab and Jew.

When Abram was ninety-nine, God spoke to him again: "I *am,* and my covenant is with thee and thou shalt be a father of many nations" (Gen. 17:1-4, Douay). Then God changed his name from Abram to Abraham, which means father of many nations, for he was to be the father of kings and the land of Chanaan was to be his and his children's forever, and "I will be their God."

God told him of a sign by which Abraham must keep this covenant, a sign which would show forth that he and his children belonged to Him, the one God. "This is the covenant you shall keep with me, thou and thine; every male child of yours shall be circumcised; you shall circumcise the flesh of your foreskin, in token of the covenant between me and you. . . So my covenant shall have its seal in your flesh, ratified to all time" (Gen. 17:10-13, Knox).

How much easier it would be to explain marriage and describe it to our children in all its majestic holiness if we meditated upon the story of Abraham. The Old Testament Israelites centered their hopes on the coming of the promised Messiah. God had told Abraham that the Messiah would be his descendant, so for generations and generations the Israelite mothers and fathers knew there was a possibility that someday one of the offspring of their marriage would bring forth the Promised One of Israel. And eventually there did spring forth from this line Our Lady, the Blessed Virgin Mary, who was to become the Mother of the Messiah, who was God made Man. The story of Abraham and the other stories of holy marriage from Scripture will help parents deepen their own awe and reverence for marriage, and will provide them with beautiful stories to choose from when it is time to explain marriage to their children.

God then changed Sarai's name to Sara, which means lady and princess and mother of kings, and He said she would have a son. Abraham fell on his face and laughed for joy that he at one hundred years would be father to a son from Sara who was ninety.

One day after this, Abraham was sitting at the door of his tent when three young men appeared standing near him. He ran to meet them and, recognizing one as the Lord, fell to the ground adoring: "Lord, he said, as thou lovest me, do not pass thy servant by; let me fetch a drop of water, so that you can wash your feet and rest in the shade. I will bring a mouthful of food, too, so that you can refresh yourselves before you go on further; you have not come this way for nothing. And when they had agreed to what he proposed, Abraham hastened into the tent to find Sara. Quick, he said, knead three measures of flour, and make griddle cakes. Meanwhile, he ran to the byre, and brought in a calf, tender and well-fed, and gave it to a servant, who made haste to cook it. Then he brought out butter and milk with the calf he had cooked for them, and laid their meal ready, and stood there beside them in the shade of the trees" (Gen. 18:3–8, Knox).

When they had eaten they asked for Sara and Abraham said she was in the tent. The Lord then said that in a year's time Sara would bear a son, but Sara, listening from behind the doorway, laughed to herself in disbelief.

"Why does Sara laugh, and ask whether she is indeed to become a mother in her old age: Can any task be too difficult for the Lord? . . ."

Then Sara denied laughing, for she was afraid. "Ah," he said, "thou *didst* laugh," (Gen. 18:15, Knox) for He was the Lord. (And I cannot understand how Zachary, the father of John the Baptist, could have failed to remember this scene at the time of his encounter with the angel in the temple.)

Leaving, the Lord said He would go down to Sodom and Gomorrha to see if the sins of the people were as deserving of vengeance as He had heard, and Abraham pleaded for the just men who might live in those two cities. Would He not spare them if there were fifty just? He would, for fifty. But what of forty-five? Yes, for forty-five. Would He not for forty? Yes, forty. But not for thirty? Yes, He would for thirty. If only twenty? If there were twenty. "Now do not be angry with me, Lord — but what if only ten?" Yes, if there were ten just men He would save the cities. Thus Abraham discovered the mercy of God by way of this bargaining.

What a wonderful passage this is for a charade. In such rich passages, read aloud to our children, we find the very words God used when He spoke, the words He inspired men to use of Him. It is different from hearing *about* Him, from reading *about* Him. We must read Scripture itself to our children.

But beyond this bit the destruction of Sodom and Gomorrha has little to do with Abraham and it is a tale of lust which is better omitted for children.

Finally, Sara bore the long-promised son, who was circumcised on the eighth day and given the name Isaac, which is also the word for *laugh.* Sara sang a pun for joy: "God has made me laugh for joy; whoever hears of this shall laugh (Isaac) with me" (Gen. 21:6–7, Knox). And Abraham was one hundred years old.

Now God was to test Abraham in a way that would be profoundly symbolic. He called to him in the middle of the night to take his beloved Isaac to a far-off mountain and there offer him in sacrifice. Rising at dawn, Abraham cut wood for the sacrifice and saddling his ass took Isaac and two young men servants and started off. On the third day they came near the place so he left the young men to watch the ass, and with a knife and the fire for the sacrifice, he bade Isaac carry the wood and go with him. As they walked, Isaac questioned his father.

"Father, we have the fire here and the wood; where is the victim we are to sacrifice?" And Abraham replied sadly,

"God will see to it that he has a victim" (Gen. 22:7–9, Knox).

When they reached the appointed place, he built an altar and on it placed the wood, then he bound Isaac and placed him on the wood, but as he put out his hand to take the knife, a voice called, "Abraham! Abraham!"

"Here I am, at your command."

"Do the lad no hurt, let him alone. I know now that thou fearest God, for my sake thou wast ready to give up thy only son" (Gen. 22:11–12, Knox).

Abraham leading to sacrifice Isaac, carrying his bundle of sticks on his back, is a figure of God the Father leading His Divine Son bearing the Cross. God was teaching Abraham as well as testing him. He had come, with his people, from a land where human sacrifice was common: now God was forbidding it. He alone would have dominion over human life. God commended Abraham and heaped benediction and praise upon him "for this readiness of thine to do my bidding" (Gen. 22:19, Knox). If only we were as ready!

In the Mass we daily liken Abraham's sacrifice to ours on the altar. We ask God that ours be as acceptable to Him as was Abraham's. Our children must know Abraham's story for a number of reasons but especially because of its significant relationship to the Mass in its example of "faith and trust and obedience." If we would teach them to love and understand the Mass, we must help them to love Abraham.

Sara died at the age of one hundred and twenty-seven and Abraham grieved for her and buried her in a double cave at the end of a field in his beloved vale of Mambre. Abraham married again in his old age and had six more children, and when he was one hundred and seventy-five he died, "having lived a long time and being full of days" (Gen. 25:8, Douay). Isaac, Ismael, all his family, gathered to bury him beside his first and best-beloved Sara in the cave that overlooked the valley.

Long before God had said to him, "Leave thy country behind thee, thy kinsfolk, and thy father's home, and come away into a land I will show thee." And Abraham went. *We* are supposed to follow God's will for us. Abraham our father — the first saint in sacred history — shows us the way. We must ask him to help us.

2

JOHN BOSCO

SAINT AND TEACHER OF SAINTS

ST. JOHN BOSCO is one of the saints children love immediately and most of all. As soon as they learn he was a juggler, a tightrope artist and a ventriloquist they are his. This is not why he is a saint, but it does dispose of a lot of stuffy notions about what saints are like. They are not bores, that is certain, and if we have one who can do all these things, it is quite fair to use him to capture children's hearts. His, which is one of the best of all saint stories for children, is even more appropriate for grownups, and especially for those who are parents, teachers or have anything to do with the forming, healing or correcting of children.

Long before the advent of child psychology as such, Don John Bosco was putting into practice what Christ taught in the Gospels which is the best, the soundest and the most modern psychology whether applied to children or grownups. St. John Bosco's techniques with children grew out of his knowledge of the eternal destiny of man, the spoiling of his nature by original sin, and the inevitable conflict of up-pull and down-drag in human behavior which is the consequence. Man was made for God and all his behavior reflects his drive for God, even when he doesn't know it. God help him if his parents and his teachers do not know it!

There is a prologue to the St. John Bosco story. He was not born a saint. He said one day to friends that if he had not become a priest and religious he would have been the most abandoned of freethinkers. If that were possible, then there is a reason why he was not an abandoned freethinker. His formation by his mother had taken place in an atmosphere so thoroughly Christian that as a child one might say he breathed the Faith, he all but ate it.

Margaret Bosco could not read but her mind was stored with riches. In the evenings she told her children stories from the Old Testament and from the Gospels, from the lives of the saints, stories which had been told to her in her childhood. She taught them Christian doctrine in terms of their daily life, formed the knowledge of right and wrong in them, drew from nature, as Our Lord did, to illustrate the truths of His lessons, to show the reality of His love and how carefully God designed the universe to serve and delight them. Morning and evening prayer, the Mass, the sacraments, the feasts, all these fed the spiritual life she nourished carefully in them, putting flesh on the bone of it.

She taught them that work well done is prayer, that play, if it is good, is prayer, that the duties of our state in life, the accomplishments and disappointments as well, can all be given to God. She was the one who took them to the village fairs where the youngest lad watched the jugglers and discovered their tricks, learned to throw his voice like the ventriloquist so the cow seemed to talk, saw with amazement the antics of the tightrope artist and vowed to learn those tricks himself (and he did, next day, in the barn). She knew boys and she taught this boy lessons he would teach to thousands of boys after him, which his own spiritual sons would teach to tens of thousands of boys.

The lessons Margaret Bosco taught, the understanding and firmness of her correction, the encouragement, the respect for work, for learning, for all the creatures of God, have gone into the Rule of a vast congregation of religious which the man founded in order to help do for other boys what his mother did for him; not what a school or a college or a business training did, but what *his mother* did for him. *There is no substitute for the teaching of parents.* And there was nothing taught by Margaret Bosco that we cannot teach ourselves.

Margaret Bosco celebrated the feast of the Assumption in the year 1815 with particular joy and the next day she was delivered of a son. Inevitably she had dedicated her unborn child to Mary on the great feast. Later she told him so. Afterward, when his unique vocation had become clear under the guidance of Mary, Help of Christians, he used to say, "I was born on the *fifteenth* of August."

When John Bosco was two, his father died leaving Margaret with her stepson Anthony, burly and unimaginative, her middle son Joseph, quiet and introspective, and this marvelously quick, inventive little son John. Terrible poverty was everywhere. They lived only because the mother was determined they should and wrung existence for them out of every least thing. Anthony was growing up to be a farmer and had no patience with anything else; Joseph helped Anthony; and little John helped when and where he could. He was all jump and spirit, this last boy, good at chores, good at games, sociable, and he played with all his might, often coming home much the worse for the wear.

His mother was chagrined. They were rough boys; he was not their match; why did he persist in playing with them when she said she preferred him not to? He *had* to. Indeed! and why? Because they were better boys when he was there! And how was that? He could get them to stop fighting and play games; he could divert them from their bad language. They had no one to teach them as she taught, to explain things as she could, he *had* to help them. Well, all right, but mind — he was not to play with the bad ones. The really evil ones were dangerous and he was to avoid them. So he went back into the fray whenever there was time, to play with all the zeal of a professed missionary. *Somehow* by being their companion and playmate, he would devise a means to teach them their religion. He was absolutely driven to it. It was a tide that would never stop rising in him, this passion to teach children to know and to love God. When he was at last teaching boys in his own school, he would stress especially this aspect of the Christian's childhood — the opportunity for an apostolate through games and play.

There is no doubt that St. John Bosco's vocation was clear to him even in the beginning, but that does not mean he was always a saint. He would work so hard to get the attention of these noisy playmates, dominating them by every fair means — with his agility which they admired, his wit, his fund of marvelous stories — and he *could* get them, and hold them too, until he got around to the catechism. Then they lost interest and teased him, even cursed to see him become angry. He *would* and pretty soon mêlée! Fists flew, there was whacking and rolling and tangling and all was riot.

Then he had a dream. It was the first of many. He dreamed he was in the yard where a lot of noisy boys were playing, laughing, blaspheming. He hated blasphemy. He rushed at them shouting, shaking his fists, swinging wildly, and suddenly there appeared a man dressed in white with a face so bright it was impossible to look at it. *"John Bosco,"* he said, *"you will not win their friendship with blows, but with kindness. Be gentle with them."* The boy was frightened. *"Teach them right from wrong, John. Teach them the beauty of goodness, and the ugliness of sin."* But that was impossible — they'd pay no attention to him, and anyway, he didn't know anything! What seemed impossible, the man replied, would become possible if he would be patient and study. The boy protested; how would *he* ever get to study? *"I shall give you a Mistress, under whose guidance alone one can become wise, without whom all knowledge is foolishness."* John Bosco grew suspicious. "Who are you, to speak like this?" *"I am the Son of her whom your mother teaches you to salute three times a day."* [1]

[1] Henri Gheon, *The Secrets of the Saints* (New York: Sheed & Ward, Inc., New York, copyright 1944), p. 294.

At the mention of his mother his wits returned and he spoke out unhesitatingly. His mother had forbidden him to have anything to do with strangers. "Tell me your name," he said. The man replied: *"Ask my name of my mother."*

And there, suddenly, was a lady as brilliant and full of light as the man. She beckoned. "Look." The boys had vanished and in their place were the most frightful beasts, goats, tigers, wolves, dogs, bears, snarling and charging. The lady spoke again. "This is the field of your work. Be humble, be strong, be courageous." She extended her hand and the wild animals became a flock of lambs. As she had transformed the animals, she promised, so he would transform her children. Suddenly he began to cry. What did this mean? If it was all about him and his work, something important he was supposed to do, what did it mean? She laid her hand upon his head. "You will understand in time." And she was gone.

She was Our Lady. He knew. His mother had taught him to salute Our Lady three times a day with the *Angelus.*

It is an episode that seems to have significance for this little boy alone or, if for more, then for those souls with whom he would work one day. But it is also significant for us that Christ Himself described His Mother in these words: "her whom *your mother teaches you* to salute. . . ." Our Lady is a stranger to a child unless someone teach him about her, and to know her is imperative. Our Lord makes this clear. She is the Mistress "without whom all knowledge is foolishness." And when she spoke to him at last, she stated the condition on which he would transform the souls he wanted for God: *be humble, be strong, be courageous.* She would repeat these same words several times during his life. They mean that the fruitfulness of his apostolate — and ours, and *our* children's — would depend upon his own struggle for holiness. It is crucially important that we understand this. It is on the interior formation of our children that we must spend our efforts first. They will be of service to God in exact proportion to their growth in holiness.

That was how it began. From that day and always he knew he wanted to be a priest. Behind all the devices he used as he set out to win souls one sees the wisdom and encouragement of his mother. The songs she had sung, the stories she had told, the lessons in doctrine she had taught, all the love she had poured into this boy was being communicated to other souls — and in such a short time! Inevitably she must have thought: "Suppose I had *not* told him!"

He conceived the idea of giving shows: juggling, ventriloquy, tightrope walking, somersaults, walking on his hands. Admission: one Rosary. His audiences were boys and girls, men and women, and if they objected he told them, "No Rosary — no show." Sundays in the summer he added a hymn to Our Lady and his own version of last week's sermon. Many of them did not walk the six miles to Mass as the Boscos did; someone had to keep them respectful of God. Winter evenings he read or recited for them, visiting their houses, keeping them fascinated for hours before the fire — but first, a few prayers? So, all right! A few prayers. A few prayers or the boy wouldn't read. When they had said their prayers, he read, and he *could* read. He was a born storyteller and a gifted and tireless reader.

One evening the priest in Murialdo, Don Calosso, questioned him after a mission and discovered to his surprise and joy a ten-year-old who had given his life to God but didn't know what to do about it. He offered to instruct him every morning in grammar and Latin, and John was never happier. But Anthony at home could not tolerate a farmhand giving himself such airs. Finally, as a temporary measure in order to keep the peace, Margaret persuaded John to seek work and lodging elsewhere. It must have cost her dear to send him off.

His next two years were spent with the Moglias near Moncucco. Here he studied when he could — out in the pasture watching the cattle; he prayed when he could not study — working in the fields, plowing and planting; he instructed when he could not study or pray — the children around the farm, in the neighborhood. In the village he held religion classes for children every Sunday afternoon. He became indispensable to everyone as usual. Here an uncle finally found him thus treading time and took him back to Becchi for further study with Don Calosso, and this development so enraged Anthony that Margaret settled the affair once for all by giving each boy his legal share of the father's little estate. Anthony left for good with a few chickens, some sheep and a cow and established himself on a small farm elsewhere; Margaret and Joseph lived on the farm; John went to live with Don Calosso. The family life even of the saints is not always smooth sailing.

John Bosco's perfect and beautiful companionship with Don Calosso had not long to last. The old priest died, leaving his bit of worldly goods to John, and in great delicacy of conscience John turned it over to his benefactor's relatives. Once again he was penniless and facing an uncertain future but this time grief added its burden and the poor lad came close to breaking under it. His mother feared for his health. God, in a dream, rebuked him for having so little faith.

Next he went to school at Castelnuova. Here he learned lessons of another kind, lessons his masters did not know they were teaching. Long before, he had met a priest on the road near home one day, and in answer to his cheerful "Good morning, Father," he had received only a curt nod of the head. It had bothered him. "If I am a priest," he told his mother, "I will never talk to children like that. I will always be kind to them, always be their friend." That was the first rule he made for himself, and it later became a rule for his Salesians: be their friend, be their friend, *always be their friend.* His experiences at Castelnuova, tasting the derision and sarcasm of the masters, the jeering scorn of the boys, taught him much. Having had less schooling than the others for his years, he was bigger than most and older, and as he was badly dressed in the bargain the masters assumed such a bumpkin must be a dolt and an idiot as well. No matter if he did perfect work, his only praise was the accusation of cheating. Anything less than perfect was held up to the class for ridicule.

John lived with a tailor who accepted produce from Margaret every weekend to pay his board so at least he learned tailoring, and, since the man had a taste for Gregorian chant as well, he also learned chant from him. At times he worked as a blacksmith's helper, a waiter, and in a bowling alley, learning lessons of one kind or another which he would use one way or another in his own schools one day. But of formal learning, he had not much to his credit by the end of the term. However, he had learned the kind of priest and teacher *not* to be. He had learned why the people sometimes lacked respect for some of their priests. He had learned humility. God's way of teaching humility never varies much. This experience of young John Bosco was like that of many young people who leave the snug security of life at home to go away to work or to school. Suddenly the years of training in the family become the key to accepting and profiting by, or being destroyed by, the new experience. At Castelnuova John was not the darling John of the people of Becchi, who would next year contribute eggs, butter, cheese, grain for him to sell so he might attend school in Chieri. At Castelnuova he was nobody's darling and he received nothing at the hands of his superiors but scorn and ridicule. Why did not this treatment embitter the boy and destroy his faith?

In part, the answer must be that God had chosen him for a special work and had given him a special grace to persevere, but there was something in addition to this. Did not his perseverance also relate to the teaching and example of his mother? Had she not patiently arbitrated the disputes with Anthony who had, time and again, loudly ridiculed the idea that such a bumpkin as John should aspire to higher learning? Had she not even sent John away for two long years, prudently bidding him to bide his time? A woman whose life is so rooted in faith, hope and charity leaves her mark on such a boy as John Bosco. Family life with its private disputes and sufferings is God's way of preparing such a child for life in the world with its public disputes and sufferings. And lastly, is not long-suffering a fruit of the Holy Spirit? This lad had striven to cooperate with the promptings of the Holy Spirit since he was a little boy. The mother, the priests at home who had taught him and preached to him, had prepared him well. He was a good tree, and already he was beginning to bear fruit.

That summer he had another "dream." The Lady appeared again and said: *"Giovannino, I am entrusting the whole flock to you."* [2] There was no doubt; he was meant to be a shepherd, a priest.

At school in Chieri John found himself once more the giant of the class. He was sixteen and the others much younger but here he worked more easily at his studies. In one year and a summer he had made up three years' work. There are stories about this period that children love to hear over and over again. Once he forgot to bring his book to school and when called on to recite, he opened another book and pretended to read the text. He read it without an error, having memorized the lesson the night before, but the boys sitting round him noticed and blurted out to the master: "He hasn't the right book!" The master, discovering this was so, forgave his forgetfulness but commented that one with such an excellent memory had better look to the good use of the gift. It could be used for evil as well as good.

Another time he was leading some boys to instructions and a sermon in the Jesuit Church in Chieri. Although they were more than average lads — they prayed and read and studied seriously enough — they liked games and fun as well. An acrobat had set up his paraphernalia in the square outside the church and the boys lingered even though it was time to go. John Bosco challenged the acrobat to a contest later after services, and the acrobat accepted. Back again, he stated he could outrace the acrobat to the end of town. The boys

<hr>

[2] *Ibid.,* p. 312.

raised a wager of twenty lire among themselves and John won the race. The acrobat, annoyed, accepted a challenge to jump the stream at the edge of town, forty lire the prize. He jumped it but John Bosco outjumped him. The dancing stick? (John had learned to do this long ago watching the jugglers at the village fairs.) His hat balanced at the top of a twirling stick, he danced the stick from finger to finger, across the palm of his hand, his wrist, up his arm, his shoulder, jumped to his chin, his nose, his forehead and back again. Perfectly! But this the acrobat could do; any acrobat could do it as well or better than any lad, however clever. And he did, until it reached his nose. Though it was a good one, it was a big one and it was his undoing. John Bosco was the winner by a nose.

Next, a tightrope-walking contest. The acrobat was jubilant. This was his *business*. This time he'd be the winner. He walked well and long, but John walked longer, better. The sum owed the student had climbed to eighty lire. In sheer frustration, the acrobat pointed to a great tree by the church and challenged the student to outclimb him. John accepted. The acrobat climbed to the top and down again, triumphant. John Bosco climbed to the top — and stood on his hands. He *had* gone higher. The boys were hysterical, the acrobat disgusted, and John grinning. He suggested that the loser pay part of his debt by feeding them all at a nearby inn; that done, he forgave the balance on condition the acrobat never again set up his show in front of the church during time for Mass or services. The acrobat gratefully agreed.

About this time John's mother and the neighbors could no longer send him enough money for board so he went to work and to live with an innkeeper. He washed glasses each evening in the public room, acted as billiard marker, and observed at close hand the poor antics of men in search of happiness in the wrong place. It taught him much; above all it increased his horror of sin and the places where it breeds. He also learned to make coffee, cocoa, ices and fine pastry and added these to the long list of his accomplishments. He slept under the stairs, like St. Alexis, and at night after chores he used to read by candlelight in his hole: Dante, Petrarch, Cicero, Virgil, Horace, many others.

But he had not yet conquered his impatience. He was hot-headed by nature and that is a thing not easily subdued. A story boys love, one especially profitable for parents and teachers, is the incident of his learning how much more is accomplished by the spirit of peace than by its opposite, anger. Our Lord had told him this in his first dream, long before, but it took him years to master it. Luigi Comollo was a new boy in the class, studious, quiet, pleasant, and neither he nor John Bosco joined the others in their ructions one day when the teacher was out of the room. The other boys were throwing chalk, books, spit-balls, standing on desks, generally turning the place upside-down, when one of them called to Luigi to get into the fun. Luigi declined. He was studying. The boy insisted. No, thank you, he was working. The boy became abusive. He'd come or he'd get hit! Who did he think he was? John Bosco began to boil. Luigi looked at the boy who threatened him. "Hit me if you like." And furiously the boy hit, twice, once on each cheek. John stared at Luigi who remained quiet and said: "Are you satisfied? I forgive you. Now leave me alone." There was nothing for the bully to do but to get out. This episode, together with one from the life of St. Dominic Savio,[3] are splendid illustrations of Christian meekness in action, of the *effect* that follows "turning the other cheek." Such meekness is part of a Christian's strength. St. John Bosco claimed that this episode taught him once for all that strength lies in self-discipline and kindness. These were not new ideas to him, but it took Luigi's example to form them into a conviction.

At last he entered the seminary. His mother wept when she said: "Remember, my little John, that it is not the habit

[3] See pp. 52–3.

that is the honour of the priestly state, but virtue. You were born under the sign of the Most Holy Virgin; I gave you to her then and I renew the gift." [4]

That day he set down some resolutions. At first glance, this list of self-denials sounds almost unnatural, a denial of things perfectly lawful, even necessary, but a soul thus far along in the love affair with God knows only that all delight is to be found in God and the sooner the lesser delights are foregone, the sooner with God's grace the soul possesses all. These things John would give up were only tastes of God. He wanted God. He resolved the following:

He would attend no public spectacle; would appear at festival dinners only when absolutely necessary; would give up acrobatics, the violin and hunting, things that accord ill with the true priestly spirit.

He would be much in retreat; would drink, eat, sleep only so much as his health required.

He had served the world by reading books not religious, now he would try to serve God by reading books of devotion.

With all his strength he would resist the very shadow of an act, word or thought against the virtue of chastity, and at the same time would neglect no slightest practice for the preservation of that virtue.

To the ordinary exercises of piety he would add every day a time for meditation and spiritual reading; every day also he would give his neighbor some example or some maxim tending to the elevation of his soul.[5]

These things he promised to Our Lady.

That summer, while on vacation, he chased a rabbit and and caught it with his bare hands. He was a marvelous runner

---

[4] Gheon, *op. cit.*, p. 321.
[5] *Ibid.*, p. 321.

and he loved it. He returned with it behind his back and one of the boys said laughingly: "You look like a poacher." Afterward he wept. It was no sin, but he wept to see how easily we fail to give up even small pleasures for the greatest pleasure of all — the possession of God. We are so eager to do *big* things. We will not until we learn to do the small ones.

During these years John had a dream which defined his vocation more clearly than ever. He dreamed he wore a cassock, rochet and stole and sat in a tailor's room sewing patches on an old garment. He asked Don Cafasso, his spiritual director (who would one day be St. Joseph Cafasso), what this meant and the saint interpreted it to mean that it would not be the new garments — that is the pure of heart — that God would give him to shape and sew, but the soiled and the worn — that is the weak, the fallen — whom he would make presentable. Still another dream repeated the lesson of his first: *gentleness, persuasion,* these were the virtues he must cultivate. He learned also that all he studied, read, meditated upon in order to help souls must, when spoken to them in sermons and instructions, be put as simply as possible.

He was ordained on June 5, 1841, at the age of twenty-five, and said his first Mass with only Don Cafasso as witness. Several days later he said Mass in the presence of his mother and the adoring friends and neighbors at Castelnuova. Knowing the life of a saint after it is over, it would be easy to make the mistake of thinking everyone else knew how it would turn out. No one knew. If any remark of Margaret Bosco's reveals her own spiritual greatness, her perfect grasp of the mystical life, it is what she said to her son this day:

"But remember what I tell you, my son. To begin to say Mass is to begin to suffer. You will see it soon." [6]

Knowing his soul well, she knew the only course for him was to go deeper into the heart of Christ and the way to this is suffering. Christ was a suffering God. We are foolish to think we can be like Him without suffering.

[6] *Ibid.,* p. 328.

John went to Turin to an Institute for young priests. There were study, prayer, the works of mercy. He went to visit the Little House of Divine Providence and saw it overflowing with the indescribably afflicted. Canon Cottolengo (one day to be St. Joseph Cottolengo) said to him: "There is work for you here," but John was sure his field was elsewhere. It was work with boys that appealed most to him.

Turin at that time had been expanding, and a building boom had called in from the country countless young boys who were certain they were on the road to fortune. Jobless, homeless, they roamed the streets, sleeping anywhere, eating what they could beg or steal, learning all kinds of vice, turning to practices too vile to name. But they had souls, and this young priest was haunted by what was happening to their souls. There was nowhere an apostolate to these uprooted boys; they belonged to him.

He walked the streets to find them, speak to them, to try to become their friends, without success. But he became a familiar sight. They recognized him. One morning, on the feast of the Immaculate Conception, he was vesting for Mass when he heard a commotion near the sacristy door. A young ruffian had come in off the street, perhaps to seek him out but more likely just to get warm, and had got himself hit over the head with the sacristan's broom and driven away. Don Bosco flew at the sacristan. "How dare you! I forbid you to treat my friends like that! What had he ever done to you!" His *friends?* "Yes, my friends! All children are my friends and especially beaten ones. Get out there and fetch him back. I want to talk to him." So the bewildered boy was fetched back and the work of the Oratory began. The following Sunday he came with a half dozen more: dirty, ragged, bug-ridden teen-agers who had souls. John Bosco loved souls.

Now the work began to grow. John was joined rapidly by boys and more boys. They met on Sunday. They outgrew the little room in the back of the church and got permission to use the playground of a girl's orphanage. But such noise and tramping about did not suit the Marchesa who sponsored it, nor her staff, nor her gardener — whose garden had died the death rapidly under the onslaught. Off to another place, and another, always being put out and told the noise and commotion were too much. In good weather Don John took them out to the country near some church where he could give them instruction, hear their confessions, say Mass and distribute Communion. Then to the fields where he fed them (heaven knows how) and played games and organized contests for the rest of the day. Home again in the evening, he to another week of exhausting clerical duties, they to their holes to count the days till Sunday.

Their numbers swelled till they began to be a subject of comment in clerical as well as municipal circles. They were wild boys. They could be a source of trouble. He carried the thing too far. The strain was beginning to tell on him; why, he had even said he would found an Order to care for them! These were the things that were being said. Even his superior Don Borel, whom he loved dearly and who returned his love, began to doubt the wisdom of such a massing of boys, and in the minds of two other priests a plan was hatched to put a halt to the thing. They arrived for a visit with Don Bosco one afternoon and after a chat suggested a ride in the open air. He never took time for recreation himself; the air would do him good. Unknown to Don John, they thought, arrangements had been made to receive him at the local asylum for, shall we say, a rest cure? But God gave this saint in the making the gift of reading souls. He agreed to the ride and bowing to their seniority, urged them to mount the carriage first. They climbed in, he slammed the door, and with a wise look to the driver called out: "To the asylum! They are expected!" Off went the driver to deliver his charges and, because arrangements *had* been made and by the time they arrived they *were* acting like lunatics, they had a time getting themselves out. That was the last time anyone undertook to prove that Don Bosco was *mad.*

Finally he leased a shed and a yard in the worst part of the city. One door opened on a tavern. The dirt floor of the shed had to be "lowered" to make room for the boys to stand. But it was theirs, and they had the Archbishop's blessing at last, and it was wonderful to be able to stay put. Their neighbors were, for the most part, every kind of rogue dealing in every kind of vice but over *their* door was written something Our Lady had told Don Bosco in a dream to write over the doorway of *her* institution: *This is my House — my Glory shall shine from it.* The boys worked to convert an outside shed into a chapel, to build kneelers, benches, tables, so they could pray, sit, study, eat; and he worked with them whenever he was free from his other duties.

Then when things looked up instead of down, he collapsed: he had ruined his health doing the work of ten men. He had spared himself nothing and he was exhausted, every energy spent, with nothing left in reserve to fight the pneumonia that attacked him. The doctors gave up hope. But God has a way of using calamities. At the prospect of losing this man who was father, mother, sister, brother, priest, teacher, saint to them, every boy in the Oratory was on his knees. They stormed heaven seeking his recovery. They wept — and they were big boys, fifteen, sixteen, seventeen years old. They begged prayers for him. They made sacrifices for him, wild promises. They vowed to reform in every way, to give up everything, to pray forever, if only God would spare their Don Bosco. Yet he lay will-less, ready to die or not to die as God saw fit. He would not pray for his own recovery. Only Don Borel, at last willing to admit that his *was* a special vocation, commanded as his superior that he pray once: "Cure me, O Lord, if such is your good pleasure, in the name of my children." God cured him.

But he was weak and had to rest. He went back to his mother's farm and stayed a while, finally persuading her to sell it and return with him to the city. He needed a mother for his boys.

How great she was. All her life was an unending giving up of her own way. This is the secret of all holiness. It must have cost her dear to pack her belongings on her back, literally, and set out for the noise and dirt and sin of a city slum after a lifetime spent in the country. And what would she be doing there? After having raised her own family, having endured the poverty and hard times, having earned her rest, what was asked of her but that she start it all over again, if not with the newborn then with those whose care is every bit as demanding, the half-grown. How like the role of a grandmother was Margaret Bosco's — although actually the boys never called her anything but *Mamma* Margaret. Older, less agile, slower in her movements, tired after a life of very hard work, content to prepare for God and heaven in the quiet and peace of the countryside, she surrendered it all, "gave it to God," and trudged to the city with this son whose vocation she had tended with her own hands, with her own heart.

She is revered now as a saint, but that does not mean this last heroic choice was easy for her. It is never easy for those on in years to uproot themselves and start all over again, even when they do it for God. Like so many grandmothers, she had lived for years in a rhythm all her own, keyed to the seasons, the sun, the dark, the good and bad weather, repeating the same domestic acts and rituals, growing blessedly, beautifully "set in her ways." Now she would exchange this serene pattern, this security of the familiar, for a life of total insecurity, a life where nothing was stable except God. This son of hers would sometimes take risks that would shake even her faith. Yet she went — because she was needed. Some must have thought she was mad, as they think grandmothers are mad to give their old age away to the service of their children's children — but that is one of the definitions of a Christian: to imitate their Master, and be as a servant.

Heaven knew what toughs asking for help this teeming, evil city would turn up at any hour of the day or night. Don Bosco brought home boys off the street and put them to bed in the loft, covering them with her sheets and blankets. They stole the sheets and blankets. He wept and she scolded, yet weeks later she took in a boy to sleep in her kitchen. He was the Oratory's first permanent boarder. That night she did something, quite unconsciously, that would find its way into the Salesian Rule. Before he went to sleep, she talked to her little stray about God. This practice of a short talk after night prayers, called the "Good Night," now is a custom in all Salesian schools throughout the world.

Finally Don John had to buy the house that went with the shed. It was a wretched one-story establishment, never worth the eighty thousand lire Signor Pinardi wanted for it. Don Bosco offered thirty thousand, which he did not have, and the offer was accepted. He had two weeks to raise the money. Before the time was up, three people made voluntary contributions of thirty-three thousand lire, thirty for the house, three for legal expenses.

He housed thirty boys, feeding them almost miraculously (sometimes he did feed them miraculously). He found tradesmen to hire them and during the day they went out to work, coming home to him and his mother at night and donating their wages to help keep "the family" going. He started evening classes, Sunday classes, teaching four and five *hundred* boys. He needed a bigger chapel, ran a lottery, begged money, and received enough to build his St. Francis de Sales church. It faced the tavern. By this time, people were done with criticism and began to watch with wonder. He built a wing for the house, saw it completed and then saw it fall to the ground under torrential rains. He built it again.

But St. John Bosco's Oratory is remarkable for more than the amazing history of its building. At a time when severe discipline and harsh punishments were commonplace in a schoolboy's life, Don John inaugurated a program (which was greeted with no little suspicion) that he called the "preventive system of education," depending upon the elimination of the time and occasion for misbehavior and the presence of teachers at all times, teachers who loved the boys and saw them soul first, as it were. Violent punishments were never used nor, as far as possible, chastisements of any kind. Don John wrote that the primary reason for this was that youth is forgetful and thoughtless and often would avoid misbehavior if only a friendly voice were at hand to give warning. He had a deep conviction, growing out of his love of God and knowledge of the soul, that good *is* more attractive to youth than evil and that half the battle of forming the young to do good was won by the loving supervision of their studies, work and play. This was a new idea at a time when repressive measures were accepted as the principal means of discipline. A repressive measure could stop disorder, he said, but could hardly make the offenders better. It was to making them better, even more to making them *holy,* that he dedicated himself.

"Experience teaches that the young do not forget the punishments they have received but often foster bitter feelings, along with the desire to throw off the yoke and even to revenge themselves. It sometimes appears that they do not heed it, but one who can follow them in their future life knows that the reminiscences of youth are terrible, that they easily forget the punishments of their parents, but with great difficulty those of their teachers. There are cases of some who in later years have in a brutal manner taken vengeance . . . The 'preventive system' makes a friend of the pupil, who looks upon his educator as a benefactor who advises him, wishes to make him good, to save him from trouble, from punishments, and from dishonour." [7]

Heaven forbid that this seem to give parents free rein in the matter of violent or thoughtless punishments! It is a valuable comment, however, for parents can profit from it as much as teachers, adapting the "preventive" principle to home as well as school. What he is saying is that love is our most powerful weapon in the training, even in the disciplining, of our children

[7] Salesians of St. John Bosco, "An Ounce of Prevention" (Paterson, N.J.: Salesiana Publishing Co.), p. 8.

and it must be the motive for all our teaching and correction. One has but to recall that Marshall Tito has said he never forgot being slapped by a priest to see an example of those "who in later years have in a brutal manner taken vengeance."

"The 'preventive system' enables the pupil to take advice in such a manner that the language of the heart, not only during the time of his education, but even afterward, presents a strong appeal to him. The educator having once succeeded in gaining the heart of his subject can afterward exercise a great influence over him, can caution, advise, and even correct him, although he may already occupy some position in the world." [8] This again, applies for the parent as well as for the teacher. The saint believed that after the eighteenth year a child's moral formation either for better or for worse was practically complete, or at least difficult to change; thus the precious six or seven years preceding it were vital, a time for parents, priests, teachers to work untiringly to form in the child a Christian conscience.

"Frequent Confession and Communion and daily Mass are the pillars which must support the edifice of education, from which we propose to banish threats and the rod. Never force the boys to frequent the sacraments, but encourage them to do so, and give them every opportunity."

Here is a saint's answer to another perennial question: should the sacraments be obligatory? We must remember, of course, that he was speaking of the relation of the school master to the child, not necessarily the parent, but there is wisdom here for both. With young children force is rarely needed, but with older ones it would seem we must make the most of diplomacy and good example, provided early teaching has been thorough and the habits of frequent Confession and Communion well established. It is almost impossible to build on a lack of early training except in the cases of real "conversions" to a more spiritual life. The family custom of weekly Confession and Holy Communion can be outside of force, as

[8] *Ibid.*, p. 8.

such, but is almost as powerful, and parents must be careful not to use it to force older and perhaps reluctant children to go publicly to confession against their wills. Children who have some serious problem to discuss with a confessor will not feel free to do so if their parents are clocking the time spent in the confessional or coercing them to go to Confession to a priest with whom they cannot be relaxed and open.

St. John Bosco said: "The first essential in the education of boys is to help them make good Confessions and good Communions." He said to the boys: "My dear boys, if you want to persevere in the way of salvation, I recommend three things: first, often receive the sacrament of penance; second, receive Holy Communion frequently (two or three times a week or even daily); three, choose a confessor to whom you can open your heart, and do not change him without a serious reason."

Very young children welcome the idea of telling a chosen Father who they are and asking his help weekly, especially if the priests available for confessions are friendly and sympathetic. Older children are somewhat self-conscious (it takes a bit of doing to tell your name) but this is because pride has already begun to stiffen them. When this is understood they will agree it is high time to overcome it before it gets worse. They conquer their embarrassment once they understand that Father is not so much interested to know what sins they have committed (he could probably guess, knowing human nature as he does) as he is *to help them not to commit sin again.* He hears so much of sin he does not spend much time thinking about specific people and their specific sins, but about *all* sin. That is his grief and he wants to help souls be rid of it. Encouragement and prayer help children over their temerity and when finally they have asked a particular priest to be their regular confessor, they are always relieved and grateful. It is well for the parents to enlist the help of the priest ahead of time, if possible, so he will pray for the success of the plan and be forewarned when a child makes his request in the confessional.

There are a number of advantages to having a regular confessor. First, he can help the pentitent single out an outstanding fault or weakness and work at it methodically week after week. Second, the continuity of such confessions makes it clear, especially to children, that confession is more than a weekly sacramental "bathing." Its *end* is *the elimination of sin* in the healing of the soul's scars and its nourishment for greater resistance to sin in the future. It feeds the growing horror and hatred for sin, the real and burning desire to please God.

These should be the effects, over a period of time, of consistent, thoughtful, frequent, well-prepared confessions. Don Bosco stressed also the importance of true sorrow for sin. Frequent confession must not become routine and automatic. Careful examination of conscience, with the help of parents when possible (children welcome help with the examination of conscience for years, even into the teens), helps to stir up true sorrow for sin and the all-important firm purpose of amendment.

Lastly, there is this advantage which no parents can afford to overlook if they care passionately about the souls of their children: the priest knows what sins may be hidden behind an awkward, hesitant, embarrassed confession, what temptations come at what ages and periods of development, and he has the Holy Spirit with him to enlighten him and to help him with the sinner. He wants to help these souls resist sin. His personal encouragement, approval and patience are needed by the child who, for all he loves his parents, one day may reach a point where he is sure they could no longer "understand." Confession must never be a weapon to be held over a child's head by anxious and disturbed parents, hurt over at last losing the confidence of their growing child. Confession is Christ applying His healing hands to their souls, and the minister Christ has chosen for this sacrament is His priest. No wonder St. John Bosco recommended to boys who would persevere in the way of salvation "a confessor to whom you can open your heart. . . ."

There were violent attacks against the Church in Italy at

this time, and the anti-clerical forces who had sworn to see her ruined went after her little ones, her poor, her miserable, her lower classes and especially these homeless boys. When this young priest began to be known far and wide as their champion, they went for him.

He was set upon when he visited the sick, and his strength and nimbleness saved him. He had a bodyguard of his boys, so his enemies tried revolvers. They shot at him through a window and the bullet pierced his soutane, but he only said lightly, "A pity, it was my best cassock." He visited a dying man and was given a glass of poisoned wine to drink. He guessed its contents to the family's great confusion. He visited a "dying" woman and somehow a brawl started among her "sons" who, oddly enough, sat around the death bed armed with sticks. The lamp went out, blows rained and he fenced his way to the door with the help of a chair. Then came Grigio.

No one ever knew who Grigio was — if he was a "who." Certainly Don Bosco never told if he knew. Grigio may have been his guardian angel. If God could make the world out of nothing, He could certainly let an angel take the form of a dog if it pleased Him. Grigio showed up one night when Don Bosco was returning home through the worst part of the city. A dog appeared to be following. He called and the dog came obediently and let himself be patted. He accompanied him to his door and left. Again he appeared, and again, whenever the priest would be going on an errand that involved danger or took him through places where danger lay. Don John gave him the name Grigio — Italian for gray — because he looked like a great gray wolf. One night he chased an assailant who fired two shots at Don Bosco from behind a tree. Another night two men threw a sack over the priest's head, to their great regret, for Grigio fastened his teeth in the throat of one and scared the other within an inch of his life. On another occasion he refused to let the priest out and lay in front of the door snarling, baring ferocious teeth. Within minutes a neighbor ran in to warn Don Bosco of a plot against his life. Often Grigio came into the house, lay by the stove, let the boys fondle him, but he never ate or drank. And when at last it was conceded by his enemies that to war with Don Bosco was a fruitless undertaking, the dog disappeared.

Ten years later the priest was about to visit the Moglias' farm and he was warned that the road was unsafe. "Oh, if only I had my Grigio!" he cried. There was a bark and a bound and Grigio was at his heels. Arriving at the Moglias, they were welcomed with joy, and Don Bosco talked and ate with his friends while Grigio lay in the corner. Supper over, the host remembered that Grigio should be fed — but Grigio had vanished. No door or window had been opened; there was no other exit. Grigio had disappeared into thin air. Thirty years later, in 1883, as Don Bosco was returning home with another priest from a visit with the Bishop of Ventimiglia, Grigio appeared for the last time to guide them when they had lost their way.

Pope Pius XI said he knew of "no life of a saint wherein the direct and miraculous action of God was more continuously manifest" than the life of St. John Bosco. There is probably no complete record of all the miracles but children love these familiar ones, and they should be so well known by parents that they can tell them at the drop of a hat. For example, there is the one about the multiplication of the loaves.

At one time the Oratory had three hundred boys to feed and owed great sums of money to the baker. The baker announced that he was not in business to feed hungry boys for nothing: no money, no bread. It was breakfast time and the boys were waiting. Don Bosco asked someone to bring to the table what bread there was. There were fifteen small rolls. He blessed them and began to pass them out himself. Three hundred boys each took a roll; there were fifteen left over — and this story was told by boys who were *there*. That was not all he multiplied when he had to. He multiplied nuts, even consecrated Hosts. Most of all he multiplied in the hearts of his boys the love of virtue and the love of God.

Then there was the time he raised the little boy from the

dead. His name was Charles and by the time Don Bosco reached the house, his parents were weeping; he was dead. "Do not weep — he is only sleeping," he told them, and went into his room. "Charles, arise." He uncovered the small corpse and the little boy opened his eyes. "Oh, it's you, Don Bosco. I've been calling and calling. I thought I was going to hell for a sin I never confessed and I could confess it only to you. But a beautiful lady chased the devils away and said to them, 'Let him be. He is not yet judged.' And now you have come to me!"

After he had gone to confession Don Bosco said to him, "Would you rather stay on earth, Charles, or go to paradise?" "Oh — to paradise, Don Bosco!" "Then good-bye, little son," and the little boy died two hours later.

He added shops and workrooms to his school. Boys who had been redeemed after wandering the streets had not yet formed the virtues to withstand the temptations of the city, so he decided to train them at their trades within the walls of the Oratory; at the same time they would be helping to clothe and shoe the others under the roof. He added classes for boys whose vocations lay along more scholarly lines, possibly even the religious life. He dreamed of establishing a seminary, but that was not yet to come. He needed helpers and knew who they would be because he had seen them all in his dreams, but neither would they come just yet.

John Cagliero would be brought by a priest in Murialdo and would one day become a cardinal. John Francesia would come to him because another small boy would whisper: "Come see Don Bosco. He's a good priest. He gives us roasted chestnuts!" John would become a Salesian and a scholar. Dominic Savio would come from school in Castelnuova. He would be canonized. Paul Albera would one day be head of the Congregation. Michael Rua was a little boy in Turin, one of a mob of small boys who rushed to Don Bosco whenever they saw him on the street. He always gave them something, a sweet, a medal, a holy picture, but for Michael he never had anything but a puzzling gesture. He would hold a holy card in one hand and make a sign with the other of tearing it in half, saying, "This is for you, Michael." It meant Michael would have half of all he had one day, half of his burdens, half of his work. He would become the first Salesian.

One night, long after, he gathered these boys into his room and they took a simple promise to live as a company, dedicated to prayer, the spiritual life and the exercise of charity toward their neighbor. They would do this under the mantle of Mary and the patronage of St. Francis de Sales, calling themselves after him Salesians. Then, as though to test their dedication, cholera struck Turin and their help was needed to nurse the sick, to bury the dead. A little scared, they and a dozen or so other boys threw themselves into the work tirelessly, working for days and nights without ceasing — and without one being infected.

Don John's mother died when he was forty-one years old and he was desolate. Shaking with grief, he told Our Lady that now he had one hundred and fifty children and no mother for them. *She* would have to be their Mother. One hundred and fifty lodged with him, but more came to him for help, and he went out to still more who needed help.

It would be a mistake to think he had nothing but successes. There were those who did not respond even to the love of this saint. He knew who they would be because he saw them in his dreams, but he could not act toward them as anything but a confident, hopeful father. Tenderness, patience, understanding — always these were the keys that opened young hearts. He set up very few restrictions for entrants and very few qualifications for expulsion. In comparison to the rules of other such institutions, his were so flexible as to seem almost non-existent. He ruled more from the heart than from the book. But he would not tolerate blasphemy and he would not tolerate impurity. The rotten apples, he said, spoil every apple in the barrel and they must go.

And he suffered. One might well be suspicious of a saint whose life was all success and no suffering. Such a one is not a saint. He had frightful varicose veins in his legs from the time he was forty. He nearly lost the sight of his right eye in a storm. He had violent headaches, bleeding hemorrhoids, a disfiguring and maddening eczema, recurring military fever (would this be malaria?) and cardiac rheumatism which sounds like rheumatic fever with its cruel joint pains. Physical pain was not his only suffering. He had enemies within the Church as well, the jealous, the suspicious, the irritated. Jealous of his friendship with the Pope, they did their best to ruin it. They calumniated him and, that failing, intercepted their letters to one another. When Pius IX did not hear from him, he complained: "Don Bosco does not write me any longer." And when Don Bosco did not hear from Pius IX, he wondered: "His Holiness does not answer my letters." The Pope died without discovering the ruse.

Then there was the devil who works hard in the making of any saint. He used the same means to try Don Bosco as he did to try the Curé d'Ars. He attacked the priest with uproars, the noise of wild storms, of thundering cavalry, of chopping wood. Don Bosco's furniture was flung about his room, his bed overturned, his bedclothes torn. Tongues of fire leaped from the coal stove to menace him, the devil sat on his face and brushed it with an icy brush. He picked Don Bosco up by the shoulders and dragged him about, tramped on him, turned wild animals against him — bears, tigers, serpents — and even took the form of a dragon, lashing about the room with writhing, scaly limbs. The frightened boys listened at the door, helpless. His friends saw him reappear each morning, exhausted, holloweyed, white as paper. They begged him to exorcise the devil but he shook his head, no. The devil would only go off and bother his boys; better to let him be busy here. What did the devil want? "Oh — just pray." Finally he was rid of him — but he never said how it was accomplished.

Added to all this there were the deaths of his two best friends, Don Cafasso and Don Borel. Even saints mourn the loss of the ones they love.

He had already established fifteen houses for his boys in Italy, three in France and one in Spain, when he had another dream; this time about homeless girls. He had never allowed himself to have any but the slightest contact with girls and women for the sake of protecting his chastity against temptation. Now he dreamed he saw little girls playing wildly in the streets. They thronged about him crying out: "Take care of us too, Don Bosco." He turned aside. They begged again. He told them to have faith — God would provide. Then his Lady appeared. *"These are my children also. Take them. I give them to you."* That is how he came to organize the Congregation of Daughters of Mary, Help of Christians to care for girls. And he formed an organization of lay helpers, the Union of Salesian Co-Operators, to help him with his children.

There were missionaries to be sent — to Tierra del Fuego, to Paraguay, to the Congo, the Indies, Thailand, China, Japan. There were cures — which he said he had nothing to do with but which belonged to Our Lady: a paralyzed woman, a blind child, a banker, a bishop, a general officer, a small boy, son of an Italian noble, many more. There were travels all over Europe to raise money, to build, to speak, to witness. He was always accessible. He appeared whenever he could, wherever he was asked. He let himself be photographed and he autographed the photographs. He let the people see him, touch him and, just as with Bernadette, they were forever snipping pieces from his soutane, stealing his handkerchief, filching little possessions to venerate as relics. He laughed; *he* was no saint but if it helped God's cause for him to tolerate such nonsense, then he was all for helping God's cause. He had lost the sight of one eye now, and was almost blind in the other. He could walk only with a cane.

Then one day he could go no longer. After years of driving himself, never sleeping more than five hours a night, traveling thousands upon thousands of miles, his poor body could no longer support him long enough to say Mass. He, who had been seen one day at Mass elevated off the floor in ecstasy, was reduced to sitting and watching and taking Holy Communion with the others. Leo XIII, dear friend, asked whom he chose for his successor and it was Michael Rua — the little boy of the halved card.

He was seventy-three and paralyzed and on his death bed. His sons wept and prayed and once more, as long ago, stormed heaven for his recovery. But this time he refused to ask for it himself. He was burned out. It was time for him to see God. He died on January 31, 1888.

What a marvelous saint. He was priest, teacher, writer, preacher, builder, confessor, virgin — and he spent himself utterly teaching children to love God. *That is what parents must do — spend themselves teaching their children to know and to love God.*

3

DOMINIC SAVIO
SCHOOLBOY SAINT

IF SOMEONE recommended St. Dominic Savio to me because he was an ordinary boy like all other boys, like our six boys, and said, "This is the saint for you people," and I should read his life to see, I should discover he is not at all like our boys — who are like ordinary boys — and I should drop him in discouragement. Of what use to us would be a saint who had no faults? We have lots of faults and the key to sanctity is not to be discovered, for the likes of us, in the faultlessness of saints but in the ways they overcame their faults. This is how I should feel if someone recommended Dominic Savio as "just an average, ordinary boy."

He was not. He was an extraordinary boy, not because he had extraordinary brains or talent but because God gave him extraordinary graces. He loved God and being good right from the beginning with a kind of passion. St. John Bosco said of him, "In the life of Dominic Savio you see *innate virtue* cultivated up to heroism during his whole life." Even *he* thought Dominic was extraordinary, as you see when you learn Don John believed that "in general children younger than twelve years of age are neither capable of great virtue nor of great evil." Well! That's encouraging, coming from a saint who knew thousands of children. Our children, at least, are not hopeless. They are simply like most other children! Knowing that all are supposed to be saints, this indicates that our children may make acts of love and virtue which will merit them an increase of grace and, coming to know and love the saints, may imitate them and pray as eagerly for the grace of sanctity.

If we do not understand this, a saint like Dominic Savio is apt to irritate more than help. He appears to be a goody-goody who was never tempted to be bad, and what's so wonderful about that? He may seem to have attained sanctity without trying. Did he simply fall into it? If so, this whole thing is quite unfair.

This isn't good theology, of course, but children's often isn't and we must be able to explain. The best answer is that it doesn't make any difference how it was with Dominic because we are *we,* not Dominic, and we are only going to be happy doing what God created *us* to do. The point to be made about Dominic is that God raised him to sanctity in the life school children live. His gift was extraordinary grace and his life shows us how to use perfectly the graces given to us — for although in one respect he was different, he was not called to do anything but what our children are also called to do.

He was born April 2, 1842, in Castelnuova, the second in a family of ten. Because Dominic was one of the "sons" of St. John Bosco, it is easy to forget that he had twelve years of preparation in his family. Saints must be given their due but such a boy could not be molded in sanctity in only three years, even by a saint, if the process had not started at home. Dominic Savio's story begins at home.

He was a sweet-tempered little boy, open and eager, and from the things he did and was permitted to do, one discovers much about his parents. They were peasants and poor and the Faith was their rule of life, the imitation of Christ their aim. Such parents are powerful in the forming of a child. Dominic accepted all he was taught in simple faith and tried to do as he saw his parents do. The love of Jesus and Mary were absolute realities to him, to offend God was a sin and sin was the worst thing possible. This is the simplicity we must recover if we would see the kingdom of heaven. Such children and saints see things clearly: God is God, right is right, wrong is wrong, black is black and white is white.

One night the Savios had a guest for dinner who would not say (at least did not say) Grace. Dominic got down from the table without saying a word and would not eat his dinner. Later he answered his parents' questions by saying he could not eat with a man who would not thank God for his food. Such a person, he said, was acting like an animal.

If this sounds just a trifle precious, it is because we have lost simplicity. Children, even *our* children, have this simplicity in the early years. Once we had guests and one very small child interrupted the grown-ups' conversation to ask a guest: "Do you want to go to heaven when you die?" He had just learned that this is why *he* is here and it was all-important. If it was why everyone is here, did everyone know it? Our guests quite possibly did not know it and although they laughed at the remark and thought it amusing, it was probably the most important question put that night. It is believable that a child who said solemn and reverent Grace every night would be scandalized by a man who wouldn't. We should at least be saddened — but we have got so used to it.

Charles and Brigid Savio doted on their children. Their only luxury was family affection and this warmed the little boy's heart. Their love and God's love secured him, and the fact that times were hard and their living poor had little effect on this security. To love God and have perfect faith keeps anxiety in its place. They moved to Riva and then to Murialdo, where Charles Savio finally found work as a blacksmith.

At the age of five, Dominic was walking alone to daily Mass. If the doors were not yet opened, he knelt on the steps of the church. Even if there were ice and snow, he waited, kneeling.

This certainly our children would not do, and I, for one,

would not ask them to do it. It is not a sin *not* to kneel on the church steps in ice and snow. God gave Dominic the *desire* to do it. Here is the difference between this boy and ours. God gave him in abundance graces He did not give to ours. Curiously, when we understand this we see that, aside from these extraordinary graces, he *was* an ordinary boy.

One wonders — why does God do this sort of thing? Because He wanted, in this instance, a *boy* saint, not a boy who would become a *man* saint. He wants many boy saints, so He made of this one a model. If, by the way, Dominic loved God so much he wanted to kneel in the ice and snow, we should rejoice, because it gave Him great honor and glory. But it was not the thing that made him a saint. St. Catherine of Siena drank the water with which she washed the leper woman, but that is not for us. It was a special grace God sent to St. Catherine. He will send us *our* kind. So much for Dominic and the kneeling in the ice and snow. It was a lovely thing to do.

He served Mass almost daily. He was so small it seemed that it should be impossible for him to stagger across the altar with the missal, but he managed. According to custom, he went to Confession often although he had not made his First Communion. The customary age for receiving this sacrament was then twelve, but Dominic's pastor and the priests he consulted agreed that this child had an unusual desire for the sacrament, was remarkably well-prepared, and should be allowed to receive it at the age of seven.

The night before his First Communion he begged his mother's pardon for all his offenses against her and promised solemnly to be good, to study hard, to be obedient and respectful from that time on, and Brigid, like all mothers, wept because Dominic was so little and so good and it was such a great and solemn occasion.

The day of his First Communion he wrote some resolutions which were to rule his life perfectly for the eight years left until his death.

Resolutions which I, Dominic Savio, took at the age of seven on my First Communion Day.

1. I will go to Confession and Communion as often as my Confessor allows.
2. I will keep holy the feast days.
3. My friends shall be Jesus and Mary.
4. Death — but not sin.[1]

Dominic finished the primary grades in Murialdo and for further study it was necessary to go to Castelnuova. He wished he could fly. Failing that, he walked to school in the morning, home for lunch, back after lunch, home in the afternoon, a total of eight miles a day every day in all kinds of weather. An old man who saw him wondered at such a small boy trudging along day after day and asked one time if he weren't a little afraid to walk so far alone. "I am not alone. My Guardian Angel is with me." But it must be so tiring, four times a day in all kinds of weather! "Nothing is tiring if you have a Master who pays you well." What master, pray, paid him for this trudging? "God. He repays even a cup of water given for His sake." The old man shook his head. He would tell the story over and over and the remark that a boy as serious and as dedicated as that would be heard from one day!

The famous swimming episode took place about this time. Some of his school friends suggested swimming and Dominic went with them down to the river. They were having the usual noisy time when suddenly Dominic realized the tone of their fun had changed and some of the boys were making vulgar remarks about their bodies. They used disgusting words. They made obscene gestures. He was stunned. Someone noticed the look on his face and laughed uneasily. What was the matter with *him?* Dominic retorted — what was the matter with *them!* Oh — *that.* Well they couldn't spend *all* their time in church. Exactly, and they didn't have to. Their bodies were temples of

[1] St. John Bosco, *Life of St. Dominic Savio* (Paterson, N.J.: Salesiana Publishing Co.), p. 7.

the Holy Spirit in and out of church. How dare they speak of them like that! The boys looked uncomfortable.

Dominic put on his clothes and went home. He felt sick. It was the first time sin had come so close. He thought of his resolution *Death but not sin,* of his friends Jesus and Mary, and it made him shiver. Sin could be simple. It could be merely a matter of choosing to go along with the rest. But they were nice boys — he had *thought.* They were his friends. Some were in his class. They didn't look evil. Swimming shouldn't be an occasion of sin. It had been. Once he had thought it would be easy not to sin if you didn't want to — but maybe he was wrong. Maybe it was going to be hard. It would mean making a lot of choices about friends and places and things. He prayed desperately for the grace never to sin.

This is a story for parents to tell in preparation for the day when their children will meet, at last, obscenity in all its ancient forms. They will meet it: on the school bus, in the washroom, on the playground, in the neighborhood. They must be prepared. Dominic met it in the same places and, while we need not expect our children to imitate his kneeling in the ice and snow, they are expected to resist temptations to impurity *exactly* as he did. There is nothing else for a Christian to do. For some boys and girls resistance is not easy. They are tempted to go along with the rest for a number of reasons: to be popular, to be "regular," to be a good sport, all the rest. God raised up this boy, who resisted the temptation to "go along," for their sake. There is no other choice. He is a model who shows boys and girls that *this is what one must do.*

One of the reasons Dominic *could* resist temptation was that he had been prepared to do so by his parents. One must take this for granted. His parents and the priests who taught him in school had formed him into what he was at that moment. We may admit to misgivings about whether our own children will resist when the time comes, but one thing we can do before it comes is prepare them. How?

First, they must understand that temptation is not irresistible.

It is a test for the will. Each time they resist their wills are stronger and more ready for the next battle. Each "no" to temptation is an act of virtue and makes the particular virtue stronger in their souls. They need to be reminded of this over and over because the *effect* of such resistance is not visible immediately, nor does there follow inevitably the taste of victory. Often one is conscious only that he has somehow been done out of something. The devil is extremely clever at making resistance to temptation seem either hopeless, or thankless, and it is our business to explain the process of grace strengthening resistance, and resistance strengthening virtue.

They must understand that the soul has a life as the body has. It is a poor ball player who does not get out and pitch, catch, bat, field. He must work constantly to develop the strength and skill he longs to display. One will make a poor Christian if he does not *practice* as the athlete practices, the virtues needed to keep him strong and holy, resisting venial sin that he may not fall into mortal sin and eternal death. The analogy may seem obvious to us but it is extremely forceful to young people universally so sports-minded.

Not only must the soul exercise its virtues (certain of which may be exercised only when God permits temptation) but it must be fed, washed, strengthened, healed when it has fallen into sin. It feeds on sacramental grace. The Holy Eucharist is its food, and holy Penance its cleansing. When this is clear, children understand better why it is so important to go to Confession and Holy Communion as often as possible. The graces of these sacraments are the key to resisting temptation, for, as the body draws its strength from its food, so does the soul — and Christ is the soul's food. Christ in the confessional washes, heals, strengthens, and Christ in the Eucharist feeds and transforms the soul into Christ-likeness.

All the while the family must pray constantly, humbly, and it must practice self-denial. All the years of "giving-up" in childhood prepare a boy or girl for the time when temptation to serious sin is going to be a reality. We cannot indulge our children year after year and expect them to be strong in self-discipline. We must help them practice self-denial ahead of time if it is going to be called on later, not only self-denial in what is harmful to their physical health, their cultural development, but self-denial also in the matter of things lawful. One will not be able to say no to a physical appetite like the temptation to impurity if one has never said no to physical appetite — to certain foods one likes, certain things to drink, sometimes to sweets, another time to an entertainment, sometimes the self-denial of "my right," or "my turn," or "my will" or "my choice." We must help them understand that it is as necessary for their wills (and *ours*) to have this exercise as it is for the muscles to have exercise. Because it is an extremely important lesson, we must season it with much love and, having explained it carefully, leave them free to choose their self-denial. If we enforce it, it is not *self*-denial (although it is possible to practice certain "family" disciplines, especially during the penitential seasons, that will be equally beneficial). They will discover for themselves the purity of heart and soul, the real freedom of spirit, that is the fruit of self-denial.

We must encourage them as well by explaining that the difficulty of self-denial will not always be the same. The soul can and will form the habit of self-denial if one keeps at it, and very slowly it will learn to control its movements a bit more easily. Temptation will not disappear, nor the need for a good fight, but at last the land appears familiar. "So! You are here again!" says the soul to temptation. "At last I know you by sight!" Best of all, self-denial is useful not *only* in the matter of resisting sin, but when it is done for the love of God it is open sesame to a deeper, higher, more glorious adventure with God.

What would be some specific examples of self-denial that children might practice — even secretly, once they have received the idea? It is better to suggest a number of possible things than one thing to be done indefinitely, for weakness in such resolves can lead to severe scruples and then the last is worse than the first. Perhaps at a meal one might, without indicating to anyone, not use salt on her food. Perhaps at another meal, one might not butter his bread. Perhaps the next day in school a thirsty boy might glance at the clock, and postpone a drink for a half hour. Still another child might eat more of what he did not like and less of what he did at each meal for several days. The silent, secret self-denials are powerful, for so many of the temptations to sin come at silent, secret times. We must not fight the battle in full view of an appreciative audience and expect it to effect great character changes. It is too easy to play at being heroic. And we must not permit a bright enthusiasm for the idea to peter out gradually and be forgotten. We must return again and again, gently and with love, to this matter — and by our own example encourage our children.

All this must be crowned by Our Lady. No struggle to resist temptation or to soar to the heights will succeed without her. Don Bosco asked Dominic in a dream, after the boy's death, what gave him the greatest satisfaction at the hour of his death: "Was it the virtue of purity, or perhaps the hope of heaven?"

"In part — but really it was the help of the lovable Mother of God. Tell your boys that. . . ."

Indeed, parents *must* tell their children that without Our Lady the best attempts will fail. The soul receives all its graces from the hands of Our Lady.

The poverty of his father's work forced the Savios to move again, this time to Mondonio. Everywhere he went, Dominic's schoolmasters were impressed with him. He was good, sincere, diligent, and always pleasing. But something happened in Mondonio which put him in a different light. Someone in the class committed a wrong and the blame was laid on Dominic. A group of boys accused him to the teacher, who berated him violently. He was a hypocrite, pretending to be so virtuous and guilty of such an offense! He deserved to be expelled and, if it were not his first offense, he would be! He had better be sure it was his last. For punishment, he was made to kneel in front of the room.

Dominic said nothing. Some were ashamed of him, some disappointed, and some pleased. It is always comforting to find the model of virtue has feet of clay. All day no one spoke to him. He went home that afternoon alone and came back the next morning the same way. That day at the noon recess, a group of boys went to the teacher, and when Dominic came back to his seat, Father Cugliero called him to the front.

"Why didn't you tell me you were innocent?"

"Because that boy had been in trouble before and would have been expelled. I hoped I would be forgiven because this would be my first fault." He looked embarrassed. "Besides, I remembered Our Lord had once been falsely accused."

Remember that Dominic Savio *had not yet met Don Bosco* when he did this. It means that he learned it from someone else — inevitably his parents, because they were that kind of parents. The sermons he had heard, his reading, the teaching he had had all contributed, but the most powerful force of all had been the teaching of his parents.

This is the kind of thing Christ tells us to do (loving enemies, doing good to those who persecute us) but that we tell ourselves won't work, if we think about it at all. We are too weak or afraid or angry or thoughtless to try it. This is too bad because not only is this the Christ-like thing to do but it is psychologically the soundest thing to do. We must forgive our enemies and do good to those who persecute us or our lives will be a violent tangle of desires for vengeance and frustration for the lack of it. Not only does Christ see what is good for *us* when He tells us what to do, but He sees what is good for our enemy as well. But being wrapped up in self, one seldom stops to consider that *His* concern is for *both* parties. Nothing could have been more surprising or disconcerting to the guilty boys than to have Dominic, the innocent one, accept the blame. It proved he had courage far and above their courage and provided them with a heavy burden of conscience. And

Dominic was quite safe doing it — psychologically speaking — because his motive was love. What one does for love of God is always nourishing to the soul. We never lose when doing things for the love of God.

The question is whether to suggest such a course to children who have had no teaching of it. Could you turn to it cold and recommend it outright to a child beset by persecutors? Would not such a child be filled with resentment and confusion when told he ought not strike back or defend himself against accusation? People like to argue this. That one should be struck by the unworkableness of the idea because "my child would not understand" is no reason for not helping him to understand. We must begin sometime, somewhere. Not all of us have thought it out early enough to begin at the beginning. Some of us must begin translating the Christ-life into terms our children will understand at whatever time we discover it. Christianity would be a poor way of life if it worked only for babies. It can transform us any time we are ready and willing to give ourselves to it. It is never too late.

When one considers teaching this ideal of behavior to a child, one imagines something like this: our child is out playing by himself when he is set upon by tormentors. He does not strike back so they maul him and make him their victim. Is this the desired effect?

This is not a fair speculation. Self-defense is a powerful instinct and, as such, does not need teaching. Some say it does, meaning that certain techniques can be taught (we are talking about children, not wars), yet most of the time even this is reduced to the permission, or encouragement to hit back. Certainly in grievously dangerous situations, or if the invitation to sin should be involved, a child must feel free to defend himself, but this is not usual. Orneriness, piggishness, aggressiveness start most frays and self-defense is not so much needed as self-control. Such imperfect behavior ought not surprise us since it is is inherited from Adam, but certainly we, as the redeemed, are bound to try to master it and to teach our children to master it. It takes most people a lifetime to do this so the sooner they begin, the better.

In the second place, it is pointless to tell or expect a child to do a Christ-like thing if he has no knowledge nor very real love for Christ. This must be carefully cultivated by parents. Love comes first before imitation.

There is need for parents to try to understand the neighborhood personalities, their difficulties, their lacks, home situations, to learn to recognize conflicts in the making and with discretion and love try to avert them when they can. Suggestions for changing play, for creative play, for changing sides, teams and, when the difficulty is not to be surmounted, for changing or removing playmates temporarily can help. Above all, there is need for a sympathetic regard for the *souls* of the troublemakers, who need help, patient teaching, higher ideals. This is hard if it is always *your* child who gets smacked! Nevertheless, much improvement could be made in neighborhood situations if parents would swallow their resentment toward the difficult children and try again to understand, teach, help, love, if they would teach their children to forgive and start loving again. Perhaps God permits such conflicts in *your* yard so this child or that may have *your* help. There are many ways to remedy such evils beside hitting back.

And there must be prayer. Time after time a child will fail in self-control, will rush in with fists flying (as the small John Bosco did) but with prayer and teaching he may one day find the courage to respond to a certain touch of grace and turn the other cheek. Our Lord was concerned with our desire for vengeance when He spoke that line, our fallen need for getting even. What we must develop in ourselves and our children — if we would understand why He said it — is the Christ-mind which sees the pity of the soul who strikes out to hurt and trouble others. How help him? Striking back may stay him for a while but it will not help him as much as love and prayer and sacrifice. We need not reason: "I would like to teach this to my child but I dare not since he is too young to grasp it perfectly and he will only become a victim." Rarely will he fail to give blow for blow — for all the teaching! But if he hears the principle lovingly taught to him in a hundred different ways as a hundred occasions suggest, one day he will have the courage to try. When and if he finally succeeds he will be stronger than he was before, and freer, because it is the strong who master self-control, not the weak. He will discover a new dimension in his relation to everyone and a thousand bits of wisdom will fall into place; he will leap one of the obstacles between himself and God. What would be the first step in teaching it? Perhaps it would be taken at family prayer, with the inclusion of the petition: "Please, Blessed Mother, help us not to love ourselves so much; please help us not to want our own way."

It has worked when it has been tried. What would Dominic Savio have done with the suffering that accompanied his turning the other cheek (there *is* suffering — the kind that goes with cutting away self-love) but pray for the boys who had accused him? The next day they confessed. Suppose they had not? They *did* — but suppose they had not. Our Lord values meekness for itself alone. "Blessed are the meek, for they shall inherit the land." "Learn of me, because I am meek and humble of heart: and you shall find rest for your souls." Meekness has its own rich rewards.

This incident in St. Dominic Savio's life is a challenge for all children. It shows a boy handling a fairly ordinary situation in the perfect way — and it is imitable.

Father Cugliero, his teacher, spoke to Don Bosco about this boy and they finally met in 1854 when Dominic was twelve. Don Bosco saw the beauty of his spirit, liked him immediately and it was agreed he would go to study at his Oratory of St. Francis de Sales.

At the new school, Dominic made friends easily. Goodness is always attractive. It is cheerful, polite, never sissified. Because he was well-liked as well as studious, his teachers often put unruly boys next to him in class knowing he could make them behave by his example and friendship. During his first year an altercation arose between two of them which he settled in a striking way.

Two of his classmates had quarreled and vowed to finish it off by throwing stones. It had started with name-calling, progressed to vile language and insults, and finally both boys were in a fury. Dominic tried to reason with them but they were older and bigger and would not listen. He told them they would break the Fifth Commandment if they persisted but they did not care. He wrote notes warning them he would tell their teachers, who would tell their parents, and they would be expelled, but the boys ignored the notes. He prayed — and God sent him an idea.

The day of the duel he waited for them after school and was permitted to go along on one condition: he must not try to stop the fight, trick them or call anyone. They got to the lot, collected their stones and were about to begin when Dominic stepped between them. He held up a small crucifix which he wore at his neck and said: "You must look at this crucifix and say, 'Jesus was innocent and died forgiving his murderers. I am a sinner and I am going to offend Him by wilful revenge.' "

The boys were stunned. He knelt before one. "Now start by throwing the first stone at me." The boy gaped. But that was silly. He had nothing against Dominic. Dominic was his friend. Dominic ran to the other boy and begged the same and the boy's reply was the same. "You! Why you? I wouldn't throw stones at *you!* I don't want to hurt *you.* I'll fight anyone who does!"

Dominic stood. "You are fools. You have enough courage to fight each other and to fight to save me, but you haven't enough courage to fight to save your souls! Christ *died* to save them. You haven't even the courage to forgive stupid insults and names. You'd rather save face than save your souls!"

One of the boys told about it later. "By that time I was shaking . . . to have forced a good friend like Dominic to go to that extreme to keep me from serious sin!" He forgave the other boy and asked Dominic what priest would hear his confession. If the two had not told the story long after, it would not be known. Dominic never told.[2]

At this time classes were not held in the Oratory, which housed the boys, but further into the city of Turin. The walk to and from class offered the same temptations boys meet today on the city streets and Dominic saw this. He tried to keep his eyes and ears from being avenues of temptation and sin. Although he kept clear of boys who were rowdy in the streets, who hung around the street corners, he was tempted, nevertheless, by the frequent suggestion to cut school. Most of the time he said he would rather get his work done, but once he agreed to go. He had gone but a short distance when he stopped. "I'm going back. This is wrong and I'm sorry I said I'd go. And if you ever ask me to go again, you'll not be *my* friends."

The astounding effect of this was that the whole crew turned around and returned to school with him. No one ever tried to get him to "hook" again. The strong and the right-minded have the obligation to lead because the weak are always looking for leaders. What great good can be done when the strong are also *good* and *will* lead.

By the end of the year Dominic was at the head of his class. "He studied hard as a duty of conscience, not to beat his classmates," wrote Father Michael Rua, a contemporary and, after the death of Don Bosco, head of the Congregation of Salesians.

It was after Don Bosco preached a sermon on being a saint that Dominic began to change. He was not as gay as before. He did not join in recreation as often. He smiled less. Don Bosco asked what was wrong. Dominic replied that he wanted to be a saint — although he wasn't quite sure how to go about it. The priest assured him that one of the things a saint had to do was be happy — no gloomy saints! Not long afterward, some of the boys told Don Bosco that Dominic was sick. He went to his

[2] Adapted from St. John Bosco, *The Life of Dominic Savio.*

room and found him shivering in bed, covered only by thin cotton blankets. "Where are your winter blankets?" He wasn't using them. No? "Why not?" Because he wanted to be a saint and one had to do penance. Don Bosco exclaimed. Did he want to get pneumonia? That's what he'd get for his penance! The winter blankets were distributed to be used in the wintertime. "Put the winter blankets on your bed!" Dominic asked, what about penance? He could do other penance. He was to be obedient to the rules of the school.

It was not long after that the boys came to Don Bosco again with news of Savio. "Wait till you see his bed!" The priest went to his room. Under the blankets were boards and on the boards gravel, tacks, nails. "What are you trying to do now — ruin the blankets?" No — it was penance again.

Don Bosco spoke gently: "First take this junk out of here and throw it where it belongs, and I will tell you about penance." There followed the whole way of perfection designed for schoolchildren.

"Listen, my boy. You are a schoolboy, not a hermit; so do the penance of a schoolboy. Your penance is to fulfil the duties, all of them, of *your* state. Do this perfectly and you will see the penance it is. There are companions who rub you the wrong way: seek them out and make much of them. There are those who are vulgar or are downright rude to you: forgive them from the bottom of your heart. Then there is the food and drink that you do not like: don't waste it. There are some subjects in class that you like less than others: don't neglect them. Other boys are chosen before you for favorite tasks in chapel: be humble about it. You find the weather is too hot, too cold, or too wet, or too dry: thank God for all of it. Then there is your internal weather — your moods, now bright and golden, now blue; ignore them all. Life is full of chances for you to show Jesus that you love Him above everything: seize these chances as they come along. If He wants you to be some kind of special martyr or hermit or something, you shall know quite soon enough —

but only through obedience. Obedience is your greatest possible sacrifice." [3]

Dominic understood at last. From that time on he practiced obedience in all things. Don Bosco noticed and kept a record of the things he did about which Dominic said nothing. In the winter he had badly chapped hands; he took no care of them and wore no gloves or mittens. The food at the Oratory was dull, often poor. There was money for nothing but the bare necessities, and sometimes even they were lacking. He ate more of what he did not like and less of what he did. He ate less than he wanted of everything. When the others had left the table, he cleared the dishes away and ate what was left on the plates, partly because he hated waste and partly as a mortification, to be rid of self-love. He was consistently gentle with his school fellows. Once a boy mistook this for weakness and after picking on him with no result, started to hit him. Dominic became angry but did not hit back. "Look, you have hit me for no good reason. This time I forgive you — but see that you do not do it again!" Could we ask for a better example of *how* a child might behave in such a situation once he understands the principle behind Christian meekness, turning the other cheek? Once again it had the startling effect of great strength and made the offense of the other boy look like weakness. Dominic practiced the custody of his eyes and his ears by deliberately choosing what *not* to look at, what *not* to hear. When asked why he did this, he answered — a little wisely — one time: "Oh, I am saving my eyes to look at Our Lady."

But he had a sense of humor. Once someone made a funny remark in class and everyone roared but Dominic, whose mind was a million miles away. Five minutes later he reacted to the joke, starting to howl. The master said sternly: "Savio! You may finish your laugh in the corner." And he did.

He had a prayer custom we might adapt for certain of Our Lady's feasts in the family. Shortly after he arrived at the Oratory,

[3] Daniel Higgins, *The Challenge* (Paterson, N.J.: Salesiana Publishing Co.), p. 58.

the dogma of the Immaculate Conception was proclaimed and everyone was planning to celebrate the feast. Nine days beforehand, Dominic wrote nine different virtues on nine slips of paper and put them in a box. Daily he drew out one, prayed to Our Lady for an increase of that virtue and tried to practice it all day. On the feast he renewed his First Communion promises before her statue. "O, Mary, I give you my heart; make it yours forever. Jesus, Mary, be my friends. I beg you both to let me die rather than commit a single sin." We might imitate Dominic's preparation for this feast and celebrate the day by consecrating the family to the Immaculate Heart of Mary.

One morning Don Bosco turned from the altar at Mass to distribute Holy Communion and was shocked to see there was not one boy at the Communion rail. The aftermath of this was the Immaculate Conception Sodality, formed by Dominic and some of his friends. Their immediate goal was to get everybody in the school to Holy Communion on Christmas, but their ultimate aim was to promote devotion among the boys to the Blessed Sacrament and to Mary Immaculate. Don Bosco had said to Dominic that boys had entrée to places and hearts where even priests could not go. Boys could do things even priests could not do. What? They could *play* — with other boys, making it an apostolate to befriend boys who needed friendship, good example, prayers and encouragement.

This idea intrigued the members of the sodality and, from among the difficult boys in the school, each chose a list of "clients" on whom they would work, first by *prayer,* second by *the sacrifices of an exact student life,* and third by *play.* If a boy played good ball, they played ball with him and praised him, were his friends. If he ran well, they joined him at that. If he sang, jumped, joked well, whittled, did feats of strength, whatever game or recreation he liked best, they joined him at it, did their best, lost — if so — cheerfully, and praised the other boy for his accomplishments. The sodalist gave good example, was a good companion, and casually, without seeming to press, began to suggest, when the time was right, that the other boy go to the sacraments with the rest. They worked on boys who never knew they were being worked on. They prayed for them, sacrificed for them, lived their lives for them and at midnight Mass the following Christmas eve, every boy in the school went to Holy Communion of his own free will.

This apostolate of child to child, boy to boy and girl to girl, is one of the things God shows us in Dominic Savio's life. There is no time when one becomes of age for the lay apostolate. As soon as he is baptized, every member of the Mystical Body, having become one with Christ, inherits a work to do. Confirmation, the sacrament of "spiritual adulthood," marks the precise moment when one takes his place in the ranks of grown-up Christians, but there is no time when one is useless or not needed. It is thrilling for a child to discover *that* he is needed, *how* he is needed. This secret working with Christ for the souls of others is something he gives himself to eagerly if we encourage it.

Dominic grew in holiness and the life of the spirit possessed him more and more. He was frequently in ecstasy (he called these "distractions"). One morning after Mass he remained for a thanksgiving in the chapel, did not show up for breakfast, class or lunch. When the others discovered him missing, they searched in vain until Don Bosco heard their talk and guessed where he was. Going into the chapel, he found him there before the tabernacle, gazing at it. He was silent, unmoving. Don Bosco called but he did not hear. He touched him. He was like stone. He shook him. Dominic turned suddenly: "Oh — is Mass over already?" Don Bosco showed him his watch. It was two o'clock in the afternoon.

Another time Don Bosco was in the sacristy finishing his thanksgiving after Mass when he heard someone talking in the sanctuary. He went out and found Dominic standing before the altar speaking, listening, speaking again. ". . . I love You and I want to love You till death. If you see that I am going to commit a sin, make me die first. Death but not sin!"

When Dominic had first come to the Oratory, Don Bosco's

mother, Mamma Margaret, as she was known to the boys, said to her son: "You have many good boys here but none are better than Savio." She would know. She had raised a saint herself.

Several times Dominic had mysterious knowledge of souls in need of the Last Sacraments. Sometimes he would leave recreation in the middle of a game, and when asked he told Don Bosco: "Those distractions — they come over me . . . and I have to walk away so I won't say things the boys will laugh at."

Once he begged permission to go home for a day. He arrived to find his mother dying in childbirth. Almost all hope for her was gone. He put a "sort of green scapular" about her neck and said: "I am going now. You will be all right." She bore her child and lived. Dominic told Don Bosco on his return: "My mother is cured now. Our Lady made her well."

From time to time he would say that he wished he could see the Pope before he died. Don Bosco asked him why. It seemed that he had had a vision after Holy Communion one morning. He saw a vast plain full of people and blanketed with fog. They walked like people stumbling in the dark. A voice said: "This is England." He was about to ask questions when he saw Pius IX, bearing a bright torch in his hands, striding through the crowd. As he walked the fog cleared before the light of the torch and the people were suddenly in daylight. A voice said: "This torch is the Catholic religion which will bring light to the English." When Don Bosco was in Rome in 1858, he told Pope Pius IX of Dominic's vision and the Pope listened with great interest. "This encourages me to continue working for England. . . ."

All the while Dominic's health was failing. It was finally recommended that he go home for a rest. He hated to leave the Oratory, knowing somehow that he would never come back. His concern was over his apparent uselessness as an invalid. What could a sick boy do to win merit from God? Don Bosco told him: "Offer God your sufferings." What else? "Offer God your life." What if the devil tempted him at the end? "Tell him you have already sold your soul to Jesus, Who has bought it with His Blood. If he keeps bothering you, ask him what *he* has done for your soul? Jesus has died to free you from sin and take you to heaven."

Thus he left the Oratory, saying good-bye with a finality that surprised his friends, asking their prayers and giving away all his possessions. He did not look as if he were dying, but once at home he rapidly grew weaker. The doctor diagnosed inflammation of the lungs and recommended bleeding. His parents, certain that he would improve with the bleeding, were disturbed when he asked for Viaticum but called the priest to please him. Ten times he was bled and he said nothing, although bleeding was painful and distressing to see — and he insisted on watching it. It only hastened his death. Though both the doctor and his parents were certain he would rally, Dominic declared he was dying and asked for the last anointing. Before the priest performed the rite, Dominic prayed: "My God, forgive me my sins. I love You and I want to love You forever. May this sacrament, which You are letting me receive, cancel all the sins I have committed by sight and hearing, and by my mouth, hands and feet. May my body and soul be sanctified by Your Holy Passion. Amen."

For a half hour after the priest left, he rested; then he opened his eyes and said to his parents, "It is time. Take my prayer book and read the prayers for a happy death." His father, weeping, read the prayers aloud and Dominic repeated them after him. When the prayers were ended, he was silent for a while, then slowly he looked about, smiled at his father, said good-by — then: "Oh — what a beautiful thing I see!" He was fifteen.

4

ST. MARIA GORETTI

MODEL OF CHASTITY

THERE IS the barest little bit known about Maria Goretti's life. Perhaps this is because it was the barest little life. Even with her mother giving the facts, only a little has been said. It could be written down in a paragraph. There were almost twelve years, surely filled with things that would help us raise our own children, yet it seems hardly any of it is known. That is odd, when she was to die a martyr and be known as the chaste patroness of modern youth. But then there are no signs posted ahead of time which say: "This way to the home of a future martyr." No one is given the insight to follow martyrs about with a pad and pencil and jot down the kind of things they say and do before they become martyrs. The challenge in such a life as Maria Goretti's is to discover, knowing how it ended, what it was made of, because martyrdom and sanctity are never an accident. They are earned.

She was born in 1890 and she died in 1902, when she was a little less than twelve years old. If she had lived she would be sixty-six today. But we may not think of her as anything but a little less than twelve. Time and years and birthdays as we celebrate them are only for this world. There is no time in the next. Maria is eternally a little less than twelve.

Her mother was orphaned at five and spent all her growing-up years working as a helper in the various families where she stayed. That she persevered to a chaste nineteen before she met and loved Luigi Goretti says much of her. Luigi was a farmer, young, sturdy, handsome, and Assunta loved him fiercely all her life. The early years of their marriage — the beginning of their family — were spent in Corinaldo, a spot both of them loved and were sad to leave. But they were poor and such a bit of land could not support them, lovely as it was. So they moved, then moved again finally to Ferriere di Conca to live in a *cascina antica* — an old dairy barn — in the most pestilent area in all Italy at that time, the undrained Pontine marshes.

They were so poor that even as tenant farmers they could not manage their holding without the help of another family, the Giovanni Serenellis. Giovanni Serenelli was a crook ten different ways, and had maneuvered all the agreements with the owner so that everything was in his name. It was not to the liking of either Luigi or Assunta that they had to share the land, much less their home, with the Serenellis.

Giovanni Serenelli was a widower. His wife had died after a series of catastrophic events beginning with the nervous breakdown of a son in the seminary. In her derangement following this shock, she was found one day by another son trying to drown her youngest, Alessandro, in a well. It was her pathetic plea that "It is better for him to die now than to live and suffer." So they took Signora Serenelli away, leaving the five-year-old Alessandro without a mother. He had loved her very much. Long years afterwards he said: "After my mother attempted to take my life, they locked her up. I loved my mother. She was a very good woman. I missed her terribly. That was the beginning of all my troubles." [1]

Alessandro went to live with his father and the Gorettis after spending several years with a married sister and her family. Nearby was the vice-ridden neighborhood of the waterfront. Unlike Maria, he was neither illiterate nor innocent when he went to farming with his father, and what he left behind in the

[1] Alfred MacConastair, C.P. "Convict Number 3142," *The Sign,* Jan. 1951.

way of amusement, his father made up for with indecent literature. The boy bore up under the rigor and boredom of their bleak existence with the help of his dirty magazines, while the father had his bottle.

These were the people who shared the Goretti's home. This is amazing. This child Maria had absolutely none of the things our society insists are necessary if one is to turn out even half well. Her environment was poor. Her education was nil. Her diet dwindled to starvation rations the last two years of her life. Her responsibilities were far above what is considered bearable for a ten-year-old, who at that age had to take over the role of mother while her mother took over the role of father. For Luigi, broken with the hard work and infectious air of the marches, died of combined typhoid, malaria, meningitis and pneumonia when Maria was ten. She had no clothes to speak of, no play to speak of, and, long before it was time for it to end, she had no childhood to speak of. Maria Goretti had absolutely nothing — unless, of course, you remember that she had the love of God. God made Maria out of His own divine love, for Himself alone, and came to dwell in her at Baptism, strengthen her at Confirmation and finally — but only four times — to be her food in Holy Communion. Maria Goretti had nothing but God. She learned about Him from a mother who could neither read nor write and from the sermons of the parish priest whose Sunday morning talks were all she ever had of formal teaching until she prepared, at ten, for her First Communion.

Heaven forbid that anyone think, reading this or any other life of St. Maria Goretti, that the key to sanctity is illiteracy. What God is showing us, among other things, with the life of this saint is that He alone *can* be quite enough. He is showing us that having nothing, we *do* have all things in Him. We need to know this saint in order to appreciate with a holy fear just how much we let *things* get in the way of what we are here for.

The whole point of this life on earth is to do God's will. This is starkly evident in the life of Maria Goretti. The Goretti's poverty served this end. More than poverty, it was destitution that insistently taught them that there was nowhere to go, no one to turn to but God. Maria learned this so well that it was she who repeated the familiar encouragements she had heard from her father, when they were needed by her mother: At least they had their health; divine Providence would help them; they would be all right.

Among the things God has given us to use in doing His will are our bodies. Maria learned God's will in respect to her body and the bodies of others. This is the lesson she teaches: our bodies are good and holy and have a high purpose, and they are to be used only for God. There is nowhere any mention of a "vow" in the life of this saint. There is nothing to lead anyone to suspect she would have grown up to become a nun. She was beautiful, as Assunta and her neighbors have said, but either she did not know it or, if she did, thought little about it. Unlike the parents of St. Thérèse of Lisieux, her parents had had no thought of entering religion, but, meeting, had fallen in love instantly. Theirs was a devoted love affair that left an indelible mark on the lives of their children. Human love, the sacrament of marriage, the bearing of babies were things Maria knew about from the example and teaching of her parents. She matured very early, as do all youngsters in southern Europe, and at only eleven her young figure was beginning to show its womanliness. Assunta, as do all good mothers, anticipated and explained things ahead of time and warned her against certain kinds of company, conversations, occasions. Yet all the time the viper in this affair was living in the bosom of the family and Assunta did not know it.

Alessandro *seemed* to be good enough. He went to Mass. He used no unbecoming language. He was present often enough at the family Rosary in the evenings. Only one thing was strange: he seemed not to know how to enjoy himself. He did not seek the normal recreations of a boy of eighteen. Assunta noticed but did not notice. These things she saw out of the corner of her eye, but he gave her no trouble so he was no cause for concern.

Until the day she went in to clean his room and saw the pictures he had put on the wall. She was shocked, horrified, disgusted. How dare he, in their home, with their children about?

"If you don't like them, don't look at them." And her protests came to nothing. He did not take them down. To the Serenellis Assunta was little more than a slave and Luigi a fool, and Giovanni held the whip.

After Luigi's death, Giovanni outsmarted her at the harvest, leaving her in debt again. He kept the key to the cupboard, leaving her children hungry. He insulted them, cursed, spat, staggered through their life and there was nothing to do but take it. This was the means by which Assunta and Maria died their daily death to self. This was the purification, excruciating but speedy, that God permitted in order that these two souls be prepared for the gift of martyrdom. The mother must willingly surrender the child who would wear the crown. Assunta was teaching her illiterate child, in her illiterate way, how to die — although she did not remotely guess it. She was teaching Maria to do everything for love, for the love of God and His most pure Mother.

As a little girl Maria had heard both from her father and her mother the story of God's love — the story of Creation, the Fall, and the Redemption. As a bit more than a *little* little girl, she told the same stories to her brothers and sisters. God's love was the only reality. The rest was to be endured like a bad dream for love of Him, and one day there would be heaven. She took over the household, therefore, and for love of Him she scrubbed the clothes, the floors, cooked the poor, tasteless meals. She was a pitiful cook with neither experience nor the knack for cooking. She swallowed down the insults and the curses from old Serenelli, and gave more of her food than was necessary to the younger children. Assunta complained to Conte Mazzoleni about the locked cupboard and got a key for herself, and for her pains the insults and the curses were doubled. There was a veritable garden of small daily deaths from which to gather: the dirt and stench of the Serenelli's clothes; the tobacco juice spat everywhere; the profanity, when the names he used were the names of Jesus and Mary; the insults, when — innocent though Maria was — she well knew the meaning of his accusations.

But she thought of the Passion and it gave her strength, and she fled daily to the Madonna as her Sorrowful Mother, and she hung on to her rosary and prayed.

She mended — miles of mending. She rocked babies, fed them, washed them, played with them, kept them out of her mother's way, settled their quarrels for them, taught them their prayers and all the doctrine she had ever learned. She walked miles upon miles, to the store at Conca, to Nettuno to market the doves and the eggs, and finally that last fateful year to the friend at Conca and the priest at Campomorto from whom she learned the Christian doctrine necessary in order to receive her First Holy Communion. She longed for Jesus in Holy Communion.

On the morning of Corpus Christi, May 29, 1902, she went to receive her First Holy Communion. She did not even have a white dress. A new dress, but not a white one, was her gift from her mother. It was wine color with white dots. One neighbor's gift was a pair of shoes, another her lovely veil, another the carefully wrought wreath of flowers. And Assunta clasped about Maria's throat her own coral necklace and presented her with the precious gold earrings Luigi had given her years before. She had prepared herself and her child for this event with every ounce of her energy and love.

That morning before she left for Mass she stood meekly before each member of her family, and Giovanni and Alessandro as well, to beg their pardon for all her offenses, according to the custom.

Assunta was in every way as anxious for this day as Maria. When the Mass was finally over, she watched her child as she remained silent and recollected in her pew after the others had left. She was satisfied. Her Mariettina would be stronger and safer now that she had received Jesus in Holy Communion. She did not know how strong, nor dream how safe.

Maria knew about human love. She knew about the things a mother explains to her daughter when it is time for that marvelous cycle of preparation to begin its monthly course in the body of a young girl. She had seen her mother and father side by side, loving companions. She had seen that they shared the same room, the same bed. She had seen her mother's body heavy with the dignity of motherhood. She undoubtedly knew something of childbirth, and she was used to the sight of mothers nursing their babies. She had some knowledge of the abuses of these great gifts of the body, enough to stand shocked, her face burning, when she heard one of her own companions at First Communion banter shamelessly about these things with a passing boy. She told her mother, and to Assunta's, "Do not listen to such words, nor repeat them," she replied, "I would rather die."

Suddenly one day she knew, with racing fear, that Alessandro's nearness and his compliments and the coaxing in his voice meant all these things put together in a way that was not God's will. She darted away from him, frightened, horrified, and he hissed after her: "If you tell your mother, I will kill you."

Not Alessandro! But he was like her brother! He was already nineteen and she was only a little girl, not yet twelve!

But Alessandro had steadily and surely fed his appetite for lust. He had trained it with his months of reading, gazing, thinking. The mind and the soul are constantly forming habits and Alessandro had formed in his the habit of impurity. He had narrowed the horizons of his imagination until Maria's charming dignity and chaste beauty did not represent to him something to admire and praise, but something to desire and spoil.

Poor Alessandro. Little did he know that in the story of the child he would martyr he would stand for all the boys and girls whose minds and souls have been ravished by dirty literature, pornographic pictures, suggestive movies, indecent entertainments, all the rest. Like so many young people, he became preoccupied more and more with passion and lust because no one had turned his mind in a different direction.

Maria had always told her mother everything, but this time she could not. With so much to worry her, so much insecurity, poverty, cheating, weariness, Assunta had already more than she could bear. And this was so shameful! How could she ever find the words to express it? Maria could not add the last and most dreadful of all worries. They were helplessly entangled in the agreement with Conte Mazzoleni and Serenelli. Their hope lay in one more harvest, one more chance to pay off their debt. Then, somehow, at long last they would return to Corinaldo; Luigi had begged this piteously for them as he lay dying. She could not tell her mother yet.

She watched carefully. She planned so she was never alone with Alessandro. She worked harder and, if it were possible, prayed more. And Alessandro changed. From the silent, un-provocative lad of the past few years, he became surly, whining, accusing, adding his complaints to his father's. He swore at her, criticized, commanded, abused, and she accepted it silently, uncomplainingly. Assunta looked on amazed, curious at the shift in their relationship.

Another time he appeared suddenly at her side, too close, his hands out to her, insinuating. And again she ran away, terrified, but not before she had heard: "If you tell your mother, I will kill you." He meant it. She knew.

From then on it was war between them, though not in any way Assunta recognized. She was too exhausted to notice any-thing. But Maria knew she would die. She was only a little less than twelve and she lived with the knowledge of her death for two, then three, then four weeks. Every morning was the morning she might die. Every afternoon. Every evening. Every parting might be the last time. Every meal, every sleep. Every kiss from Assunta might be the last kiss. Every child tucked in, rocked, blessed, might be the last. Every Mass, every Commun-ion.

Some people go mad waiting like this, but not Maria. She was prepared. Her mind and her soul had formed habits too. Her courage and endurance and sanity were made of the hours and days and weeks of grinding work given to God, the hardship, hunger, damp, sorrow, the prayers, the songs she had sung to the little ones, the patterns she had stitched with her mending, the burned *pasta,* the smell of the scrub water, the slime of the tobacco stains, the shame of those pictures on the walls of that room. All these things she had given to God through the hands of His Blessed Mother, her darling Madonna in front of whose picture she had burned so many stumps of candles, arranged so many bunches of wild flowers, and cried so many tears.

She had been preparing for this years before when she began to learn the story of God's love and that His will alone is perfect; when she learned to respect her body and the bodies of others, to clothe it modestly, to care for it reverently. She had been preparing for this when she saw her mother and the other mothers she knew growing big with life; when she sometimes heard cries in the night and learned that a child had been born; when she saw the women nurse their babies at their breasts. She grew up knowing that God had made her body and the bodies of others for His holy will.

Priests give their bodies to God to do His holy will. She knew this. They have a sacrament of their own, which elevates their gift of life-giving all the way to heaven. *Their* sacrament gives them the power to bring Him down to be the food of the souls begotten by the married.

Maria Goretti knew the married had *their* sacrament, in which to beget with God's help the bodies and souls He has known forever, for whom He waits until each two give their consent. She knew the horror of sin — *any sin, not just sins of the flesh.* The secret of her holiness was that she loved God with her whole heart and whole soul and her neighbor as herself. Not only was she willing to die rather than sin, but she was willing to die rather than permit her neighbor to sin.

It was bound to happen. Alessandro had moved steadily in

the direction of the goal the devil had contrived for him, while Maria had grown in the likeness of Christ.

It was a hot day, the sixth of July, in the year of her First Communion, 1902. It was five weeks after she had received the Body of Christ for the first time.

After lunch, Maria sat mending on the landing of the outside stairs leading to their home with the sleeping baby Teresa beside her. Alessandro was threshing beans in the field with the others. He excused himself and ran to the house. Upstairs he went, past Maria, then downstairs and into the tool shed. Then he ran upstairs again. Would he never be done and get back to the field? She sat with her head down, concentrating on her mending.

"Maria. Come here."

"What do you want?"

"I said come here!"

"Not until you tell me what you want."

He reached out and dragged her into the kitchen. A dagger was in his hand. Now she would consent or he would really kill her this time. But she would not.

"No! Alessandro, no! It is a sin! You will go to hell, Alessandro! God doesn't want it!"

She didn't die *just* defending her purity. She died defending her purity in defense of God's law. Many good girls have died defending themselves but they are not martyrs. Maria Goretti died a martyr.

The neighbors used to call her *poverina,* poor little one. But Maria was not a *poverina.* Who is poor who knows that possessing God she possesses all things, and that in doing His will is all perfection? This is what St. Maria Goretti teaches our children. She is not just a saint of purity. She is a saint whose love and obedience and prayer *bore fruit* in sublime purity. She is the child of parents *who knew they were supposed to raise saints but had no way of knowing they would.* They knew little else but that to do God's will in all things is the secret of sanctity. How well they taught this child!

This is the beginning for us, too, if we would teach our children about chastity. We cannot *start* with chastity. We start with the love of God, with doing His will in all things.

The first lesson in chastity comes when children are very small, and we find they explore their bodies with their hands. Although this is innocent and there is no grave fault, it must be corrected, gently and lovingly, not ignored. And they can begin to pray for the grace to love purity.

Through the many phases of their growing curiosity it must be explained again and again. They learn that it is not amusing to laugh at their bodies busy about bathroom functions. "God is wise and good to give us bodies that keep us well so easily." They learn to guard their conversations, to correct their playmates. "It isn't very nice to laugh about things like that. God made your body and it is good." They learn that a baby is in its mother's body before it is born. God even chose to send His Son to earth in this way, as we recall in the Hail Mary with the words, "blessed is the Fruit of thy womb, Jesus."

They learn that mothers feed their babies from their breast. They learn by seeing it done in the family, or, if it cannot be accomplished there, by seeing it done in other families, or perhaps by seeing it reverently portrayed in works of art. They must learn. "Our Lady fed her Baby that way. She is praised for it in the Gospels."

They learn soon enough that much of the world has a very different attitude.

With regard to modesty in dress, this will come up long before adolescence, especially since fairy tale heroines are so often portrayed in strapless evening gowns with plunging necklines. To little girls, this kind of revealing attire easily becomes synonymous with femininity, with beauty, with being dressed up. It is our task to instill the Christian outlook, helping our daughters, by word and example, to understand that modesty does not detract from femininity, but rather is one of its most beautiful adornments. They will realize this to some extent by instinct, if their sense of modesty has not been destroyed. And if there are older girls who understand these things whom the younger ones look up to with admiration, a huge step forward will have been taken.

The young must learn that we are meant to be, by the right use of our bodies in marriage (if that is to be our vocation), sharers in God's work of creating. From the time they are very young, in the ways best suited to their years, children must be formed in the conviction that God made us male and female for the purpose of raising up children, and that offspring are a blessing. Otherwise they will fall victim to the lamentable state of mind which concerns itself only with the secondary and even self-seeking aspects—pleasure, romance, excitement. That this state of mind is widespread today is all too evident. This must not be if we would raise children who will be strong in chastity. The primary purpose of marriage is to bring forth the souls God loves, the future saints of Heaven.

So—*that* is why we do not approve of ladies who are photographed in immodest dresses and appear on the covers of magazines. "Boy, that's awful! Letting them take her picture in that and then putting it on a magazine. That's not what God wants." This is the understanding of the nine-year-old. This is his preparation for one day choosing, judging, rejecting, certain movies, television shows, magazines, reading *and* companions.

Why do people do such things, if God does not want them to? Because with every beautiful thing God has made that has a right and a good purpose the devil will try to tamper.

"That is why we must be careful to dress modestly, not to wear tight sweaters and blouses, low-cut necklines, suggestive designs in our clothes—not because there is something wrong with a beautiful figure. Indeed there is not. God designed and made each young body and each is good. But the devil will try to make others sin with their eyes and their thoughts, so we must do our part in guarding *their* purity as well as our own."

But in all our struggles as parents with the spirit of the world, the flesh and the devil, we must not rely on our human efforts and strategies. Catholic mothers and fathers know that help from heaven is the "daily bread" of raising Catholic children. We need the Blessed Virgin Mary to give us the courage to protect our children from temptations—even when "everybody else" sees no harm—and to neutralize those temptations that are truly unavoidable. She will also help us with the right words when we have to explain purity to our children. But we must *ask* her, and with real confidence—and every day!

Sooner or later we must explain the monthly process which is the sign of the great creative gift God has given every girl's body. This has been so degraded by undignified terms, by slang words, by innuendoes that strip it of all purpose, that much of womankind is convinced it has no reason beyond being a nuisance. We must be careful to give our daughters the sense of awe and wonder that this great manifestation deserves.

"This process will begin some time soon, dear, and when it does, you must remember that it means you are growing up, becoming a young woman. God has only one end in mind for the whole race of humankind: He wants us to be with Him forever in heaven. In order to have the souls He has planned, they must be born in bodies. They are born of men and women who marry and become parents of families. The mysterious process that will take place soon in your body will be a sign that you would be able to bear a baby. It is a sign of the privilege and duties of motherhood.

"Sometimes there may be a bit of discomfort during menstruation. Sometimes it may be slightly painful. Think of the discomfort or pain as part of the great privilege that goes with being a girl, whom God has given the gift of life-bearing. Guard your body carefully. Be careful of your health as well as your thoughts and conversations. All must be kept in careful custody until God's plan for you is clear. He has had a plan for you since before He made the world, since He has had you in His mind, since forever. If you are to be a mother one day, He already knows who your children will be!"

But what if one is not meant to become a mother? What if one is to become a nun? The gift of life-bearing, so great, so nearly divine, is the young nun's wedding gift to her Beloved, her Bridegroom, the Son of God, not a rejection of it, but an offering of it, in exchange for which she asks to be made fruitful in bringing forth Christ in the many souls she will teach, nurse, watch over, pray for. Man is not a pure spirit without a body. He is body *and* soul and with both he must serve and praise and worship God. Whether in marriage or virginity, whatever his vocation, always he must make God the gift of his body.

Lifelong purity of heart and soul and body is God's law and will for everyone, both children and adults. We will never ever outgrow this virtue. Without purity one could never be a good wife and mother, nor a good husband and father, nor a good priest or good nun, for it is part of every vocation. Thus, the immodest magazines that one unfortunately sees too frequently on newsstands and even at grocery-store checkout counters are not only wrong for children to look at; they are wrong for *anyone* to look at. And "adult" bookstores are no more a proper place for adults than they are for children. God wishes our purity to grow deeper and stronger with each passing year, as we grow in Sanctifying Grace—no matter what age we are.

It is God's will that mothers and fathers who love purity will bring up children who love purity. We can explain to a child, "It will not be hard for you to understand the wisdom and goodness of God's plan if you think about how it is when people get married. First, God lets them know, in answer to their prayers, that the vocation He has planned for them is marriage. He lets them meet each other and get to know each other well. They think about how it would be to marry and live together for the rest of their lives. He helps them understand this is right for them in a number of ways, among them the feelings of love and affection which grow stronger between them all the time. So they pray about it some more, and think about it carefully, and when they decide finally that they want to live together and raise a family for God, they marry.

"Marriage is God's way of making new saints, by entrusting babies to good parents who will, first of all, have them baptized, so that their souls become beautifully pure and holy with Sanctifying Grace. Then good Catholic mothers and fathers will carefully raise their little ones to love God and to avoid sin, all sin—lying, disobedience, immodesty, and anything else that would offend God and dim the beauty of their souls. Many times this means that parents must not allow their child to watch some show, or read some book, or play with some playmate. Parents have a *very* important task, a task that goes far beyond bringing their children into the world and providing food and clothing for them."

Parents can expect their children to ask further questions about the vocation of marriage and procreation. The Church's traditional approach has always been one of great modesty, so as to avoid at all costs the arousing of the passions. The subject should be unfolded to the boy or girl by the parent of the same sex, in a delicate and reverent manner, with constant reference to spiritual truths and a minimum of physiological detail.*

As children grow older, they start to realize that, unfortunately, not everyone loves purity. Some people do not dress, or act, in a pure and modest way. And this is where temptation comes in, for all sins have an *appearance* of attractiveness; otherwise, no one would commit sin.

---

*Two classic little books to help the Catholic father and mother in this task are *Listen, Son* and *Mother's Little Helper,* currently available from Angelus Press, 2918 Tracy Ave., Kansas City, MO 64109.—*Publisher,* 1995.

That is why we must pray for the grace to love God's will. If we love it, it will be easier to do it. This is why we must pray for the grace to love purity. If we love purity, it will be easier to resist temptations against it.

All this Maria knew. All this was why she would let Alessandro kill her rather than commit a sin. He wanted her to break God's law. He wanted to do something that was not God's will. Her love for purity was the fruit of her love for God and His holy will.

Heroic love of God comes with prayer and long training in self-denial and surrender to God's will. This is the one step on the way to sanctity that it is easy to miss. Whatever the circumstances of our lives, we see only that our plans are thwarted, disadvantages are our lot, and we suffer a number of afflictions not of our own choosing. Strangely enough, if we would accept and use them, we would grow in the precise heroism that is needed by us if we would be saints.

In the end Maria bore heroic suffering. Alessandro stabbed her fourteen times, each in a vital spot. Her heart was pierced, and her lungs. Her intestines were severed. The surgeons in the hospital at Nettuno could not explain why she was not dead. By necessity, they performed surgery without anaesthesia. She cried: "I thirst," but even in their pity they could not give her water.

She lived thus for twenty-four hours. She received the Last Sacraments, her fourth Holy Communion. She was made a Child of Mary. Would she forgive Alessandro, the chaplain asked? Our Lord forgave His murderers and promised the Good Thief paradise. Of course she forgave Alessandro . . . "and I want him with me in Paradise." Dying, she warned him again in her delirium: "You will go to hell!" Thinking she was back in the kitchen lying on the floor, she cried: "Carry me to bed because I want to be nearer the Madonna . . ."

Assunta stood and watched and waited—and realized she had raised a saint.

Alessandro was tried and convicted and imprisoned, unrepentant. Then, years later, he saw Maria in a vision in his cell and finally surrendered to remorse and began his life of reparation. He asked and obtained Assunta's pardon. Together, the old mother and the man who had murdered her child attended Christmas Midnight Mass. Thus Maria Goretti can truly be called the spiritual mother of Alessandro's soul. Her purity was shot through with charity.

Purity has always been difficult, but never before, it has been said, have there been so many temptations to impurity. The devil must be winning many souls through this means. But besides the devil, there is our own weakness to contend with. Young people must understand that the emotions and desires which rise up to tempt them ought not take them by surprise, because this struggle is part of man's fallen nature. And of course, in addition to the devil and the flesh, "the world" is the other source of temptation.

St. Maria Goretti triumphed through fervent prayer to Our Lady, Holy Communion, and a will strengthened by the faithful fulfillment of God's Will each day. By these same means, all youth can win the same victory.

Note: Parts of pp. 74-81 above, as well as of pp. 10-11, have been adapted by the Publisher.—*Publisher*, 1995.

5

ST. BERNADETTE SOUBIROUS
Model of Humility

From the time of the apparitions at Lourdes until the end of her life, there is scarcely a word from St. Bernadette or about her that is not recorded. There is an embarrassment of riches, so much comment, so many books. As far as was possible, everyone who knew her from birth to death was interviewed and every shred of evidence was collected. There is almost as complete a record of this saint's childhood and maturity as it is possible to have, and there are surprising lessons to learn from it.

The first seems to be the same old thing: God does make it clear that *things,* position, success, the respect of the world, have little to do with serving Him. They are the setting and the accessories but that is all; we use them well or badly. They are not essential to grace. The lives of saints like Bernadette show us immediately that, even when we understand all this, we continue to be prey to the old phony values. We yield to pressures, cultivate haves and knows, confuse having and knowing with virtue, feel that to be on the right side of the right people must be to be on the right side of God. For all we may do it unconsciously it is lamentable, for such sentiments are not God's. He seems to have a predilection for the poor and the miserable and underscores their nothingness as though to show us how unimportant are all the things the world holds dear.

He is forever choosing saints from among the poor and the miserable like the Gorettis and the Soubirous, neither of whom most people would be likely to go out of their way to cultivate.

St. Bernadette is loved by those who know her — few seem to really know her — for many things but probably best of all for her humility. With marvelous hindsight, now that it is done, we can see the ways by which God perfected her humility.

It began with the kind of stripping He often effects in order to invite souls to sanctity. Everyone has such invitations in his life and calls them by a number of names: misfortune, bad luck, scandal, suffering, or the cross. We can use them or resist them. They rarely *look* like the cross. With the Soubirous it looked like shiftlessness, but it hastened them down the distance between pride of possession (which is everyone's) and the complete poverty of those at the bottom of the heap. God stripped Bernadette of any and all pride by a process so unattractive that her situation looked abominable, but it put her in a position of distinct advantage — which is not to say, of course, that the stripping did not hurt nor that she did not suffer, nor even that she understood exactly what He was up to.

But she did understand that He was always up to something. We know this from a conversation she had with her cousin, Jeanne Védère. Bernadette believed quite simply that everything that happened had some meaning and was permitted by God for some reason. The perfect thing to do was to accept and wait. She and Jeanne were together one day when a priest stopped to talk to them. After he was gone, Jeanne asked who he was.

"That is my foster-mother's brother. He was so good to me at Bartrés. I like him so much. He came during his holidays to spend a few days. . . . As long as he was there he took my side and I had nothing to suffer . . . after, the person who was unkind to me went on as before."

Jeanne asked her why she did not tell her father if she was unhappy.

"Oh, no. I thought that the good God wished it." And she

forebade Jeanne to speak of it. Jeanne, afterward a Trappistine, testified to this conversation only after the death of Bernadette.

It would be wonderful to know who taught her this abandonment to Divine Providence, but that is not as important as knowing she learned it early. One might hear a thousand times, "God's will be done. He has a reason," from elders hardly conscious they have said it, but the marvelous thing is that when they have said it in the presence of children, and the children *have* heard it, they believe it. They act on it and let it act in them. The first years of faith are most important and profound truths can be learned then which cannot be drummed into older heads full of skepticism. This is not because young children are more easily persuaded (in some matters, indeed, they are not!) but because Faith, the gift, is in them after Baptism and it wants only Truth in order to become concrete. The child who does not learn these things when he is small must stumble through the growing-up years only half equipped to make sense of what is happening to him and in him and around him. Perhaps only after some frightful struggle with suffering or serious sin will he be moved to piece together the bits of Christian truth he knows and fill the gaps in his knowledge of God's ways. It is terrible to waste the early years.

So — Bernadette knew how to accept when she was small. It is good she did. She had to accept much before her childhood was half over. God was preparing her and it was hard. Not only did she suffer poverty and cold and hunger but humiliation also. They became to some "those Soubirous."

Her mother was a member of the Casterot family, who long had been operators of the mill of Boly in Lourdes. Her father, although not quite on a par with the Casterots, qualified well enough to suit the family, whose principal concern after a good match for Louise was that the family mill continue to turn. The father of the family had died leaving it to his widow and children and since Louise, at sixteen, was the daughter next in line to marry, it was plain a good marriage would be one with a miller. François Soubirous was a journeyman miller and, although much older than she, he won her heart and they were married. Financially they were quite secure and married life for them was as married life for any other couple.

But François was not a businesslike miller. He was not deliberately *bad,* just irresponsible and lazy, a gregarious soul who enjoyed the sociability of the cafe as much or more than the call of duty at his mill. It is easy to justify waste of time as "good for business"; one might be "entertaining customers." But it wasn't good for François *or* his family.

Louise, like her husband, was sociable, and she entertained at the mill. In itself this was a custom of the district. Women who brought their grain to be ground were offered a bit of refreshment, which would have been all right had it not taken so much time and had they paid for their milling. Jeanne Védère, in later testimony, describes touchingly the woman, the custom and the situation which contributed so much to their misfortunes.

"Louise was a very good Christian woman, gentle, of a pleasing disposition, hardworking. She had, to my mind, all that one could wish to see in an excellent mother of a family. However, I had noticed at her home, at the mill of Boly, a practice which I certainly did not approve. I remember having spoken of it once to my parents. My mother answered that it was the custom at Lourdes and my father told me that it was that expense which put the family into sore straits. From morning till night women would come to grind grain: no one would leave without taking something to eat: there was always prepared for them some bread, wine, cheese, when there was nothing else; so that it often happened that they spent more than they gave in recompense to the miller. I saw in that only the most complete disorder." [1]

And Louise had apparently neither the experience to know a custom that was good for business from one that was its ruination, nor the courage to end it. Even Bernadette at one

---

[1] Père Cros, *Histoire de Notre Dame de Lourdes d'apres les document* . . . p. 45.

point asked Jeanne to speak to her mother about the extravagant entertaining, but Jeanne forebore from correcting her aunt, a woman so much her senior.

Testimony referring to this period of their lives treats of Louise's possible overfondness for wine itself. The question is debatable although it is true that she did drink wine, according to the custom of her country. Some witnesses infer she drank too much, others insist she did not. Her brother-in-law said she "used to sell her linen in order to drink." André Sajoux, her cousin, admired her but also testified: ". . . she used to touch wine a little . . . she sometimes lost her reason." (One cannot tell from this whether he meant she was very drunk, or just a little tipsy.) Basile Castero, her sister, said: "In her youth Louise was always well-behaved: at that time she did not like to drink: that habit came to her after marriage." This claims only that she did drink; how much it is impossible to tell. The gendarme, Bernard Pays, said: "I knew the Soubirous before the apparitions; the mother had been a virtuous girl. Much later she became a drinker, but she did not drink every week and there never was a public scandal." On the other hand, Isodore Pujd testified: "Sure, Louise now and then would rather do without bread so as to have a little wine. She had no decent food, she worked hard, she tired herself out, and still she had to breast-feed her infant. She felt that she had to strengthen herself with something, and a little wine revived her." Père Cros, in whose official three-volume work the various testimonies are collected, has this to say: "Louise . . . used wine rarely and little. Her poverty never permitted her to take as much wine as the hardships of a wet nurse and a field-laborer called for. . . . Those who had a better knowledge of Louise's misery, privations and maternal hardships would have compassion for her, not scorn." [2]

Precisely — and to scorn Louise by revealing even the debate over her drinking habits has never been our intention. Whether her drinking was only the usual amount found among all Latin

[2] *Ibid.,* p. 45.

people or whether it was more is of concern to us only insofar as the family situation was desperate and many things (perhaps this among them) contributed. *Some* combination of the good and the weak, of wisdom and folly contrived to reduce the Soubirous family to a state of destitution. Just such combinations of goodness and weakness, wisdom and folly continue to afflict families. Yet, as we see from this saint's story, such misfortune may be the means of sanctity if one will use it. "It is all very well," a family might say, reading the life of St. Thérèse of Lisieux, "to point out how the Martins raised *their* saint, but they were probably saints themselves. *We're not* in our family." The Soubirous weren't either. However one sees their struggle, they were quite ordinary people at this time, with some good qualities and some not so good, and they were not saints.

It is tragic to be the children of a ne'er-do-well, but not so tragic that God cannot use it. Alcoholism, mismanagement, irresponsibility, all the afflictions that lead families into disgrace, God can work to good. Such sufferings can be recommended in the making of saints in only one respect: some cross is inevitable. *It is the cross* even when it looks, to the family involved, like nothing so much as a *mess.*

Little by little the stripping went apace. When she was ten Bernadette spent the winter with her godmother, Aunt Bernarde, living in her household, helping with the children. At twelve she returned to her foster-mother at Bartrés where she helped out as shepherdess. At neither place was there time for her to attend school, join the Children of Mary, or enroll in the catechism class in order to prepare for her First Communion. It is hard to believe, but at fourteen the neglect of Bernadette's First Communion seemed not to impress anyone but Bernadette herself.

She had chronic asthma, with a habitual cough and periods of frightful suffocation. She contracted cholera during an epidemic that hit Lourdes and this left her so debilitated that her growth apparently was affected, her height remaining at four feet seven inches all her life. She could always be identified as the smallest in any group. But she had spirit and knowing this, the appearance of submissiveness again and again is all the more striking. It can be seen in Aunt Bernarde's testimony before the official investigator: "She was small and timid and when scolded did not answer." When we learn that she was gay and had a temper, a sense of humor and a strong will, this tells much about both Bernadette and Aunt Bernarde.

Once destitution really struck, Louise and François tried hard to pull things together and make some kind of home out of the dismal hole where they finally came to live. André Sajoux owned a house with a room called "the dungeon," which had once served as the town jail and was described locally as unfit for animals. Abandoned in favor of a more habitable jail, it was variously rented, used as a flophouse for migrant workers and, finally, it became the home of the Soubirous family, rent free. This was after Sajoux had boarded up one of the two windows, dug a cesspit outside it and established a manure pile on top. The room was about ten by fourteen feet. They arrived, after five evictions, with a box containing their linen, a bed and one chair. They had in addition a few pottery dishes. André Sajoux supplied the following detail for the official investigation:

"Needless to say, none of the usual results of such destitution were wanting. If the vermin were destroyed today, they would return tomorrow." And we know from further testimony that Louise worked endlessly to destroy them. Later, after the apparition of February 25, one of Mlle Estrade's friends in the crowd noticed that Bernadette pushed her hand under her kerchief and scratched her head. Said Mlle Estrade: "It is very probable that an unwanted family had established itself there. It is certainly true that she scratched with all her might! My friend drew my attention to her and said: 'You want me to believe that *that* girl sees the Blessed Virgin?'"

Bernadette was the oldest of the Soubirous children and at home she took care of the others. She tidied the house while her parents tried to find work and in her spare time she went off, sometimes taking the younger children along, to find faggots for the fireplace and rags and bones to sell the rag-and-bone man. This was after she finally left her work of shepherding at Bartrés to prepare for her First Communion. When one reads that Justin, her younger brother, was found scraping wax off the floor of the church and chewing it to assuage his hunger, it is not hard to believe the accounts of their destitution. But they were proud and would not beg.

Sometimes, when she could, Louise would spend a few sous for white bread and wine for Bernadette, the slightly more delicate fare recommended by the doctor because she was sickly, but often when their mother's back was turned, the younger children would take it away from her. Bernadette never seemed to care enough to make a fuss about it. This is told on herself by Toinette, her youngest sister. "She told us off when we did wrong and never allowed me to wander off and leave the baby. This used to annoy me, but all the same we loved her and my brothers were fonder of her than of me." Submissiveness to God's will is the beginning of not wanting your own way.

No amount of searching turns up a valid claim to extremes of piety in Bernadette as a child. She could not remember having said the rosary in the fields while watching her sheep, but one can suppose she did. Many pious Catholics carry rosaries about and snatch the time for a decade or two as they work. Perhaps she was too busy watching sheep to remember when she prayed, but watching sheep in itself is prayer when you accept it and offer it as the work God has sent you to do. Her companions at the time did not remember her making or decorating little outdoor shrines, though people say now that she did; and she herself denied parting any waters so sheep could cross dryshod, or multiplying any cornmeal. These claims can logically be dismissed as loving embroideries when one discovers that, as far as is known, she performed no miracles while she was alive — ever.

Although a number of people thought so, Bernadette was

not stupid. Things worked to give this impression, however, and it would seem that, since she was quite convinced of her own stupidity, God permitted this to guard her against any spot of intellectual pride. Marie Laguës Aravant at Bartrés tried in vain to teach her the catechism; it never occurred to Marie that to learn by memory lessons taught in a foreign language would be impossible for many people. French was the language of the catechism and was as a foreign language to Bernadette, who spoke only Lourdes *patois* which was more Spanish then French. Indeed, Our Lady showed better sense than the obdurate Marie; Our Lady addressed Bernadette in *patois*. But not Marie. " 'She was thick-headed,' said Madame Aravant many years after, smiling with affectionate remembrance. 'It was useless for me to repeat my lessons; I always had to begin again. Sometimes I was overcome by impatience, and in temper I threw the book aside and said to her, ' "Go along, you will never be anything but an ignorant fool." ' " No wonder she remained humble. She was a little nobody, they all agreed, who knew next to nothing and she meant quite sincerely the remark she made years later: "If the Blessed Virgin could have found someone more ignorant than I, she would have chosen her; she picked me up under a pebble."

So, on the threshold of the apparitions, at the age of fourteen, Bernadette was not a saint. What she *was* should encourage parents who pray they will be able to raise saints, because she was quite like most nice ordinary children who love God sincerely and try to serve Him as best they can. It would not be the apparitions that would make Bernadette a saint, but her faithful struggle to overcome herself. Take away the apparitions and you still had a girl to whom God would send the grace for sanctity as He sends it to everyone. She had one advantage (anyone in his right mind would call it a disadvantage): she had been stripped of everything including family reputation. Shortly before her first meeting with Our Lady, her father had spent a week in jail on an unproved charge of thievery. The Soubirous were indeed a sorry lot! But later when she showed remarkable courage it was the fruit of this stripping. If only we had enough faith to believe God knows what He is doing!

Bernadette had nothing left to risk. She had nothing left to fear — except sin. All the other fears had been met and lived with. If courage is seeing what must be done and doing it, Bernadette already had the courage to obey the commands of the Lady at the grotto. If now she was to make a fool of herself, she could do that too. She had looked foolish so many times. Crawling in the dirt, smearing her face with mud, eating grass, all the things that would make people turn away in disappointment and murmur, "She is mad," would not be her initiation to humiliation. She had already had it. How precious are the lessons we learn from the sufferings we fear most. If only we could teach this to our children.

It all started on a cold morning in February, 1858, as she stooped beside the river Gave to remove her stockings so she could wade across to gather wood. The sound of a wind came to her and she looked up, but the trees in the meadow were still. She began to remove her stockings again, and again she heard the sound of the wind. Strange — the trees were still. Puzzled, she looked around; then she saw it. Opposite her, standing over a wild rose bush which grew from a ledge in the grotto of the rock, stood a young girl slightly smaller than herself, possibly seventeen years old, dressed in a white dress with a blue sash and wearing a white mantle on her head. Her hands held a rosary of pearl-like beads on a gold chain and at the tip of each small bare foot was a yellow rose. Bernadette reached for her rosary and tried to make the Sign of the Cross but she could not. Then the girl in the vision made it, and Bernadette could. Afterward people said that if the Sign of the Cross is made in heaven, it must be made the way Our Lady taught Bernadette to make it. They said the rosary together, the girl moving the beads between her fingers and saying only the *Gloria* with her lips. Finished, she beckoned Bernadette to come closer but the child was too frightened, and the girl disappeared. This was the beginning.

For our purpose, a day-by-day account of the apparitions is not necessary. There are excellent books on these, of which my favorite is B. G. Sandhurst's *We Saw Her.* Bernadette told her sister and Jeanne Abadie about the vision and they told her mother. Her parents forbade her to return to the grotto and she obeyed them. Later, when she was permitted to go, the Lady asked if she would come for a fortnight and she said she would — *if her parents would let her. There* is respect for the authority of parents! Certainly Bernadette suspected who the Lady was, but obedience to her parents came first. Obedience and humility are born of simplicity and simplicity is knowing Who your Father is, trusting Him and doing exactly as He tells you. Now, after a decade or so of unchecked expression by the uninhibited children of overly permissive parents, it is being discovered that obedience *to* parents and discipline *from* them are not bad things after all but rather some of the stuff of which character is made. The Church has been teaching this for centuries. Moses told it to the Jews after he received the Ten Commandments from God. It means simply that one surrenders his own will to God's will, which is manifested for a child through the will of his parents. It reveals the will of God at the present moment for any child, as well as for Bernadette. God was testing her obedience.

When her parents gave her their permission to return to the grotto she did, and when they withdrew their permission later she stayed away. Then one day something happened and she could not resist it. It was as if she had been taken by the shoulders, turned around and *made* to go back. Her parents accepted it as a valid sign from this child who never disobeyed and they never interfered again. Her mother said to a friend at this time that Bernadette was a truthful child, always obedient, always believable. Wasn't that precisely the kind of child God wanted for this task?

Very soon the word was out and the controversy began to boil. People took sides and Bernadette had not only the curious of the town to cope with but also the annoyance of the priests and the incredulity of the nuns at the school. "If it is really the Blessed Virgin you see, then ask her to teach you your catechism!" But one thing the doubters could not explain: such a transformation came over her when she talked with the apparition! This made people cry. Another thing was the way she bowed so beautifully. "Where did she learn to bow so?" they asked each other. Sometimes she smiled; sometimes she was sad. Why did she look so sad? One time, she said, it was because the Lady had looked off across the distance, then sadly at Bernadette and said, "Pray for sinners." One day the Lady said to her, "I cannot promise to make you happy in this world, but in another."

The police badgered her, and her pastor, and the neighbors, and their relatives and friends. The curious flocked to see "the visionary." The police took her testimony and read it back garbled, trying to catch her in inaccuracies. The Abbé (her pastor) called her "You little liar!" People crowded the street in front of her poor home and tried to see her, touch her, get her to bless them and their children. She said to them, sometimes crossly because it was all so ridiculous, "But I am no priest who wears a stole! I cannot bless!" They tried to give her money for her rosary, for her medals, her scapular, and she refused. They tried to make her family accept money and she forbade it. They gave her little brother a few sous for fetching a pail of grotto water and she slapped his face — harder than it had ever been slapped in his life, he said later.

Wherefore this imperturbability? How is it she could not be distracted, confused, bribed, wheedled, discouraged, or even made to disregard authority in view of such divine favors? Henri Petitot, O.P., in *The True Story of St. Bernadette,* says this is how the gift of Fortitude is given by the Holy Spirit to help with the work at hand. It would be a mistake to think "character" alone could have held Bernadette so purposefully to the point. There is no character without the grace of God. How much more intelligently we might work at the forming of character in our children, did we understand that it is, above all, a work of grace. The better we know the work of the Holy Spirit, the better we can cooperate to help Him form our children.

It is thrilling to see this example of fortitude as shown forth in the steadfastness of Bernadette. It helped her keep the three secrets Our Lady told her which, some guesses have it, possibly had to do with these very trials by badgering. Even though it was the Blessed Virgin who gave the commands, Bernadette had still to obey. She was not suddenly a puppet without a will. Little enough preparation it was, all the suffering in lowliness. A short time before she had been a wretched slum child. Now she had need not only for fortitude but understanding, to remember that nothing *she* had done had wrought this change. The only possible qualification for her new role *was* her lowliness.

It is not hard to see why God does such things as exalt the humble and humble the exalted. Oddly enough, both are part of the making of a saint. It is easy to have only the most ignoble grasp of His point here, seeing the humbling merely as a promise to put everyone in his place! But the end of God's work is not to get even with man. He is a lover — wooing. It is essential that the exalted be humbled, else they are lost to Him. He is delighted not by their humiliation but by their self-knowledge. He simply wants them to discover who they are — or better, who they are not.

Because He must use fallen creatures, He exalts the humble in order to teach the proud ones that He is not a respecter of persons. That is *our* weakness, and that is why such wretched slum children as Bernadette teach us best that we are great not because of anything we have or do but because of the price paid for us on the Cross. Our only claim to greatness is in the indisputable fact that God loves us.

No one is beyond the need of humbling. It is one's safety. Even Bernadette, after all the hubbub died down and she was in the convent, said quite sincerely, "At Lourdes I was too much esteemed . . . I shall work to correct myself. . . . Yes, I will

pray for you, but pray also for me, for I am very proud." God
alone knows if she were proud. It is not necessary to know, only
to be afraid of it.

But at fourteen she was still one of the weak ones He was
using to confound the others. It cost her. Her life was never
hidden after this, not even in the convent. She was always
"Bernadette," even after she became Sister Marie-Bernarde. She
was a public witness right up to the end and this was sometimes
almost unbearable. Even before she left Lourdes for Nevers,
she learned what a nightmare the role would be. She said Our
Lady had chosen her to be a servant, and indeed she was called
to the parlor to serve her more times than any parlor maid.
Everyone came seeking information or to look at her, the lowly,
the great, the hierarchy, all who were curious. Regrettably, not
even the highest ecclesiastics could resist flashing their rank to
get in to see her. As many as *thirty times a day* she was called
out of her classroom at the hospice to go to the parlor for
interviews. Sister Victorine said she would stop before the door
to the parlor and tears would stream down her cheeks as she
cringed before the ordeal. "Courage," Sister would say, and she
would dry her eyes, smile her small, neat smile (see it in her
photographs) and walk in. Thirty times a day! Say the day,
for purposes of interviewing, began at nine in the morning
and ended at six. That would mean on such a day she was called
out of class on an average of once every eighteen to twenty
minutes. No wonder she was no scholar!

She never volunteered information, only answered questions.
Skeptics came and went away convinced. Skeptics came and went
away unconvinced. "You have not persuaded me," one said. "It
is not for me to persuade you, only to answer your questions,"
was her tart reply. Perhaps one of the things Our Lady said to
her at the grotto was, "You will have to give me your privacy."
One of the most touching things Bernadette ever said was to
marvel at the way the goldfish in the botanical gardens at
Bourdeaux, where they stopped on their way to the convent
at Nevers, could swim about unconcernedly before the eyes

of the crowds staring at them. Would it were that easy for her! But saints are saints because they do what God wants, not what they want.

Withal, she was an adolescent and a number of comments on her adolescence have been confused, it seems to me, with faults. To the mothers of teen-age daughters these sound less like faults than like "the nature of the beastie." She was found one time "in the act of altering a skirt in order to enlarge it and give the effect of crinoline." Another time "she was found inserting a piece of wood into a corset to do duty as a staybone." Teen-age girls rarely make the connection between the vagaries of fashion and the pitfalls of the spiritual life. They must be helped to see the relation of the one to the other, to see how the one can reflect the other, how it can help or hinder the development of the other. I, personally, think this had to be done for Bernadette as for any other young girl.

Sister Victorine at the hospice said her most prominent faults were "self-opinionatedness and obstinacy." She was also inclined to reply quickly and impatiently when she was teased or pestered, sometimes hurting someone's feelings by the passion of her retort. "From the environment in which she had lived so long [the worst part of town, in other words] she had acquired the habit of answering back rather violently, and without toning down her language in the way a more refined upbringing would have taught her to do." And, like St. Thérèse of Lisieux, she was extremely affectionate, which is dangerous if one is tempted to offer creatures the affection that belongs to God. She was not a saint yet.

She had a longing to join the reformed Cistercians but her health was too poor and at last she decided to enter the convent of the Sisters of Charity of Nevers who had kept her as boarder and scholar at the hospice in Lourdes. Her last visit to the grotto was heartbreaking. To the astonishment of the nuns, she broke down and sobbed. Her farewell to her family was equally difficult and her first days at the convent were filled with weeping. She wrote: "The good Sisters encouraged us (another postulant was with her) by telling us it was a sign of vocation." And for their part the Sisters rejoiced, loving her sincerely but also, it must be admitted, jubilant over their famous catch. None of them knew that Mother-General Josephine Imbert had delayed an unconscionably long time before admitting her, to the annoyance even of the Bishop. In the process of canonization there appeared this statement by Mother Josephine Forestier: "Monsignor Forcade (the Bishop) was annoyed about it when he preached the retreat to our Sisters at Toulouse, at which Mother-General was present. Everything leads me to think that he had to insist upon her giving him a final answer."

But now that she had arrived, Mother Imbert asked her to tell the Congregation the story of the apparitions once for all, then no one was ever to mention it again. It has been said the Sisters' obedience to this order was "heroic" considering the feminine nature, but this puzzles me. The years to come were to hold all manner of exceptions, at least in spirit, to this rule. There would be inspecting, touching, whispering over and displaying of Bernadette until the end of her life. Still, she would go to the depths of humility. God was about to begin perfecting in humility the little one He had permitted to be exalted.

The perfecting of saints comes often at the hands of people who are sure they are doing God's will — which of course they are, but sometimes not in the way they think! Père Petitot warns his readers that before they jump to any conclusions about the actions of Mother Josephine Imbert and Mother Marie-Thérèse Vazous, mistress of novices, they recall what Our Lord said to St. Margaret Mary about *her* sisters in religion. "I do you much honor, my dear daughter, in making use of such noble instruments to crucify you. . . . I am using in your case persons who are devoted and consecrated to me."

Both Mother Imbert and Mother Vazous were outstanding religious with many remarkable qualities, and were well loved by their spiritual daughters. That they were severe with Bernadette neither tried to deny, but they were severe, they insisted, to protect her from pride. This is probably quite true as far as it goes, but their motive seemed mixed with a little animosity. It is God's business to judge, not ours. But it is impossible not to see how they behaved.

Beginning with a normally cordial relationship with the superior-general and novice mistress, things for Bernadette soon began to grow colder. On one occasion the superior returned from a journey and her novices gathered to greet her according to custom. She kissed each one and gave her some word of greeting — except Bernadette. A kiss in silence was all there was for Bernadette. The only way to approximate the effect of this is to imagine warmly greeting all but one of your children. It was a deliberate cut for no good reason since she was an ideal novice.

One would think she would please any superior. She kept the rule perfectly and her faithfulness in small things has been compared to that of St. Thérèse of Lisieux. The other novices had taken her as their model and tried to imitate her, but in vain. She performed no unusual penances yet her mortification was constant. She mortified her natural preference at table. She refrained from drinking for an hour or more when she was thirsty. She fled from those who would break silence with her "like one fleeing the plague." And she always came as soon as the bell rang. Yet she was not a dour religious but very gay, making pleasant talk at recreation and even once inquiring if they ever skipped rope here at Nevers? No? What a pity. She had loved to turn the rope for her companions to skip when she was at the hospice in Lourdes. But it cost her. She used to say, "By continually whacking the beast, you end by mastering it." Still she could not please the two Sisters. One day she was mending an umbrella and bent down to hide herself as the superior approached, whispering to Sister Henri Fabre: "Mother Josephine! Oh, how I fear her!"

One of the explanations for Mother Vazous' coldness was that as novice mistress she desired the "entire spiritual confidence" of her daughters; she wanted entrée into their souls. But Bernadette could not let anyone into her soul any more. Our Lady had stopped there and given her three secrets she was bound to

tell no one, and never again could she lay bare her soul to anyone. Apparently Mother Vazous resented this. Her influence
was strong with Mother Imbert. An incident that happened before Bernadette's profession shows the severity of their feeling.
The ill-health which had plagued Bernadette constantly seemed
about to take her life. The Bishop was asked for permission to
admit her to profession, and came to conduct the short ceremony
himself. After his departure, she revived, sat up in bed, and said
to the mother-general: "Mother, you have made me make my
profession because you thought I should die tonight; well, I shall
not die tonight." Mother Imbert's reply was: "What! You knew
that you would not die tonight and you did not say so! You are
nothing but a little idiot! I declare that if you are not dead
tomorrow morning, I shall take off the black veil of the professed that you have just been given, and send you back to the
novitiate with the simple novice's veil."

It is hard to imagine *anyone* making that speech to someone
just beyond danger of death, much less a responsible religious,
and especially when one suspects the reason for the hasty death-
bed profession was to be sure the famous Bernadette was, after
all, a professed Sister of Charity of Nevers. Knowing Bernadette
had a quick temper, and taking into account her very real weakness, it is astonishing to hear her say: "As you please, dear
Mother." It would have been so understandable if she had rolled
up in a little ball and cried.

On her clothing day, she had said to her sisters in religion,
"I have come to be hidden. I want to be forgotten, to be esteemed
as nothing." Such a soul has tasted blood. Only one satisfaction
exists for it and the way to it is hidden and dark and lonely.
The road turns inward and self must be hacked away until nothing is left but Christ. She wrote, "The love of Our Lord will be
the knife to cut and do away with the tree of pride and its evil
roots. The more I abase myself, the higher I shall raise myself
in the Heart of Jesus." She had been just a little girl when she
picked up the scent of God, accepting things because "I thought
God wished it." She hadn't quite understood *why.* Now she

knew. He wanted her to draw near to Him, and the things He permitted to happen to her were the *way*. Now she not only accepted them, she embraced them.

But it would be wrong to suppose that because she had a great desire for God, she did not suffer from these rebukes. She was intensely affectionate. She suffered terribly. She cried, the others noticed, but she did not complain. She wrote in her little note-book: "O most holy Mother of my Lord, who has seen and felt the loneliness of thy dear Son, help me now in mine! And you, saints of Paradise, who have passed through this trial, have compassion on me who suffer it, and obtain me the grace to be faithful unto death." She wrote: "I beseech Thee, O my God, by Thy loneliness, not to spare me but not to abandon me. . . . Give me grace to recognize Thy hand in it, and not to desire any comforter but Thyself." His hand — in those loveless reproaches! But she had the saint's sanity. She knew what it was for: "The love of Our Lord will be the knife to cut and do away with the tree of pride. . . ."

There was a saying among the novices: "It is not well to be Bernadette!"

St. Thérèse called her hurts "pinpricks." Bernadette used to say: "I've just had a sweet." "What sort of one?" asked Sister Marcelline Durand one time. "Oh, that is my business." When she committed faults, she accused herself of them before night-fall. While she was still at the hospice at Lourdes, the Sisters noticed that her spells of stubbornness, her other faults, were always followed by an attack of physical suffering. They used to say, "She will soon be ill," and she was. It seemed to them God willed to make her expiate her fault immediately. One wonders, also, if it might possibly have been a physical manifestation of her own remorse. Man is body *and* soul. Great delicacy of conscience often affects a delicate constitution. Our Lord has told the saints that remorse for sin pleases Him, because it shows us clearly how weak and helpless we are without Him. It is the seed-bed of humility and we might explain this when we must punish our own children, helping them to make their punishments *expiation,* helping them to be glad to *see* their weakness that they may not trust it again. If there is to be any good come after sin, it must be our knowing, better than ever, our poverty without Christ.

Sooner or later a Christian who is really struggling along the way of perfection finds himself forever on the receiving end, either at his own hands or at the hands of others or of God. Meekness does not come naturally, nor does it become meekness if we are not absolutely honest all the way. Saints like Bernadette can teach us, and help us teach our children, how to "take it" and not "suck sorrow." Her struggles are like everyone's, child or adult. The jealousy, coldness, nipping, biting of her superiors in religion are not unknown in the classroom, the play yard, the neighborhood, nor in the office, the factory, the PTA, the sodality, the household. The constant judging of her, jumping to conclusions about her, deciding what she must be, must think, must mean, must want, are faults children and grown-ups alike suffer from one another. The awful suffering at the end of it and her discovery of her part in the work of the Sacred Heart of Christ must be our discovery too, if we are to fulfill our vocations as members of the Mystical Body.

It was not that her superiors should not have suspected temptations to Bernadette's pride. The ignominies she bore were almost too outrageous to believe. Practically everyone was convinced she was a saint, so practically everyone was in search of a relic! The clippings from her scissors in the sewing room were surreptitiously picked up and saved; snips of her hair were saved; things she touched were treasured; her old shawl was mysteriously exchanged for a new one and carried off to another convent to be cut up for relics. She distributed some candied nuts to some children one day and hardly were they out of her presence than the candies were coaxed away from them and carried off as souvenirs. Because there was a prohibition laid on discussing the apparitions does not mean that the interviewing ceased or that the same superiors were above showing her off to visiting hierarchy or distinguished guests.

Once a bishop came to see her when she was sick, and as he leaned over her as she lay in bed his *zuchetto* — the little violet skull cap bishops wear — fell off. She knew what he was up to and did not move to hand it back. Finally the superior laughed and said: "Come, *Mademoiselle,* give his cap back to *Monseigneur."* On another occasion one of her superiors was showing a visitor about and approached a group including Bernadette. "You see," she said, "these veils differ. This one is a novice's; this one is of silk; this one," pointing to Bernadette's, "is of *Béarnaise."* With which Bernadette pulled the veil down over her face, the better to display it for the visitor! The novices devised all manner of means to be near her, touch her, get her to straighten their veils (she did not like a crooked veil). Once she barely controlled her anger when she discovered a young novice silently kissing her veil in the back. *"Mademoiselle!* You know that is forbidden!"

Who would claim that all this and more did not pose a danger to pride? But she did not want it or like it. If only people would let her alone! "If only I could see without being seen!" She had mountains enough to level and valleys enough to fill without their adding difficulties. Someone asked if she did not feel her present role was too insignificant considering she had been the one to whom the Virgin appeared. She startled them by asking what one did with a broom when one was finished with it? Why — put it behind the door. Precisely; Our Lady had used her and finished with her, and now she was put behind the door where she belonged. "I only acted the part of the oxen at Betharram who turned up the statue by chance when they were plowing . . ."

It is touching to read this and then read what Mother Marie-Thérèse Vazous said of her to the chaplain at the Mother House *twenty years after her death.* She was then superior-general of the Congregation. "If the Blessed Virgin willed to appear anywhere on earth, why should she choose an uncouth, ignorant peasant girl, instead of an educated, virtuous and distinguished nun?" She had said as much to her secretary, Mother Bordenave (who wrote one of the earliest biographies of St. Bernadette). "Oh, Bernadette was a little peasant. I do not understand how the Blessed Virgin could have revealed herself to her. There are so many others, so refined, so well brought up. However!" This ought to show us once for all the folly of trying to please people instead of God. Even the saints failed to please all of the people all of the time.

Before she died, Mother Vazous worried about having been too hard on Bernadette. "I was afraid I had been too severe in her regard, and that was tormenting me." She consulted a monk who bore a great reputation for sanctity and came away convinced she had done right. She said just before she died: "God permitted that Mother Josephine and I should be severe with Sister Marie-Bernarde in order to keep her humble." And God knows they did. Bernadette must thank them for it in eternity.

But because humility was her outstanding virtue does not mean Bernadette would never have felt the sting of pride. God permits temptations in order to strengthen the will and make it strong in virtue. If this is so, then Bernadette must have suffered from the rebellion of pride many times, and must have had to fight it with all her strength. Indeed, she admitted that the public humiliation served up to her on the day of her formal profession was as bitter a trial as she had known, even though she did not let her emotions show. On this day each young nun is called up by the bishop after profession to be given a letter of assignment. It had been pre-arranged that there would be no letter for Sister Marie-Bernarde. The bishop asked: "Why has not Sister Marie-Bernarde been called?" Mother Imbert replied: "My Lord, it is not possible to assign her an obedience. She is a little dolt and good for nothing." He called her forward. So — she was a little dolt, good for nothing?

"Mother-general is quite right. It is quite true."

"But then, my poor child . . . what was the use of your entering the Congregation?"

"That was exactly what I said to your Lordship at Lourdes, and you answered me that it did not matter."

The bishop had no answer. It was quite true. Mother Imbert said,

"If your Lordship is willing, we can keep her at the Mother House, out of charity, and find something for her to do in the infirmary. As she is nearly always ill, it will just suit her. To begin with, she will simply be employed in cleaning; then, perhaps, later on we might set her to preparing herbal drinks, if we can ever find the means of teaching her."

And *this* must have been very hard to take — precisely because Bernadette was *not* a dolt and everyone knew it. She possessed a number of talents, and, as for finding some means of teaching her to mix herbal drinks, the domestic things were her forte and they knew that too. She had been mothering the little ones in her household, or the little ones in her aunt's household, doing just such tasks as this, ever since she was a small child. "Given her quick temperament, sickly and highly strung as she was, it must have needed heroic virtue under the circumstances to resist the secret temptations originating, as she said, 'from the human *I*,' and encouraged by the devil who, according to St. John of the Cross, St. Teresa, the Curé d'Ars, and other leading lights of mystical theology, never fails to exercise his deleterious influence in the weaker parts of man's nature, above all in the cases of those whom he feels are predestined to sanctity and to a mission of general atonement."

How would she have rebelled? My guess (one can only guess) is that all this persecution must have looked suspiciously like jealousy, and what would have been more discouraging and humiliating for Bernadette to discover than her own unspoken, "they are *jealous*," rising up again and again? It could give a soul such vicious comfort, and one constantly weak and sick would be such easy prey; to find *some* comfort *somewhere* is so imperative then. She did not take credit for having been involved in the apparitions. How bitter to have to be punished for having been chosen! Now she was paying the price, and she had to fight to love it.

She was made assistant infirmarian. She was a gifted nurse,

loved dearly by her patients and commended warmly by the doctors. Finally she was too sick to do anything. She had come to the understanding that her vocation was to suffer as a victim in reparation for sin. Our Lady had told her at the grotto to do penance and over the years she had developed great devotion to St. Francis of Assisi and St. Margaret Mary, both of whom Our Lord chose to share His suffering. The agonies of her illness were without end: asthma, haemorrhages, abcesses in the knee and the ears, immobility, deafness, caries of the bone, almost constant insomnia as her tuberculosis progressed. She sat sometimes all night on the side of her bed in constant pain, because to lie down was to suffocate. That she understood this vocation to suffer is borne out by the answer she gave one of her superiors who came into the room one day and asked jokingly: "What are you doing here in bed, lazybones?" She replied: "I am working away at my calling, dear Mother. I am being ill." One of the Sisters expressed her pity one time to see her in excruciating pain, and she said: "The Blessed Virgin told me that I should not be happy in this world."

But affliction was not her greatest pain. She wrote in her notebook: "Oh, of course it is very painful not to be able to breathe; but it is far more so to be tortured by interior sufferings. That is terrible." Her superiors did not relent their "purification" of her pride. "On a painful occasion," wrote Sister Marcelline Durand, "Sister Marie-Bernard, suffering from a tumor on her knee, met Mother Marie-Thérèse, who addressed some sharp words to her. Bernadette gave a sigh. 'Oh, our Mistress,' as though to say: 'She is always after me!' [Technically, she was no longer Bernadette's *mistress* as Bernadette was no longer a novice.] Then Mother Marie-Thérèse rejoiced: 'Ah! We have touched her self-love!'" Père Petitot remarks that whereas it is often self-love that is touched and hurts, in this little nun, at this time, it was rather her gentle heart that was wounded — but Mother Vazous could not see there was one, nor that she had hurt it. But everything, even this, can be an instrument for our perfection.

One would never have thought of Bernadette as a saint to teach us humility through suffering. She has always been the little girl in the pictures and the grottos who kneels looking at Our Lady. She did more than that. She lived the doctrine that we reach Christ through Mary and going by way of Mary she shows us how little nobodies knowing nothing can climb the highest peaks of contemplation. She wrote in her notebook:

"O Mary, my Mother, take my heart and bury it deep in the Heart of Jesus!" She carefully copied down the counsel of her Confessor: "Remember often those words . . . Our Lady spoke . . . Penance! Penance! You must be the first to put them into practise, and in order to do so bear in silence everything you have to put up with from your companions and your Superiors, in order that Jesus and Mary may be glorified. Ask Our Lord earnestly to make you understand the cross He wills you to carry this year, and carry it lovingly, faithfully, and generously . . . Do not be afraid. Keep always very close to Our Lord in His tabernacle, and following His example carry the cross hidden in your heart bravely and generously."

This is how she learned humility. We can teach these things to our children, and learn them ourselves. "Do not be afraid . . ." Most of us are afraid of humility because it comes so dear, but Bernadette would keep us company and help us to learn if we would ask her. Our lives and the other spoiled creatures who share them with us will provide the opportunities, just as her life and her companions provided the opportunities for her. In the end her humility was perfect and beautiful. What would you guess would be the last words of St. Bernadette?:

"Holy Mary, Mother of God, pray for me, a poor sinner, a poor sinner."

6

THÉRÈSE OF LISIEUX

STUBBORN SAINT

THÉRÈSE MARTIN was a darling child. She was also spoiled.
She says she was not but then she is a poor judge because, when
you have been spoiled by gentle, loving parents and sisters, it
never quite looks like spoiling, or being spoiled, and you find
other words for it.

It was to be expected. Even the Martins suffered a certain
prejudice in favor of their youngest and let prudence be the victim of indulgence and possessiveness humor misbehavior. The
Martins could spoil their youngest without meaning to just like
everyone else.

This is intensely interesting and helpful to families trying
their best to raise saints, for it shows that faults and defects ex-
isted in even such a child as Thérèse Martin and that is not what
one has been led to believe. Though the faults of a saint should
not be of undue concern when it is their virtues we are supposed
to imitate, nevertheless to know they had some is a relief to us
who have them also. It is also interesting to see that many of the
lovely childhood virtues assumed to have been exclusively hers
are common to almost all small children and common to childhood. Our children share with St. Thérèse the riches of the
baptized and will be given as good a chance to be their kind of
saint as she was to be hers. God does not so much want more
St. Thérèses as He wants more saints. This has to be understood,

or parents cannot search her life for practices that helped form her with any conviction that they might also help form *their* children. Their children have more in common with St. Thérèse than they ever dreamed.

What was she like?

She was very pretty, very intelligent, had captivating ways and was the youngest of nine, the one God sent them in answer to their prayers for a priest. For a family dedicated to the raising of saints, this meant the attention, love and effort of all were focused on this one child in an intense way. She was everybody's darling. "I had always been the most petted and loved by my parents and sisters, and if they too [her two brothers and two sisters in heaven] had remained on earth, they would no doubt have given me the same proofs of affection."

She sometimes was naughty and at other times, although perhaps not deliberately naughty, she was certainly surprised by imperfection. She tells of these things herself. Even her remarkable spiritual perception, her feats of self-denial, did not change her temperament, and faults cropped up clearly enough for her to remember them when she looked back.

She was almost exclusively in the company of her parents and older sisters, and because of this she learned many things other children quite as intelligent might not have occasion to learn until later. It is important to remember that although other children are not as spiritually gifted as St. Thérèse, many are as intelligent. Hers was spiritual genius: the genius to love God heroically. It is not to be confused with a high I. Q. This undoubtedly she possessed but it is not especially pertinent. The point to make is that had her spiritual training been neglected by her parents, she might *not* have been a saint. This poses a question: how do we know we have not had more spiritual giants in the potential? Perhaps there have been thousands of souls with such promise who have not become giants because no one bothered to teach them how. Indeed, St. Thérèse wrote later that had *she* not been raised by *her* parents, with their fine sense of duty toward the care of her soul, she might have become a hardened sinner. She said the soul of a child is like softened wax, waiting to receive the imprint of good or evil from the parents who care for it.

That the love of parents is the medium through which the love of God is taught is perfectly demonstrated by the following tale. When Thérèse learned that heaven was the best possible place to be, she immediately wished both her father and mother would die and go there. (This is not unusual; many children say the same thing.) But what about herself? Would she go to heaven too? Her mother said she would if she were good. But if she were not good? Would she go to hell? Without waiting for an answer she said:

"I know what I will do — I will fly to you in heaven and you will hold me tight in your arms and how could God take me away then?"

Her mother wrote: "I saw by her look she was convinced that God could do nothing to her if she hid herself in my arms."

What power parents have! God is at their mercy. They may reveal Him to their children or not, as they wish. We need not worry about His loving them. We know He does. The danger for us lies in taking such love for granted and doing nothing about it when it wants teaching, illustrating, pointing out. Thérèse's family saw everything in relation to God. When they were not consciously teaching it, they were unconsciously teaching it. She wrote of many things in her childhood that show the effect of this. She used to go to the river with her father to fish, and while he fished she spent the day picking flowers, sharing a picnic lunch, day-dreaming about life and death, earth and high heaven. This kind of day-dreaming is common to childhood. Children who have talked much about God and thought much about Him, will daydream about Him. "See the bug God made? See the flower God made?" One child, picking stones from the brook, said: "See the stones God made that He washed for me?" This is not especially remarkable from a child who has been *taught to see.*

We must leave children time for such things. It is so easy

to over-organize them. One mother said recently with amazement, "I have just realized that my daughter belongs to so many organizations that she no longer has left an afternoon to take a walk." No time is left for solitude, for meditation. Yet everyone says at one time or another, "I have the best times when I am alone." Children say it often, revealing one of their important needs — a healthy, necessary aloneness. Who knows what secret things God works in them when they are alone with Him?

One child said: "When I am alone and having a good time outdoors, sometimes I think about God and that makes hot tears come to my eyes." And this child is no saint! Neither is this an imagined experience, nor something he says to attract attention. He is like every other child God made who is still unspoiled by the world. It is a sign of the homesickness in his soul, the instinct for heaven. It is also one of those hasty, embarrassed confessions small boys are apt to make to their mothers or godmothers or favorite aunts, or teachers, and afterward they are sorry because it probably "sounded dumb." Such avowals embarrass grown-ups and they are suspicious of their sincerity because they no longer know what children are like, nor the quality of the child-likeness we must reacquire if we would enter the kingdom of heaven. How rarely we stop to consider the reality of God dwelling in our children. But the Martins never forgot!

The first time Thérèse saw the sea, she sat with her sister Pauline on a rock and watched the sun sink leaving a path of gold across the water. She gazed for a long time on this symbol of grace lighting up the way for her tiny ship with its white sails. She promised never to steer out of sight of Jesus so as to sail on in peace to the homeland of heaven. Too sentimental? Not at all — it is exactly what she did.

But her family, while cultivating her piety, did not neglect doctrine nor asceticism, both of which are necessary if piety is to last and put on flesh. Doctrine is essential for a strong faith and self-denial whets the appetite for God. Her mother wrote of her at the age of three: "Even Thérèse is anxious to practice mortifica-

tion. Marie has given her little sisters a string of beads on purpose to count their acts of self-denial, and they have really
spiritual but very amusing conversations together. The other
day Céline asked: 'How can God be in such a tiny Host?' and
Thérèse answered, 'That is not strange because God is Almighty.'
'And what does Almighty mean?' continued Céline. 'It means,'
said Thérèse, 'that He can do whatever He likes.' "

Not all three-year-olds would give such an answer, but they
could if they had been taught it. We must not conclude that
since Thérèse became a great saint she came into the world
knowing the answers. That was not necessary. *She had a family
to teach them to her.* Other children have families to whom the
answers are available, and who have the same *obligation* to
teach.

Another time, when she was several years older, she was
upset to learn that not all souls enjoy the same glory in heaven.
This did not seem right. (Questioning to see if God is really as
fair and as good as He is supposed to be, as fair and as good as
they, is constant from young children.) Pauline told her to
get her thimble and her father's water tumbler and fill them
with water. She asked Thérèse which was fuller. But neither
was fuller than the other; one simply contained more because
it was bigger. Oh! *That* was it. Each soul in heaven is filled
to its brim and can hold no more; each, being full of God, is
completely happy. "My Father's house has many mansions."

Mme Martin continues from her letter about the string of
beads: "But it is still more amusing to see Thérèse continually
putting her hand in her pocket and pulling a bead along the
string for every little sacrifice."

St. Thérèse wrote of these self-denials later (she counted
them into the hundreds) and was quite honest about the ease
with which she accomplished them. She despised the quasi-
humility that pretended it had received no great gift when it
had. "I made it a practice never to complain when my things
were taken, and if at any time I were unjustly accused, I preferred to keep silence rather than attempt an excuse. There was,

however, no merit in all this for it came to me quite naturally."

Still, she was not *quite* perfect. When discipline was called for, her mother was the disciplinarian; her father was hopelessly her slave. Her mother used to say laughingly that he always did whatever Thérèse wanted, and he would answer, "Well, why not? She is the Queen!" He called her his Queen, the Queen of France and the Queen of Navarre. Yet Thérèse did not think he had spoiled her. But there is a fine line between spoiling and not-spoiling and parents must always be on guard. One day Thérèse was swinging when her father passed by and called out, "Come give me a kiss, my little Queen." Contrary to her usual way, she did not stir but answered rather pertly: "You must come yourself for it, Papa!" He took no notice of this and went into the house. Thérèse thought this very wise of him. Speaking as a parent, I disagree — or should I disagree as a *mother*? It is exactly the kind of thing doting fathers will do, and mothers will protest. Marie in her motherly way thought it needed notice also. "You naughty little girl, to answer Papa so rudely!" And the reproof took effect. Immediately Thérèse jumped down from the swing and ran into the house, crying out to her father that she wanted to apologize.

The desire to run quickly and beg pardon may not be developed in all children but it is *in* them. It is in everyone. Some need to save face so badly they must be coaxed to apologize — but even then they *want* to be coaxed. Often children will act on their need to "make things right again" quite spontaneously, but where there is a situation which is tense and they are caught off balance, they must have help. The immediate confession of faults and a sincere apology must be encouraged not only for the obvious reasons, but because it prepares a child for one of the sweetest of all his relationships with Christ — that of penitent.

Thérèse seems more like our children when we discover what faults she confessed so quickly. "Mamma, I smacked Céline, I pushed her once. I am sorry and I will not do it again." Once she pulled some wallpaper off the wall "without meaning to." My! *That*'s familiar.

But even Mamma, with her keen eye for little signs of petulance and pride, sometimes capitulated to the utter deliciousness of this child. She wrote this when Thérèse was quite small: "The dear little thing will hardly ever leave me; she is with me continually. She loves to go out to the garden but if I am not there, she cries till they bring her back to me." This sort of thing is so flattering to us! No wonder parents miss the little fault in it. She was not to overcome these baby tears — indeed, they were baby tantrums — for a long time. The weakness of human nature cost her, as the rest of us, and she had to struggle. She wrote that to her great displeasure on their Sunday walks her father thought it wise for her to return before the others lest she be overtired, but she obeyed nevertheless. Céline used to bring home a basket of daisies to reward her on their return.

Yet her statement that she had never denied God anything from the time she was three has made it seem to most parents that, past three, she was not only faultless and sinless but without any need to struggle with even the slightest weakness. This implies it was no fight for her, but if it was no fight, how is she a saint? Sanctity is *heroic*.

She never consciously denied God anything, then; but in her as in the rest of us there were reflexes that reacted to certain stimuli and it was a long hard battle to unseat these. In her comfortable home, among her parents and sisters, the ever-present love and admiration could not help but make her vulnerable to suffering which would not even be suffering to those less accustomed to the atmosphere of approval. She was like a little hothouse flower. Her struggle for holiness would be increased a thousandfold because the chill winds outside would be so much chillier to her. How differently God permitted the childhoods of St. Bernadette and St. Maria Goretti to form them! But not everyone is asked to suffer public disgrace, or destitution, or martyrdom in attempted rape. Each one is asked, however, to suffer the agonies of trying to live with self, with others, to survive hurt feelings, self-pity, misunderstanding, judging, the battle with softness, and so on — and on and on and on. In the Martin family God was preparing a sheltered, loved, admired child to be the saint of the "little way," not a way with only a little suffering, but a way in which there would be terrible suffering from little things — or so they would look beside such poverty and disgrace as the Soubirous', or such a terrible death as Maria's.

Thérèse would go to Love taking Him sufferings which in other lives are not even felt. Maria was probably as cold, as tired, more hungry and certainly more outrageously insulted than Thérèse ever was, but this — with the exception of the final, terrible surprise — was about what she expected of life, and the same was true of Bernadette — at least for a while. They accustomed themselves to it and accepted, hardly murmuring. But Thérèse was different. One dare not try to measure whose suffering was the greatest. No ruler exists to measure suffering. One of the things we must renounce is the comparing of sufferings, mine to yours or his or hers. Suffering is God's gift, His invitation. Each one's is exactly right. God makes no mistakes, giving too much to one, neglecting to give enough to another. Each one is free to suffer it willingly, or to hate suffering it. St. Thérèse has made entirely credible the possibility of crucifixion at the hands of insignificance. After her, we may never judge suffering. The value of it does not lie in *our* measure of the suffering but in God's — and the measure of the love that accepts it.

Thus, one does not rejoice to discover her weaknesses but to discover the roots of her suffering because they are so familiar. The suffering in all lives — as in hers — that costs us most is the denial of our own will. She wrote later: "My God, I choose everything — I will not be a saint by halves. I am not afraid of suffering for Thee. One thing only do I fear, and that is, to follow my own *will*. Accept then the offering I make of it, for I choose *all* that Thou willest!"

This is what our children are made for: to choose God. If only we would always remember, we would care so much more about preparing them!

"I had another fault," Thérèse related, "that of strong self-love." And she told of the episode of the long sleeves and bare arms which showed the seedling of self-love in even this little girl. The family was going to the country and her mother asked Marie to dress Thérèse. "Be sure her arms are not bare because of a possible sunburn." Thérèse said nothing while she was being dressed, "but in my mind I was thinking, 'I would be much prettier with bare arms.'" Anyone but a saint would underestimate self-love in its baby form, but a saint *knows*. This saint in particular knows, for her whole battle was with this weakness. It is *the* enemy. It lost us Paradise. It is not wise to ignore the first signs even in the little ones. As for bare arms, they are not quite the threat to modesty and reserve they were once held to be, but we *do* have *our* customs and they must be resisted on better grounds than bad taste.

Our nature is spoiled. Surrenders to it call only for more surrenders. It is no cliché to say that if you give human nature an inch, it wants a mile. It is a bald comment on the state of man after original sin. We have disapproved of certain improprieties on general principles, yet when the local customs include bare midriffs, baton twirling (in itself inoffensive but not so its prancing and its costumes) and daring formals, we have capitulated weakly because "everybody wears them," and "they're such nice girls." It is not because they are *not* nice girls that they should be modest, but because, as nice as they are, they are weak as all of us are weak and it is possible for them or someone else to think or do or say or be far from nice — for blinking at this weakness. The very statement *"I trust my child"* is overconfidence. The most "trustworthy" child in the world is born into it with Adam's weakness, and *that* cannot be trusted. Our *strength* is in *Christ*. Only if we keep His word, ask His help, imitate His life, will we be strong; only if we will *be* Christian.

St. Thérèse as a little girl pouting because she could not have bare arms was in the mood of our daughters when they want to wear something that is not appropriate to their vocations as Christians. And Mme Martin was wise. She understood very well that even *her* good little girl was not safe from the danger of a devouring pride. Once she offered her a penny if she would kiss the ground and the stubborn little thing would not, even for a penny. Imagine the spectacle had such pride and will and genius been turned in the direction of self instead of God.

Books, reading, reading aloud helped to form this saint. They were an important part of the Martin's family life. Thérèse loved being read to. This is absolutely universal among children. She loved especially liturgical readings that explained the feasts and seasons of the Church year. Like all children, she loved to celebrate the feasts. "The *feasts!* What precious memories these simple words recall. I loved them and you (Pauline) knew so well how to explain the mysteries hidden in each one." And she loved Sundays.

"What a glorious day . . . Almighty God's feast and a day of rest." Every Sunday she went to High Mass with her father. When she was still too little to follow the Mass, he would lean over and whisper to her from time to time, pointing out things of special interest. "Listen attentively, little Queen. He is speaking of your holy patroness." All children love the stories of their patron saints.

The first sermon she ever understood was about the Passion. She was five and a half, an age when children are quick to fill with anguish, even weep over it, vowing if they had been there they would not have let it happen. She remembered watching her father's face at Mass and thinking how great his love for God must be when it could make him look as if his soul had already taken flight. How much we teach at the times we do not know we are teaching!

She received a profound love of the poor from her parents,

who gave alms generously and showed the greatest reverence for even the least admirable of God's family. One time her father helped a drunken man to his feet in the street, took his bag of tools, and supporting him on his arm led him home. Another time he gave alms to a poor epileptic stranded in the railway station, then begged alms in his own hat from the passers-by until the man had enough money for a ticket home. One time Thérèse was walking with her father when they met a poor old man painfully dragging himself along on crutches. Thérèse, accustomed to give alms to the beggars they met on their walks, quite innocently offended him by offering a penny. He smiled at her sadly and shook his head. A few moments later her father bought her a little cake, and with all her heart she wished she might run back to him with it. She turned to look; he was at that moment turning to gaze at her. She vowed to remember him on her First Communion day because it was said that God grants all the wishes a child asks on that day. Five years later she did.

This tremendous sympathy is another of the properties of childhood. The hearts of children are vast, willing to receive anyone, any cause. Grownups are fond of observing how cruel they are to one another, but this need not be. Children are as quick to be compassionate. Which they will be depends entirely upon the teaching of their earliest years. What giant steps they could take with their sympathy if we would teach them from the beginning to see Christ in all men. Parents have but to accept the standards of the world to pass them on to their children. The communicating of values is, for the most part, a process that is not even seen. A child who wanted to give away his mittens to a poor boy hesitated for fear of displeasing his parents. How marvelous if he had been sure his parents would be pleased, knowing he had seen Christ in his friend. What might have happened in the souls of the two boys had the mittens changed hands for Christ's sake? The desire in the heart of the one was precious and pleasing to God, but how visible it would have made Christ's love had he felt free to act!

Thérèse was four years and eight months old when her mother died of cancer. An incident that occurred just before her mother's death makes an important point about family prayer. Thérèse and Céline went each morning to spend the day with a family friend and one morning Céline wondered if they should tell their hostess they had not said their prayers. "Certainly!" said Thérèse. When Céline timidly made this known, the lady replied: "Well, children, you shall say them," and led them to a large room where she left them *alone*. They were amazed! Thérèse exclaimed, "This is not like Mamma; she always said our prayers with us. . . ." The warm, happy, togetherness of family prayer (and the togetherness even during the sessions that are not *perfectly* warm and happy) prepares a soul for prayer alone. God invites each soul to a life of prayer. Family prayer prepares the climate where the habit of prayer will grow.

Her mother's death marked a new period in Thérèse's life, "the most sorrowful of all." "I became timid and shy, and so sensitive that a look was often enough to make me burst into tears. I could not bear to be noticed, or to meet strangers, and I was only at ease with my dear ones at home. . . ."

Life at home, however, seemed to be quite sunny. She did not like dolls much, but she loved to mix colored potions from seeds and the bark of trees and when they "turned out pretty," she would pour some into a little teacup and offer it to Papa. She played hermit with her cousin Marie (the way other children play priest and nun) in a "pretend" hermitage in the back of the garden. One would potter about the "pretend" vegetable patch, while the other would pray (not pretend). One day coming home from school they decided to imitate the hermits' custody of the eyes. Jeanne, her cousin, and Céline were walking behind; little did they know the two in front had their eyes closed. *Crash!* They had run into a display of merchandise on the sidewalk. The shopkeeper ran out bawling, the hermits, now wide-eyed, took off on the run and Jeanne, panting behind them, filled the air with scolding. After a lifetime of hearing none but the most saccharine stories of the Little Flower, it is a joy to discover this little scrape. As a punishment for their folly Marie and Thérèse no longer were allowed to walk together; it was Céline with Marie and Jeanne with Thérèse thereafter. Thérèse had referred at one point to "union of will" between Marie and herself, so she closes this little story with the humorous comment: "This mishap put an end to our *union of wills*. It was all for the best anyhow that partners were changed because the two elders (Céline and Jeanne) were never of the same mind and used to dispute all the way home. So now the peace was complete."

Her sister Pauline prepared her carefully for her first Confession which she made long before First Communion as was the custom. "You had told me, Mother dear, that it was not to a man but to God Himself that I was going to tell my sins, and this truth so impressed me, that I asked you seriously if I should tell Father Ducellier I loved him 'with my whole heart,' since it was God I was going to speak to in his person." This story should never be left out of any child's preparation for Confession.

After her Confession was finished, she passed her rosary to Father Ducellier so he might bless it, and on the way home she stopped to look at it under a street light. "What are you looking at, Thérèse?" asked Pauline. "I am looking to see what a blessed rosary is like."

When she was ten, she became ill with a malady that has been described in various ways, from something diabolically inspired to a severe nervous breakdown. The saint herself thought of it as an "illness in which Satan assuredly had a hand." Satan *would* be interested in such a soul as this. A nervous breakdown would be a very good way to disturb it. She was seriously ill, sometimes semi-conscious and rigid, sometimes delirious, imagining about her all kinds of weird shapes which filled her with fear. Prayers, a novena of Masses, all seemed unavailing. She only grew worse. One Sunday as she lay in a more desperate state than ever, unable to recognize her sisters when they spoke to her, they threw themselves on their knees and prayed fervently before a small statue of Our Lady. Thérèse with her last strength begged Our Lady to have pity on her, and instantly the statue seemed to her to become living and smile. She was cured instantly.

She prepared for her First Communion by following a plan written by Pauline and published later as "Two Months and Nine Days Preparation for First Communion," by Mother Agnès of Jesus. The plan could be adapted to the imaginations of boys and girls in a number of ways. Thérèse imagined she was filling her soul with blossoms to make a bower for the Christ Child. "Every day . . . I made a number of little sacrifices and acts of love which were to be transformed into so many flowers: violets, roses, cornflowers, daisies, forget-me-nots. . . ." Marie talked long and earnestly with her every evening, training her "as the warriors of old trained their children in the profession of arms. . . . She spoke . . . of the imperishable riches which are within our daily reach, and of the folly of trampling treasures under foot, when one need but stoop to gather them." It was a preparation that bore fruit in a sublime First Communion day, and a ceaseless longing for the Holy Eucharist afterward. The plans, the rehearsals, the catechism lessons, the finery — these are not the whole of it. It takes long intimate talks such as these to nourish the heart in its anticipation of the Bread of Life. Parents can do this.

At this time she told Marie she would like to be taught the practice of mental prayer but Marie discouraged her, not realizing that she had been at it for a long time, unknowingly. This should be a fairly common thing in children who have been taught about the love of God. It is not unusual to hear a child say he has been thinking of God. If he has, it is mental prayer, "lifting the heart and the mind to God." The reveries of childhood are very close to it. In answer to one of her mistresses at school, Thérèse described the process exactly. Sister had asked her what she did on holidays at home. "I often hide in the corner of my room, where I can shut myself in with the bed-curtains and then I think." "But what do you think about?"

Sister asked, laughing. "I think about God, about the shortness of life, about eternity — in a word, I *think*." She continues, "It is clear to me now that I was really engaged in mental prayer."

During retreat before her solemn Communion, she fell prey to severe scruples which lasted two years. This was a period where melancholy and insecurity with people, at school, in the world outside her home, made her so ill she had to be taken from school. This is known, in our time, as "failure to adjust to the group." (It is interesting and credible to hear St. Thérèse credit this with the preserving of her vocation.) And she felt sorry for herself too. "True, I sometimes felt sad because of the indifference shown me, but I would console myself by repeating this line from a beautiful poem Papa often recited for us: 'Time is thy barque and not thy home.'"

M. Martin may have been hurt by his daughter's failure to shine amid her associates at school but he did not waste any time trying to ensure it. He was concerned most of all with her eternity. For that matter, even if one does not have the same preoccupation with eternity, how do we *know* all children are supposed to adjust to groups? Who said the normal and right adjustment for every child is *popularity?* How much of the suffering of "ill-adjusted" children might not be part of a tender and solicitous plan by which God wishes to protect them for more important work than being popular? Some are designed to adjust to groups and they will and their work will be as apostles in the groups. Some have other work to do. If we would start implanting this conviction in children from infancy, we could eliminate much of their seeming need to follow the pack.

Then Marie entered Carmel and Thérèse resigned herself to weeping. "I no sooner heard of her determination than I resolved to take no further interest in anything here below, and I shed abundant tears. But tears at that time were nothing unusual; they flowed for the most trivial cause. I was most anxious, for instance, to advance in virtue, yet I went about it in a strange way. *I had never been accustomed to wait on myself or do any housework, and Céline always arranged our room."* (Italics mine.)

And this, without doubt, was a terrible mistake. It is incredible that a family that took so seriously the training of a soul should neglect *work*. The role of the Christian is servant, in imitation of a Master who acted as servant. The neglect of this surely accounts for many of her difficulties. It explains, for example, the enormous heroism of her acceptance of the splashings in the face at the laundry at Carmel. Instead of reproaching the one who splashed her, or indicating her displeasure, she accepted this despoiling and offered it as an act of love. But what is so difficult about that? The mothers of babies, washing diapers, have been splashed in the face with far worse than water in which the handkerchiefs were washed!

But — Thérèse had never done any washing.

She continues: "Now, however, with the intention of pleasing Our Lord, I would sometimes make my bed, or, if Céline happened to be out, I would bring in her plants and cuttings. Since it was for Our Lord's sake that I did these little things I ought not to have looked for any return. But alas! I did look for thanks, and if, unfortunately, Céline did not seem surprised and grateful for my small services, I was disappointed, as my tears soon showed."

This should be one of the most valuable passages of all for us, because it shows the terrible imbalance that can grow in a child who has not been taught to work for the love of God. Undeniably, St. Thérèse was indulged by God as well as by her family, and given many graces other children do not receive, yet even this did not overcome, in her life at home, the lack of training in work. *Work* was the one thing the Martins overlooked.

Thérèse learned that "love and a spirit of self-forgetfulness" are the ways to happiness. Nothing teaches this better than work. If we would have our children learn this, we must give them, together with the other things that make up the Christian life, tasks at which they are obliged to work hard and well for the love of God.

"Again, if I unintentionally offended anyone, far from making the best of it, I would weep like a Magdalen, thus increasing my fault instead of repairing it. Then when I began to be reconciled to the blunder, I would cry for having cried."

This is a great comfort to the parents of adolescents who go from brightest sunshine to intense gloom with the speed of light. Adolescence, even in the saints, looks like nothing quite so much as adolescence.

The cure of her sensitivity and inclination to tears came on Christmas eve in 1886. "I was far from meriting the graces showered upon me by Our Lord. I had a constant and ardent desire to advance in virtue, but how numerous were the imperfections that were mingled with my acts! My extreme sensitiveness made me almost unbearable. . . . All arguments against it were simply useless. I could not correct myself of this miserable failing . . . and how then could I entertain the sweet hope of entering Carmel soon since I was still in *my swaddling clothes!* . . . I must tell you here the circumstances under which I received the priceless grace of my complete conversion. On reaching home after midnight Mass, I knew I should find my shoes in the chimney-corner. During our childhood, this custom filled us with such happiness that Céline now still treated me as a baby, being the youngest in the family (she was almost fourteen) . . . but the hour had come when Our Lord desired to free me from the failings of my childhood, and even its innocent pleasures. He permitted that Papa (fatigued by the midnight Mass), instead of indulging me in his usual way, should feel annoyed and as I went upstairs I overheard him say: 'Well! — let this be the last year!' These words cut me to the very heart, and Céline, knowing how sensitive I was, whispered: 'Don't go down just yet, you would only cry if you looked at your presents before Papa.' But Thérèse was no longer the same — Jesus had transformed her. . . ."

She went down, opened her gifts, praised them and never

hinted that she had heard her father's remark. Céline was amazed. It was so unlike her! "But happily it was a sweet reality and Thérèse had once and for all regained the strength of mind which had left her when she was four and a half (the time of her mother's death). . . . *Satisfied with my good will,* Our Lord accomplished in an instant the work I had not been able to do after ten years of effort. . . . Love and a spirit of self-forgetfulness took complete possession of my heart, and thenceforward, how happy I was!" (Italics mine.)

Good will — that is what God wants. If we will give Him that, He can do something with us. Here is the key to the relation of the faults to the gifts. A great disservice has been done to the Little Flower *and* the generosity of God by ignoring her faults (such as they were) and writing of her as though she had been entirely perfect from her cradle on. What her faults teach especially is that faults are as nothing to God if we give Him our hearts. Parents worry so over faults, and rightly too (one cannot ignore them), but a child's love for God is far more important than his faults, and the love can be the remedy for the faults. All the while we are watching carefully to help them prune away their faults, we should be watching twice as carefully for opportunities to feed their love for God.

Not long after this a picture of the Crucifixion brought to a climax all the desires that had been forming and becoming clearer in Thérèse as the years drew on. "I was consumed with an insatiable thirst for souls; this time it was not priests' souls that enkindled my zeal but the souls of *great sinners,* whom I longed at any cost to snatch from the everlasting flames of hell." She asked for a sign from God approving her desire for souls (a practice we should not encourage in our own children's imitation of the saints). The sign she wanted was the conversion of a notorious criminal, Pranzini, condemned to die on the guillotine. She prayed and made sacrifices for him daily and waited anxiously for the day of execution. "My prayer was granted to the letter. Though Papa never allowed us to read the newspapers, I did not consider it an act of disobedience when, on the day following the execution, I hastily opened the paper, *La Croix,* and looked for the part concerning Pranzini. . . ." He had repented at the last moment and kissed the Sacred Wounds three times.

I confess that when I first read this passage I thought to myself, "But that was disobedience!" I was grateful to learn that her father, hearing about the incident later, was glad Thérèse interpreted his wishes rather than the letter of his prohibition, and I rejoiced to discover *why* he forebade their reading newspapers because I think it is a principle that we must apply to radio, television, movies, popular magazines, and the offerings of the entertainment field. He excused her seeming disobedience thus: "But the motive was in this case a spiritual one and, timid as she was at the time, it would have embarrassed her to be obliged to disclose the reason for wanting to read about Pranzini." His explanation of the prohibition appears here: "She realized that I did not want them (his daughters) to be *wasting their precious time* reading the news of the day — a cause of distraction." (Italics mine.) So often our concern over the good or evil or indifference of radio, television, movies, certain forms of popular music and entertainment gets trapped in an attempt to analyze the offerings themselves, and we fail to see that even if we had the very best in all these fields, we would have to discipline our use of it.

M. Martin was not condemning newspapers in themselves — inevitably useful to him as a means of keeping track of the affairs of his day — but he was implying that the first use of the mind is to listen to God in order to be led to the contemplation of Him. Understanding this, one constantly must be on guard against "wasting precious time" for God in fruitless diversion, whether it be entertainment in newspapers, magazines, radios or television sets. These things are made to serve man, but man is not made for them. His end is God and he must spend more of his time developing this relationship than any other. We defend so often our legitimate need for relaxation, recreation — not quite saying, but almost saying, that we even need to get away from God once in a while! *This is not true!* He is the source of the peace, rest, joy, relaxation, recreation we need. "Come to me, all you who labor and are burdened, and I will give you rest. Take my yoke upon you, and learn from me, for I am meek and humble of heart; and you will find rest for your souls" (Matt. 11:28–30). This is a promise to us — if we will give up distraction.

Freed from her extreme sensitivity, Thérèse developed a passionate desire for learning. She read and studied furiously, learning more in a few months than she had in the whole of her formal school life. "It was to *history* and *science* that I devoted many hours. . . . The chapter from the *Imitation* concerning such study often came to my mind at this time but in spite of that warning, I managed to continue all the same, persuading myself that at my age, it was my duty to study and therefore I was doing nothing wrong. I do not believe now that there was any offense to God in all this but I do admit that there was a good *waste* of time because I set myself a limit of time (to which I was faithful) so as to mortify my desire for knowledge." The chapter she refers to is *Against Vain and Worldly Learning. . . .* "When thou shalt have read and shalt know many things, thou must always revert to the one beginning. I am He Who teacheth men knowledge, and Who giveth a more clear understanding to little ones than can be taught by man. He to whom I speak will quickly be wise and will profit greatly in spirit."

She had loved the *Imitation of Christ* for years and knew most of it by heart; now this and books of spiritual reading became her food. Thérèse and Céline, confidantes in their teens as in their baby years, had long intimate conversations about God as they gazed nightly at the stars out their wide window. "The practice of virtue gradually became sweet and natural to me. In the beginning my looks betrayed the effort, but little by little self-sacrifice grew easy. . . ." It was *work.* But she had been preparing for this "conversion," as she called the Christmas eve experience, ever since childhood. Everyone has such conversions, and each time the old truths seem brand new, as though one had just understood them. "Oh! *That* is what it meant!"

Now she determined to enter Carmel. She was not yet fifteen and her plan met strong opposition. Her father fell in with her, as always, and Céline, the older and therefore the one entitled to go first, generously stepped aside and encouraged her as did Pauline in the convent. But Marie, also there, was determinedly against it and "did everything possible to thwart my plans." Her uncle declared that "to enter such a severe order at the age of fifteen seemed contrary to all human prudence," and said that nothing short of a miracle would make him give *his* consent. Thérèse prayed for the miracle and he changed his mind. Thinking that with her uncle's consent the point had been won, she was shocked to discover that Canon Delatroitte, the ecclesiastical superior at Carmel, thoroughly disapproved of her entry before she was twenty-one. "Of course," he said, "I am only the Bishop's delegate; should he allow you to enter, I shall have nothing to say."

Thérèse was cast into the depths and "Papa was at a loss to console me." He offered to take her to Bayeux to see the bishop. That morning in October 1887 she put up her hair for the first time in order to look very mature, and in answer to the bishop's question about how long she had wanted to enter Carmel, she said, "A very long time, My Lord." The vicar general doubted it had been *all* her fifteen years, had it? She answered solemnly: ever since she was three. But the bishop thought perhaps she should stay home a while longer, to which her father replied that he supported her in her determination, adding that they were going to Rome on pilgrimage and if the bishop should not give his permission, they would not hesitate to speak to the Pope. When the bishop said he would not give his decision before he had spoken to the superior of Carmel, Thérèse began to cry. Taking her head he placed it on his shoulder and caressed her, "in a way, I was told later, he had never done with others." And they returned to Lisieux. "It seemed to me as though my future were forever shattered, for the nearer I drew to my goal, the greater my difficulties became. Yet all the time, deep down in my heart, reigned a wonderful peace, because I knew I was seeking only God's will."

Those who did not know why the Martins were going to Rome suspected it was in an effort to change Thérèse's mind about Carmel. A trip to Rome was *that* worldly. Not that the Martins undertook it in the spirit of the world, but their traveling companions seem not to have been entirely dedicated pilgrims. They were people of rank, moneyed, very gay, reasonably devout, and Thérèse says the whole affair would have injured a vocation less firmly established than hers. But she was not dazzled. It only increased her desire for the cloister. She wanted to be at the business of saving souls. During this journey she discovered the need to pray for priests. She understood for the first time that for all the grandeur of the priesthood priests remain men and subject to human frailty. She was beginning to understand her vocation.

Passing through Switzerland, she marveled at the Alps and promised herself to remember these splendid heights later when life in the convent shut out all but a little space of sky. "I will recall this day and it will encourage me. I will make light of my own small troubles by thinking of the greatness and majesty of God; I will give my heart to Him alone and avoid the misfortune of attaching myself to fleeting trifles. . . ." She was in her teens. It is true she was not a "typical" teen-ager, but one whose baptismal innocence had never been lost; alas, this seems not to be typical. But in her cannot one see one's children's zeal and dedication to causes usually far less exalted mirrored as they might appear had these children's growing-up been guided and nurtured as carefully, as sacramentally?

Perhaps, if Thérèse comes anywhere near being "typical" of anyone, she is typical of those children who discover they have a vocation to religion, who discover they are in love with God. How sad that, with a few exceptions, this kind of love seems not to be typical of the rest. Thérèse was certainly gifted and graced in unique ways, but it was not to Thérèse alone that the invitation to live an intensely spiritual life has been given. We have all been invited. Is this how — granting her unique role *was* different — our teen-agers might tend, did we try as hard to teach as her parents did, to love as her parents did, to be holy as her parents did? Would their great passion for their causes "come out like this" if their lives had been lived as consistently on a supernatural plane as hers? It is easy to say *no, she was different*. That is no answer. We do not know if our children are not as different in their way as she was in hers. There is only one way to know: by bending all our energies to knowing and loving and living for God as she did. If we would have the supernatural life be *the* reality for them, it must be for us.

Rome next, and still on the morning of their audience with the Pope no word from the bishop. Thérèse determined to speak to His Holiness, Leo XIII, on her own behalf, when, unexpectedly, the vicar general of Bayeux announced in a loud voice that he absolutely forbade anyone to address the Holy Father. Thérèse panicked. Céline whispered: *"Speak."* And she did, asking that she be allowed to enter Carmel at fifteen in honor of the Holy Father's jubilee. The Holy Father did not understand what she was saying and asked the vicar-general what this was all about and he, in turn, said the matter was being looked into by the superiors of the Carmel. Thérèse spoke again: "Holy Father, if only you were to say 'Yes,' everyone else would be willing." (Was there ever a more stubborn child!)

The Pope looked at her affectionately and said, "You will enter if it be God's will." Thérèse was about to coax again when she was told by two of the Guards to rise and move on. When she refused to leave, they had to take her by the arms, lift her to her feet and lead her weeping to M. Martin!

Her original plan had been to enter Carmel on the Christmas before she was fifteen because it was the anniversary of her "conversion." She entered at the age of fifteen and three months, on the following April 9.

Out of the context of religion, without sanctifying grace and the obvious operations in her soul of the gifts of the Holy Spirit, she might have been a prodigy of another order acting typically fifteen. The same determination and passionate dedication are seen in the lives of child tennis stars, child actresses, child singers — *and also in their parents.* Thérèse's gifts, her mind, her heart, were trained first on God, as her parents' were before her, and she was determined to give them to *His* service. It happened that He wanted her a nun, but this kind of concentration on God is not only for those who will become nuns. She had a number of gifts; indeed, she ended by writing a book. To look to God for direction is the only way to go about discovering how to use one's gifts whatever they are, and *if* they are playing tennis, or acting, or singing.

From the time she was a little girl, Thérèse felt she was "born for great things." She understood that her "personal glory would never reveal itself before the eyes of men, but would consist in becoming a saint — *a great saint.*" But this is in everyone, not just those who know that God is man's end. Man is the center of his own universe first of all. He *knows* in his heart that he is meant for something great. He waits for it momentarily. If he doesn't discover it, if it doesn't "happen," he tries to prove it anyway and then he ends up in sin — or sickness. But he is right all the time: he is created for union with God and this is greater than his wildest dreams. However, if he is not taught it is this, he will try union with everything but God, knowing ecstasy is to be found somewhere. It is to be found lastingly only in God. It is terrible not to know.

And it is terrible not to understand these things when we are raising children because it explains so much about them. Especially, it explains teen-agers who are sometimes driven to such heartbreaking or ridiculous ends in their effort to find something but they don't know what. People say "to find themselves," and in a way that describes it, but then no one has *really* failed to find self. We are full of it. It is more to the point to say we need to get rid of self, or to know what to do with self. It is useful and fills a need, has a work. Teen-agers suspect they are important and they are quite right. Since the Redemption they are needed by God to help with the work of bringing all men to Christ. Whatever their individual vocations, this vocation is common to all. Only *this* is worth giving your*self* away for. "I will give my heart to Him alone and avoid the misfortune of attaching myself to fleeting trifles." What they need most of all is a *cause*. Lo — they have one, but too often no one has told them what it is.

Thérèse was tempted to spend the last three months before her entry into Carmel leading a life less strict than usual, but she resolved to be even more more mortified. "When I say mortified, it is not to give the impression that I practiced corporal mortification. I have never been attracted to such penances. Far from resembling those heroic souls who from their childhood practiced all kinds of mortifications . . . I made my mortifications consist simply in checking my self-will, keeping back an impatient answer, rendering a small service in a quiet way, not resting my back when seated, and so on. . . ."

She entered Carmel on April 9, 1888, to pray and suffer for souls.*

Trials began immediately. Spiritually arid, she suffered much at the hands of Mére Marie de Gonzague, the superior. She was excoriated publicly for leaving a cobweb in the cloister, for going daily to the garden to weed (she was under obedience but it looked like "taking the air"), and for her "slow ways and want of thoroughness." When she spent an hour with the superior, she was scolded most of the time. Her struggle to please — and nothing was so certain but that nothing would please — was like a child trying to please a difficult teacher, a wife trying to please a difficult mother-in-law, a mother-in-law trying to please a difficult wife, an employee trying to please a difficult boss. She was learning to work for Jesus alone.

"I thank God for having provided me with so sound and valuable a training: it was a priceless grace. What should I have become . . . if I had become the pet of the community? Instead of seeing Our Lord in the person of my superiors, I might have

* St. Thérèse herself said, "I have come to save souls, and especially to pray for priests." — *Publisher*, 1995.

considered only the creature, and my heart ... would have been ensnared by human affection in the cloister."

This is the answer for all the rebels, whether in their tens or teens or twenties — or sixties. It is the invitation to cut the heart free of dependence upon human approval. It is terribly hard anyway — and for her it was more than that. She had lived the entire fifteen years of her life surrounded by approval.

To be told at the close of her novitiate that she could not be professed for another eight months was a bitter disappointment and very hard to accept. But one day at prayer she was given the grace to know "that my too eager desire to take my vows was mingled with much self-love." For a long time she had thought of herself as Jesus' plaything, a little ball, to amuse Him as He pleased. Now she saw that "since I belonged to Our Lord and was His little plaything to amuse and console Him, *it was for me to do His will and not for Him to do mine.*" This is a great triumph for anyone — and especially for a girl whose wishes had been granted in abundance so many times in her life. She decided she would use the months of waiting to make a wedding garment of love and self-sacrifice, much as she had prepared in her soul the bower of blossoms at the time of her First Communion.

She discovered this: "He does not disclose everything at once to souls, but as a rule gives His light little by little." Self-knowledge comes rapidly — whether to parents or their children — once we begin to surrender our wills. "At the beginning of my spiritual life — between the ages of thirteen and fourteen — I often wondered what greater knowledge of perfection could come to me later on, for I thought it impossible to acquire a better understanding of it than I then had. (Oh, the thirteens and the fourteens — they know it all!) It was not long, however, before I learned that in this matter the more one advances, the farther one seems from the goal, and now I am not only resigned to seeing myself always imperfect, but the thought of it even affords me joy."

She had liked having nice things about her as a postulant.

Now she began to work at breaking her desire for such satisfactions. She would once have pitied herself, she wrote, if someone took her lamp by mistake and she had to sit in the dark, but God taught her that the meaning of true poverty was, "being deprived of not only what is convenient, but what is necessary. . . ." It made her happy to spend her hour for work sitting in the dark. (Not long ago a young mother wondered how, even in holy poverty, one justified the neglect of trips to the dentist. St. Thérèse touches it here.)

She grew in her preference for the least rather than the most, the worst rather than the best, frightening lessons when read from St. John of the Cross but quite within reach as St. Thérèse demonstrates them. The point, of course, is not to be *miserable* but *free from self-love* and more happy than ever (the effect of being freed from self-love). For example, she was glad when a pretty water jug was taken from her cell and replaced by a large, badly chipped pitcher. A tiny thread it was, an attachment to pretty things cut. She crushed the head of a pretty pin for the same reason, another thread cut. It was not necessary, of course. Neither the pin nor the water jug were occasions of sin. Neither does this mean that every Christian seeking perfection must cease to take pleasure in pretty water jugs nor crush the heads of pretty pins. These are but two examples of what were probably thousands of such acts performed by Thérèse in her determination to stamp out self-love. Each child, each adult, will meet as many thousands of opportunities to counter self-love, and each vocation frames them differently. Her example here is meant, not to set us on our guard with water pitchers and pins, but to show us the minutiae of which the way to perfection consists. It is not for the most part a dazzling display of anything, unless *love* — but the love is often uncomprehended; it is consistency that is the characteristic of the saint. Long after others have lost their zeal the saint is still stubbornly fighting. She had vowed: "I will not be a saint by halves! I choose all that Thou willest!" So she determined to give all.

She began trying not to excuse herself when she was accused, "but I found this very difficult." The impression has been given too many times that she found it easy. Her first victory cost her a good deal. A jar had been left beside a window and was found broken. The novice mistress was very displeased and believed Thérèse to be the culprit. She scolded her for being untidy and careless. Without explaining, Thérèse promised to be much more careful in the future — but it was hard. She was still very little advanced in self-renunciation, she wrote. One could believe it would be hard for *that* will to renounce itself. "I found it necessary to console myself with the thought that all would come to light on the day of Judgment." Just like the rest of us.

Most of all she tried to practice "little hidden acts of virtue, such as folding the mantles which the Sisters had forgotten and being on the alert to render them help." Bless her heart. This is the sort of thing a good housewife does by second nature. Every young girl's training should include such tidiness and consideration merely as part of daily duty and always for the love of God.

She had an attraction towards penance but after a few efforts ended in failure — like wearing a spiked cross that caused infection, and putting wormwood (a bitter herb) in her food — she was not permitted to do anything unusual beyond leading the rigorous Carmelite life. She was not even allowed to keep the fasts until she was twenty-one; therefore, for practically two-thirds of her religious life she was dispensed. "Indeed, the only mortification I was permitted was the overcoming of my self-love, which did me far more good than any bodily penance could have done." With the help of Our Lady she prepared her wedding dress and she was professed at last on September 8, the feast of the Nativity of the Blessed Virgin.

The following year on retreat she learned something important to the making of her *little way*. She frankly admits she did not enjoy preached retreats, but this retreat master was an exception. Not only did he launch her "full sail upon the ocean of confidence and love which had so long attracted me," but he also told her that her *faults* did not grieve Almighty God. She had never before heard that it was possible that faults should not give pain to God, and the idea filled her with joy. It fitted her picture of Our Lord's tenderness. She had felt He must be more tender than even a mother, and she knew — having had many a "mother" in her short life — how ready a mother is to forgive the involuntary small faults of her child. It was a key. "Fear makes me shrink, while under love's sweet rule I not only advance — I fly."

At the end of her eighteenth year an epidemic of influenza struck Carmel and *Soeur* Thérèse helped nurse the sick and bury the dead, working endlessly, exhaustingly. During this period she was able to receive Holy Communion daily, a rare privilege at this time. But far from increasing her consolation, there never was a time when she felt it less. Now, however, she did not care, for it was her desire to give satisfaction to Jesus, not receive it from Him. She pictured her soul as a rubbish heap and asked Our Lady to raise a pavilion there to receive her Son, calling on the angels and the saints to come and praise Him with her. Yet even this did not stay the distractions or the drowsiness, so she practiced making thanksgivings all day long — to make up for having done so badly in choir. "You see . . . my way is not the way of fear; I can always find means to be happy and to profit by my failings, and Our Lord Himself encourages me to do so. . . . How sweet is the way of Love! True, one may fall and be unfaithful to grace, but Love knows how to draw profit from everything, and quickly consumes whatever may be displeasing to Our Lord, leaving in the heart only a deep and humble peace." This utter confidence of a little child is her way of spiritual childhood.

Now she got no satisfaction from any spiritual reading except the *Imitation* and Holy Scripture. No matter how beautiful a book might be, it did not help her. More and more Our Lord instructed her from within her soul. She did not "hear" Him in the manner of that mystical grace, but rather learned from Him silently. "The Teacher of teachers instructs without the sound of words, and although I have never heard Him speak, yet I know He is within me, always guiding and inspiring me; and just when I need them, lights hitherto unseen break in upon me. As a rule, it is not during prayer that this happens but in the midst of my daily duties." She is showing busy parents how the interior life works. He is present like this, waiting to speak, in every soul in the state of grace.

But how, Thérèse wondered, could she achieve sanctity when she had so many imperfections? She would have to find a short way, a little way, since she was too weak to climb like the big saints did. She found in Holy Scripture, *"Whosoever is a little one, let him come to me,"* and she knew she could be a saint if she were content to remain as a child, simple, unquestioning, obedient, giving what she could give, accepting what she was asked to accept.

One of the things Thérèse was asked to accept was the role of assistant mistress of novices, with almost entire responsibility for the training of the young nuns. She taught them lessons she had learned painfully herself. Here, strangely enough, she is like a natural parent. She teaches wisdom that applies to family life as well as the convent, lessons we might well learn from her and apply to ourselves and our children. One of the most important concerns dependence upon human affection. It applies to the need for affection and the demonstrations of it which entangle so many young people in both light and serious love affairs. The temptation to seek affection is common to every vocation and the devil will lay a trap for such hunger wherever he finds it, seeking to bar it from reaching its end in God. Although St. Thérèse was teaching her novices that to seek satisfaction for self in human affection builds a barrier to knowing fully *God's* love, the principle applies to lay life as well as to the religious.

What our society has come to look upon as something *due* the young, i.e., frequent and heavy dating, involvement in high school and college love affairs as a prelude to marriage, is neither a good nor necessary preparation for choosing a life mate. We have been sold the diabolical idea that sampling many possible partners gives one a better chance of finding the right one, rather than resisting the allure of pleasure with the *many,* and waiting for prayer and God to lead to the *one*. Since love is meant to serve God, not merely satisfy man, it makes much better sense to put one's chances for a happy union in His hands. Nor will love satisfy man for long unless it does serve God, because that is how God made it to be. That is one of the laws He made that operates inexorably, whether we like it or not.

St. Thérèse writes of her own relationship to her mother superior in Carmel (and remember, *sin* is not involved here, but the indulgence of natural cravings for conversations, select friendships, signs of affection and so forth): "I remember when I was a postulant there were times when I was so violently tempted to seek my own satisfaction, some crumbs of pleasure, by having a word with you, that I was obliged to hurry past your cell and cling to the bannisters to keep myself from turning back. Many were the permissions I wanted to ask; pretexts for yielding to my natural affection suggested themselves in the hundreds. How glad I am that from the beginning I learned to practice self-denial! Already I enjoy the reward promised to those who fight bravely, and I no longer feel the need of refusing all consolation to my heart, for my heart is set on God. Because it has loved only Him, it has grown, little by little, till it can give to those who are dear to Him a far deeper love than if it were centered in a barren and selfish affection."

These words, written of the love-life of a young nun with God, apply stunningly to the love-life of a young layman. The setting is different but the application to the human heart is the same. "Pretexts for yielding to my natural affection suggested themselves in the hundreds." How exactly her allusion to the affections which could entrap a religious and divert her from the pursuit of God applies to the liberties young people in the world would sanction for themselves and which would divert their attention from God. The object of both vocations — marriage and religion — is God. The means is love: the love of God in marriage, and the love of God in religion. For the religious to spend her love on attachment to persons is a risk which could defeat her purpose in leaving the world. For the layperson to dabble in love affairs is the same risk. The very fact that marriage is his vocation means his struggle will be partly with his body. Both vocations demand, for all their differences, *supernatural* love. Both have temptations which make the same appeal to natural love: "These are only natural affections, after all . . . it is only reasonable that one indulge them. . . ." The words apply to the temptations in both vocations.

"How glad I am that from the beginning I learned to practice self-denial!" The time for learning self-denial begins just beyond babyhood; it is all the years leading to this.

Her joy, as a young virgin freed of all attachment to self-satisfaction is the same as the joy of the chaste lover: "Already I enjoy the reward promised to those who fight bravely . . . for my heart is set on God. Because it has loved only Him, it has grown . . . till it can give to those who are dear to Him (whether one's Sisters in religion or one's sweetheart, fiancée, husband, wife) a far deeper love than if it were centered in a barren and selfish affection."

She is like a parent speaking to parents when she writes of guiding her novices. "Our own tastes, our own ideas, must be put aside, and in absolute forgetfulness of self we must guide souls, not by our way, but along that particular path which Our Lord Himself indicates. . . . I have been like a watchman on the lookout. . . . Nothing escapes me. . . . I would prefer a thousand times to receive reproofs rather than inflict them on others, yet I feel it necessary that the task should cause me pain, for if I spoke through natural impulse only the soul in fault would not understand she was in the wrong and would simply think: 'The Sister in charge of me is annoyed about something and vents her displeasure upon me, although I am full of the best intentions.'" How like family life! We must pray for the grace to correct our children from a supernatural impulse, else they, like her novices, might think: "The mother and father in charge of me are annoyed and vent their displeasure although I am full of good intentions!" We must not confuse blunders with faults, mistakes with sins. Only if our motive is supernatural can we overcome our irritation and always differentiate between them; correction and punishment must be dictated by our concern for our child's soul, not our embarrassment in front of the neighbors!

She was severe. She writes that if they could read how it pains her to correct them, they would say "so far as they can see, it does not in the least distress me to run after them, to point out how they have soiled or torn their beautiful white fleece." She was a real mother. "But in their hearts they know I love them. . . ." They were like all children.

She gives invaluable information to parents about their guidance of the souls of their children. "From the beginning I realized that all souls have more or less the same battles to fight, but on the other hand I saw that since no two souls were exactly alike, each one must be dealt with differently. With some I have to humble myself and not to shrink from confessing my own struggles and defeats; by this means they have less difficulty in acknowledging their faults, being consoled by the discovery that I know their trials from my own experience. In dealing with others, my only hope of success lies in being firm and in never going back on what I have said, since self-abasement would be mistaken for weakness."

Again and again her experience with the novices mirrors family life. One novice said: "You did well to be severe yesterday. . . . At first I was indignant but after I had thought it over I saw you were right. I left your cell thinking all was at an end between us and determined to have nothing more to do with you. Then . . . the light began to shine and now I have come back to hear all you have to say." So the young mistress served "some food less bitter." But she soon discovered she must not go too far! "If I let fall the slightest remark that might seem to soften the hard truths of the previous day, I noticed my little Sister trying to take advantage of the opening. . . ."

But most important of all — *parents note* — was prayer. "My whole strength lies *in prayer and sacrifice:* these are my invincible weapons, and experience has taught me that the heart is won by them rather than by words."

She tells about her prayer: an uplifting of the heart, a glance toward heaven, a cry of gratitude, and love, in times of sorrow as well as joy. ". . . there is no need to recite set prayers composed for the occasion [all the time] — were this the case, I should indeed deserve to be pitied!" Aside from the Divine Office, she had not the courage to search books for beautiful prayers. They were so numerous, so beautiful, she could not choose between them; they only made her head ache. "Unable either to say them all or to choose between them, I do as a child who cannot read — I say just what I want to say to God, quite simply, and He never fails to understand me." When she was so dry of soul no good thought would come, she repeated very carefully one *Our Father* and one *Hail Mary* and these were her food.

Compliments came to her from the novices and from others for her success with the novices, "but the remembrance of my weakness is so constantly present to me that there is no room for vanity." When she wearied of the oversweet diet of compliments, Our Lord served her "with a salad well-flavoured and mixed with plenty of vinegar." Then He let her novices "see me as I really am and they do not find me altogether to their liking. With a simplicity that is delightful they tell me how I try them and what they dislike in me; in fact, they are as frank as though it were a question of someone else."

A strange and marvelous transformation had taken place in her. She had reached the point of loving that lies *beyond* the frightening words of St. John of the Cross: "Strive always, not after that which is most easy, but after that which is most difficult . . . not most pleasant, but most unpleasant . . . not after great things, but after little things . . . not after which is higher, but which is lower. . . ." That it *has* a point seems to elude some. The point of it — the prize to be won — is to be rid of *self.* She says of herself: "How can anything so contrary to nature afford such extraordinary pleasure? Had I not experienced it I could not have believed it possible!" The writings of St. John of the Cross had always been her favorite, after the *Imitation* and Scripture. At seventeen and eighteen these alone satisfied her. She had always followed him but she was almost surprised to see that his teaching worked!

What did she do that God should work this wonder in her soul? Here are some of the things.

There was *Soeur* St. Pierre, the most crotchety of invalids. Someone had to help her into the refectory nightly but no one wanted to — not even *Soeur* Thérèse. She offered, however, because she could not bear to miss the opportunity promised by Our Lord: *As long as you did it to one of these the least of my brethren, you have done it to Me.* Even so, it took all her courage. Her help was accepted only after considerable persuasion. "First her stool had to be moved and carried in a particular way, without the least hurry, and then began the journey. Supporting the poor old Sister by her girdle, I tried to acquit myself of the task as gently as I could; if by some mischance she stumbled, I was told I was going too fast and that she would certainly fall; when I tried to lead her more slowly she would say: 'Where are you? I don't feel your hand. You are letting go your hold. I am going to fall! I was right when I said you were too young to take care of me!' "

When they reached the refectory she had to be installed in her place "with some maneuvering." That done, she had to have her sleeves turned back "always according to her own special rubric." Then Thérèse was free to go. But she noticed it was very difficult for her to cut her bread, so she offered this last little service willingly, and old and cranky as *Soeur* St. Pierre was, she could not help be touched. This last service and her smile won the old nun's entire confidence in the end.

There was a Sister near her in the choir whose presence Thérèse could always identify by a peculiar little noise (which was special to this particular Sister) and during meditation this so irritated *Soeur* Thérèse that at times she was wet with perspiration from the effort to resist silencing her. She knew she should bear it patiently for love of God to avoid hurting the Sister, so she struggled to find pleasure in the noises. She waited for them, listening as one expecting music, and offered this strange suffering to Our Lord as her prayer.

Another nun was a constant source of annoyance to her and she was sure the devil was accentuating the nun's bad points in her eyes. She knew charity ought not only to be in the heart but should show itself in deeds; so when she met the nun she prayed for her, offered her virtues and merits to God, and tried to do her some little service. If the nun tried her in conversation, she made herself smile and change the subject. Yet sometimes the irritation was beyond endurance. Then she had to slip away quickly in order not to reveal her struggle to be pleasant. The outcome of these tactics was that one day the Sister said, "Tell me, *Soeur* Thérèse, what it is that attracts you to me so strongly? I never met you without being welcomed with your most gracious smile!" St. Thérèse writes: "What attracted me was Jesus, hidden in the depths of her soul, and I answered that I smiled because I was happy to see her (not adding, of course, for spiritual reasons only)."

One time it was necessary for her to enter the cell of Mère Marie de Gonzague, who was ill, to return the keys to the sacristy. Another Sister, afraid of disturbing the superior, tried to take the keys from Thérèse, who insisted, however, that it was *her* duty to return them and that she too wanted no noise, and she tried to push her way in. Their genteel tug-of-war over the keys awoke the superior and the blame was laid on *Soeur* Thérèse who was "burning to defend myself." But it occurred to her suddenly that if she did she would lose her peace of mind, so she "ran away." And this was so hard to do that she had to sit down on the stairs to quiet the beating of her heart. I love this incident, especially. She *was* partly to blame, and seeing her impulse to defend herself, even so, and save face brings her very close. Before we can begin to take injustices silently, we must learn to accept justice! It is hard to admit you *have* been wrong.

When starting to paint, if she found her brushes in confusion or a ruler or penknife missing, she was tempted to lose patience and had to firmly resist the impulse to "demand, and sharply demand," her possessions. Then she remembered Our Lord's words: "If any man take away thy coat, let go thy cloak also unto him," and tried to appear glad to be rid of them. If she had to ask them back, she tried to do so as one of the truly poor in spirit who expect nothing, who are content with the role of servant, and who are happy to discover that when one *is* relieved of his coat and his cloak, he can now run — not merely walk — to God.

She ruthlessly exposes our imperfect poverty of spirit. We are so often kind for the sake of being considered kind, or in the hope that our kindness will be returned; sinners do as much. We take a natural delight in pleasing friends; sinners do the same. We have little ways of showing that we know an imposition when we see one, instead of giving or serving an importunate seeker with a generous heart. And what if we *think* of something wise or something funny and say it, and we hear someone repeating *our* words later as though they were their own! Ah, but don't we find an opportunity to let all know that that was our thought first, as though the Holy Spirit, who sent it, could not send us another.

It was hard to love the way she wanted to love. She found the secret of love in the ever-presence of Jesus.

"Oh Lord! Thou dost never ask what is impossible; Thou knowest better than I how frail and imperfect I am; Thou knowest that I could never love my Sisters as Thou hast loved them, unless Thou, O my Jesus, *lovest* them *Thyself within me.* It is because Thou dost desire to grant me this grace, that Thou hast given a *new* Commandment. Oh! dearly do I cherish it, since it proves to me that it is Thy will *to love in me* all those Thou dost bid me love."

There is our answer. None of this is beyond any of us. The secret of our strength lies in our weakness. St. Paul said that was *his* secret — for Christ is the strength of the weak ones and we are the weak.

Here is her practical instruction if we would really love:

"When I show charity towards others I know that it is Jesus Who is acting within me, and the more closely I am united to Him, the more dearly I love my Sisters. Whenever I wish to increase this love, and the devil brings before me the defects of a Sister for whom I may feel but little attraction, I hasten to look for her virtues and good motives. I call to mind that though I may have seen her fall once, she may have gained many victories over herself which in her humility she conceals, and also that what appears to be a fault may very well, owing to the good intention that prompted it, be an act of virtue. I have all the less difficulty in persuading myself that this is so because of one of my own experiences that taught me that we must never judge."

Then she tells of an occasion when the portress came to ask if one of them would do her a certain service. Thérèse was eager, but she knew her neighbor was as eager, so she deliberately folded her sewing slowly to give her neighbor the opportunity first. The portress noticed the deliberation and said, laughingly, "Ah! I thought you would not add this pearl to your crown: you are too slow." And the community was left under the impression that she had acted imperfectly. Because it showed her once and for all how an act of virtue can look to others like an imperfection, she reasoned that it would be as easy for an imperfection to look like a virtue. It helped her not to judge others. We dare not: "Judge not and ye shall not be judged."

In these lessons taught by St. Thérèse are the remedies for all our problems. There are applications to every child and every grownup. The passion to possess things, to follow fads, to dress as the rest, to do as the rest, all these are treated here. The remedies for pride, stubbornness, smugness, selfishness, respect of persons are revealed here. Strangely enough, these are the answers that suggest themselves to all souls at one time or another in flashes of simplicity (touches of grace), but often they are rejected because they seem *too* simple, "unreasonable," not in accord with the behavior and customs of the rest of the world. Thérèse's way seems too simple and we pass it by looking for something more complicated. *We* have become complicated so we reason that God must be complicated too. God is only complicated to *us*. How we wish it *could* be this simple!

For example, how often have we wished praying were not so complicated, but there are so many to pray for, so many intentions, so many things we should say in our prayers. Thérèse wrote that she could not possibly remember all the names of those who wanted her to pray for them, nor their intentions, nor the things she wanted to remember herself. She would have been awake most of the night had she tried to remember, and then she might have fallen asleep and forgotten someone (she sometimes did fall asleep at her prayers). So she prayed in the words of Solomon: "Draw me; we will run after Thee to the odor of Thy ointments. . . ." In drawing her, she reasoned, He would draw also all the souls she loved, since she could not separate herself from them.

She thought of those Christians who offer themselves as victims in reparation for sins against God's goodness, and thought that she would rather be a victim of His *love,* loving Him for all those who do not — who neither know His love nor return it. With her characteristic childlikeness, she assumed the position of the *heart* in the Mystical Body, reasoning that if each one is some member of the Body, she would choose to be the heart for she wanted to love *all* the members and *feed love* to all the members. Her prayer, her life, she would pour out into the entire Body, feeding the missionaries afar, the priests at home, the Sisters, the laity, all, as the heart pumps life into all.

Thérèse put out her arms and gathered up the world and offered herself for each one in it. We can do the same, and we can teach our children to do the same. They are childlike *now*. We can teach them the way of love before the world has a chance to spoil them.

One of the most poignant of all the episodes toward the end of Thérèse's life was the night she went to bed and felt something hot and thick surge up in her throat. She guessed what it was. "As our lamp was out I knew I must wait till morning to make sure of the happy news, for I suspected that I had vomited blood. Morning was not far off and as soon as I arose, I remembered that I had some good news to learn: going over to the window I found I had guessed right." It does not mean, as some have believed, that she thought it was a good thing to have tuberculosis. It was a welcome portent to her because she longed to go see God, and this meant that it was His will she go soon.

But she died hard. She suffered the black desolation of the night of the soul, the trial of faith that seems to be desertion. The devil tempted her as she lay dying, daring her to believe that there was really a heaven waiting for her and a God who loved her. There was a constant stream of nuns making pointless conversation, asking if she suffered, if she were a saint, repeating bits of community gossip on the subject of her sanctity or lack of it. Thérèse heard one nun wondering what the Prioress would write of her when she was dead, since "she had done nothing." She heard another say, after she declined some beef tea, that not only had Thérèse done nothing, but she was not even a good religious. The Sisters brought the straw mattress for her corpse downstairs, put it in the hall outside and she saw it. The artificial lilies arrived for her funeral and she asked to see them also. She answered questions about her supposed sanctity in various ways: "No, I am not a saint;" again, "No, I am not a great saint;" and once, "You know very well you are nursing a little saint." She did not say she had had a revelation but she might have been divinely inspired, nevertheless; she might have been speaking of the state of sanctifying grace; and she might have been speaking as a soul who has tried to live in union with the saints. More than anything else, it sounds like the remark of a child who has put her trust in holy Hope and has taken God at His word. *He can* make such souls saints, if they will become as little children.

She endured horrible agonies during the last three months. Haemorrhages, violent intestinal pain, fits of choking, coughing, suffocation. Almost daily she maintained a high fever in the afternoon and again and again she said she felt herself in Purgatory. Finally, her lungs were entirely gone. "My little Mother," she said to Pauline, who describes her last illness, "I should despair unless I had faith. I can well understand how it is that those without faith kill themselves when they suffer as much as this. Take good care not to leave any poisonous remedies within the reach of any sick people you look after if they suffer such agonies as these. For I assure you that when pain reaches this pitch, one could lose one's reason any moment."

Finally, on the evening of September 30, 1897, reduced to a little, emaciated, burned-out bit of a thing, she died, saying: "Oh, I love Him. . . . Dear God, I love You!"

Long before when she was very tiny her mother had written letters about her in words that should warm the heart of every father and mother, words to store away against the time when things have gone all wrong and bitter discouragement makes them wonder if their children could possibly "turn out right." Her mother had written about her pretty ways, her tiny mouth, her gaiety, her fond nature, but she also wrote the following about her disposition:

"I find it necessary to correct our poor baby who, at times, goes into dreadful tantrums. Whenever she is crossed, she rolls herself on the floor like someone in despair who believes that everything is lost. There are times when she almost suffocates from emotion. She is a very nervous child."

And she wrote this: "Céline is naturally inclined to be good . . . as to that little puss, Thérèse, one cannot tell how she will turn out, she is still so young and thoughtless. She is more intelligent than Céline but has not nearly so sweet a disposition as her sister. Her stubbornness is almost unconquerable. When she has said *No* nothing will make her change; you might leave her all day in the cellar without getting her to say *Yes*. She would rather sleep there than do so."

So her stubbornness was an important part of it all. Stubbornness built upon by grace, together with immense love, is what St. Thérèse is made of. What made the difference? What happened to transform the stubbornnesss this way? I think the answer is to be found in one line she wrote about her childhood:

"As I grew older, my love of God grew more and more, and *I frequently offered Him my heart, using the words Mamma had taught me:* O my God, I give You my heart: take it, I beseech You, so that no creature might ever possess it but You alone, O my sweet Jesus."

7

THE HOLY FAMILY

IT WAS an amazing thing God did when He created the family, although how amazing it is impossible to say since we are too small to know *all* about it, and our words place us at a disadvantage to say even the things we do know. Past, present and future are poor ways of expressing something that happened where there is no time at all. But one must try.

God did not, we know, create the universe and then decide to put families in it. He thought of the families first. What happened can be explained in this way to most children, to, say, a child named Philip:

"Close your eyes and think of who you are. Do you see yourself in your mind? Now say the word that is your name. As best as I can explain it, Philip, that is how it was when God the Father saw Himself in *His* mind and spoke the word that was *His* name. Who He saw was God the Son. That is why God the Son is called *the Word* by St. John in his Gospel — the part that is used most days as the last Gospel in the Mass. God the Father looked at the Son and loved Him, and God the Son looked at the Father and loved Him, and their love was so great that we call it another Person in God: the Holy Spirit.*There they were since forever, loving one another, when out of their love came the idea: 'I am going to make *Philip* — because I want him!'"

Philip was loved into existence, as were Stephen and Christopher and all the others who ever were in the world and who ever will be in the world. Each exists because he is wanted. God made the world in order to have a place to put them.

---

*Catholic teaching affirms that while the Holy Spirit is the Divine Love between the Father and the Son, He is nevertheless truly a *Person.* — *Publisher,* 1995.

After the world was made, beautiful and orderly with all things in their places, He made Adam (out of clay which He had made out of nothing), and out of Adam He made Eve. Then He changed His manner of creating. Instead of creating the rest from clay or from one another in that fashion, He promised Himself to let them help Him forever, and with that He made the sacrament of marriage and the family. Ever since then He has had to wait for the consent of each mother and father before He could create the souls He has wanted since forever.

God does only what is perfect so there is no improvement to be made on the idea of marriage and the family. It is true that since the Fall, families are far from perfect, but even in a fallen world there is no better way for man to begin than in a family. It is his frame. Once God chose to become Man, it became *His* frame. Therefore, to examine His life in His family should yield us all the secrets of perfection, for the Holy Family's was a perfect life in a fallen world.

I confess I once resented being told that if we would live perfect lives we should model ourselves after the Holy Family. Not, you must understand, that I did not admire them, but I considered them inimitable. Our Lady's privilege of Immaculate Conception made her so different from us. She did not have even our inclination to sin. We are never safe from temptation. We are always able to fall. How could we imitate her — *pretend* we are not? In the same way I considered the Christ Child inimitable. It is a nice thing to say, "imitate the Christ Child," but it is a bit more than impossible. *He was God.* St. Joseph, too, was chosen and prepared as no one before him or after, to be the husband of the Immaculate Virgin and the foster-father of God. Imitating them, I considered, was a manner of speaking. One was not meant to take it literally.

I was quite wrong. We are meant to take it literally and strive with all our strength to imitate the Holy Family, and it is precisely because they are who they are that this is so. The imitation of anyone else is a psychological thing which will produce a certain likeness simply because we are rather clever at aping one another and picking up manners. The imitation of God is psychological too, *but most of all it is mystical.** When we try with sincerity to imitate Christ, His Holy Mother, His virgin father, *something happens in us.* We have begun at last to move in the stream of our supernatural life and the current starts to carry us closer to God.

There is another thing, not a matter of imitation but of *being. We live with Christ as they did.* He has said so. *"Whatsoever you do to the least of my brethren, you have done it to me."*

We are in the habit of thinking of the "hidden life" of Our Lord as the period of thirty years the Gospels hide from *us,* but they were not hidden from anyone else. The Holy Family was quite visible to its relatives and friends. They all knew what His life as a Jewish boy was like, and we might see it for ourselves if we traveled to Palestine today, so little have some of the customs of His people changed. The books the Evangelists wrote (and which leave out so many things we would like to know) were written to contain His teaching, not the familiar details of His life.

I suddenly understood why all I thought of as "hidden" was left out of the Gospels when I thought what *I* would say if someone asked me about *our* life. "It is really no different from anyone else's life," I would say. So when they were ready to put down His life, the Evangelists had no need to write what everyone already knew. A few things about His childhood *were* unusual: the time the Magi came, the flight into Egypt, the time He was lost in Jerusalem, but everything else in His life was like that of every other child's. His childhood was unique because *He* was the Son of God — only because of that. Otherwise it was quite ordinary. The Christ Child was hidden in ordinariness.

He looked no more like God to His neighbors than any one of the little boys in our family looks like Christ to us.***Only those who had been told who He was knew He was God. It is only because He has told us He *is* here that we see Him in our boys and girls, husbands and wives. Outwardly they are the same familiar faces. *This is the hidden life.*

---

* That is, it has to do with the Divine Life of the soul which is Sanctifying Grace. — *Publisher,* 1995.

** Here, of course, one enters the realm of speculation. — *Publisher,* 1995.

The word *imitation* limps in its attempt to describe what our family life should be, for it must *be* the life of the Holy Family. There is mystically in us the same divine life that lived in the little house at Nazareth. This is the key to our perfection: to be who we are, other Christs, perfectly, as indifferent as possible to our circumstances for holiness is not to be acquired from these. It comes from within in that life with God that we call our "interior life," and that governs our use or misuse of circumstances and our living with Christ in each other.

The Holy Family seemed no different from any family around them. They were poor, but probably not the poorest, and they had common names. Jesus, Mary, Joseph — lots of people had those names. They had common occupations. To be a carpenter was not rare and all the women who married were housewives. The children all played the same games. They drew in the dirt, tagged at their mother's heels, ran up and down the outside steps to the roofs, shouted at play in the courtyards. Young boys went to the synagogue school where they sat around the teacher and learned by heart passages from Scripture, prayers, things about the Law, how to read and write and compute. The girls learned things at home from their mothers. They carded and spun the wool from the sheep and the linen thread from the flax and helped to weave the family garments at the loom. They mended, cooked, cleaned. They carried water on their heads from the village well, as their mothers did, and probably did their washing there the same way they do it today. They helped their mothers gather twigs and brush for kindling, pick the fruits and herbs, dry them, preserve them: olives in jars of salt, raisins dried or pressed into cakes, figs in vats. The boys helped their fathers and learned their trades, cultivated with them the little gardens each family kept on the hillsides outside the town and tended the goats and sheep if they had them.

The house Mary kept smelled of olive oil, like the others, and wood smoke, and in hers there was always the pungent smell of wood shavings from the workshop in front on the street. The sounds that drifted in were the sounds everyone heard, voices, bells, cries, the braying of donkeys, barking of dogs, and that most ordinary sound of a hammer hitting wood. Mary heard it for years. One day she was to hear it on Calvary when the timbers of the Church were being nailed to God and she was bringing forth, with her Son, mankind newborn.

Their house was partly hollowed out of limestone, cavelike, and partly built on earthen walls with beams for support. It was dark and cool inside with only one doorway and perhaps a small window for daylight. The smoke from the little fire stung their eyes and sometimes made tears come. Joseph made the wooden utensils she used — the spoons, bowls, stools, the table at which they took their meals — and brought from his shop the wood for her fire. Her cooking ware was clay and the family's diet was simple: vegetables — lettuce, onions, cucumbers, legumes, olives — and sometimes mutton or veal. There was cheese from the goat's milk, and figs, grapes and nuts, with water and wine for drinking. Her bread was made in round flat cakes, baked from flour she ground herself, leavened with dough from the previous day's baking, baked in the ashes or in a simple clay oven. In nice weather she probably cooked outdoors. In the colder months — November through March — she probably had a little fire inside near the doorway.

In her wooden bridal chest Mary kept their treasures: their woolens, their feast-day clothes. The sleeping pads were rolled up by day and kept on a shelf along the wall. They said morning and evening prayers and Grace before and after meals and numerous other prayers and blessings — as did everyone else. They went to the synagogue on the Sabbath, where Mary sat with the women and Joseph and Jesus sat with the men. There they heard Scripture read, prayed the Psalms, sang together, said prayers. They celebrated the feasts with their relatives and neighbors, going to the synagogue to hear the story of Esther at Purim, to Jerusalem for the Pasch, the feast of the Dedication, the harvest Feast of Tabernacles when the children delighted to dwell in little huts or arbors, decorated with branches and fruit, as part of the celebration of this feast. On these journeys they

traveled with their relatives, made the same offerings and returned home with them.

This was the life led by all the people of their class. What do
we learn from it? We learn in a more stunning way than we
have understood before that *family life* was the means chosen
by God for the forming of Himself as a man. It is with great
difficulty that we shake off our ideas of the forming of Christ.
Father Leen wrote in *In the Likeness of Christ* that we persist in
seeing it as a stage play with all the parts memorized ahead of
time and the main characters "written in," knowing what to do
and how it will turn out. Jesus would have been imperfectly a
man had this been so. It is part of the mystery of the Incarnation
that Christ, being God, could assume the human condition and
learn — as our children learn. Family life is the first teacher.
It is the means God chose for teaching His Son.*

In the Gospels, Christ's teaching is expressed again and again
in words and lessons His mother and earthly father taught Him.
They not only saw things as they are, as we are fond of saying,
but they also saw in all things the signs of God, of holiness, of
truth. And they spoke of them to God in their prayers and to
each other in their conversations. One of the things that happens in us as we draw closer to God is that our enthusiasms,
desires, hungerings are concentrated increasingly upon Him. He
becomes increasingly the source of our joy. We have eyes only
for Him and all things become, for us, things in some relation
to Him.

The vision of parents teaches a child more certainly than
anything else and it can never be successfully camouflaged. How
grown-ups see the world, whether in terms of God, or power, or
advantage, or money, or success, is what their children read in
them and how they too look at the world. It is all there is for
them to imitate, so — the innocents — they imitate it. And it is
not so much the great and self-evident faults of parents that do
the damage, for soon enough children see these faults and with
their own disapproval as their shield they will often resist the
obviously *bad,* the bad from which they may actually, visibly

---

* As God, Jesus Christ had the complete knowledge of God. As man, He
had 1) the knowledge implied in the Beatific Vision, 2) infused knowledge,
and 3) experimental, "learned" knowledge, acquired through sense and intellect;
this acquired knowledge would increase from day to day, but was perfect
of its kind and not liable to error. (See Attwater: *A Catholic Dictionary,* 1958,
p. 277).—*Publisher,* 1995.

suffer. It is what empties out of the smallest nooks and crannies of their parents' minds and is insidiously, certainly, spilled into the minds of the children that stains them, teaches them, forms them. No one with a heart that really loves money best can successfully pretend that he does not. He will betray himself a thousand, thousand ways. It is so with all the loves we would substitute for love of God. If we would teach our children to love God best, we must love Him best ourselves.

It was their love of God that formed the attitudes and thoughts of Mary and Joseph and molded the attitudes and thoughts of their Boy. It is no good to say, as I might once have said, "But *He was God* . . . these things were already in Him." He was perfectly *human.* Humans learn these things from their parents.

Once He was dining with His disciples and the Pharisees protested to see that Christ and His followers did not fast as the Law proposed. He gave them two answers, neither of which they could understand because their hearts were crabbed for lack of loving the truth. First He said it was fitting that when they had the bridegroom with them they rejoice — there would be time and a reason to fast when he was taken away. Then He said: "Nobody uses a piece taken from a new cloak to patch an old one; if that is done, he will have torn the new cloak, and the piece taken from the new will not match the old" (Luke 5:36, Knox).[1] He meant that the new teaching He had for them would not mix with the old, and it would be better for them if they would leave the old; and He illustrated His meaning with a commonplace from His mother's life. How many times had He seen her, in her holy housewifely way, mending garments thus? Perhaps He had asked her one day: "Mother — why do you do it that way?" Maybe she had answered Him in these very words. He learned from her that the old is for the old and the new for the new and they do not go well together.

He continued with another example that brings St. Joseph

---

[1] Scriptural quotations from the *New Testament* in English, in the translation of Monsignor Ronald Knox, Copyright 1944, Sheed & Ward, Inc., New York.

to mind. As a child did He learn about wineskins and their properties from some excitement among the families on the courtyard? Joseph — any father — would have explained to his startled child, "Nor does anybody put new wine into old wineskins; if that is done, the new wine bursts the skins. And there is the wine spilt [did he point discreetly to the evidence?], and the skins spoiled. If the wine is new, it must be put into fresh wineskins, and so both are kept safe" (Luke 5:37, Knox). New wine ferments and old skins were not strong enough to hold it. Many a child grows up and hears himself one day repeating the words of his father before him.

Once He said to His disciples: "You are the salt of the earth; if the salt loses its taste, what is there left to give taste to it? There is no more to be done with it, but throw it out of doors for men to tread it under foot" (Matt. 5:13, Knox). What made Him think of this? Did He ask His mother one day where the salt came from, as He watched her preserving the olives in jars of salt in her little house? It is possible the salt she used came from the shores of the Dead Sea, so heavy with salt that it lay on the shores like sand. All boys everywhere ask their mothers such questions, and all good mothers explain, musing aloud on the goodness of God to provide such things as salt, the need of men to respect it. Imagine the joy of God, learning about His own creation, salt, from Mary's beautiful mind. Her personality and wisdom and reverence would form His human learning*— about salt, and patches and many things.

That day He had been teaching them the Beatitudes, and after He had told them the parable of the salt, He told them this one: "You are the light of the world; a city cannot be hidden if it is built on a mountain top. A lamp is not lighted to be put away under a bushel measure; it is put on the lampstand, to give light to all the people of the house; and your light must shine so brightly before men that they can see your good works, and glorify your Father who is in heaven" (Matt. 5:14, Knox). Was it not His house He was remembering, its cool gloom and how His mother lit her little oil lamp and set

---

*It is legitimate to speak of God as *learning* because Jesus Christ as man learned, and Jesus Christ is God. This flows from the theological principle known as *communicatio idiomatum*, or "interchange of attributes," whereby both divine and human properties can be predicated of the one Person, Jesus Christ. Though Jesus Christ be designated by a name which connotes His

it on the lampstand as she began to prepare the supper for Jesus and Joseph? Undoubtedly, she praised God for the light as she did it, she who was so accustomed to the images of the Psalms, to seeing the signs of God about her, to the beautiful prayers of benediction that blessed the works and the fruits of God all through the Jew's day. "Blessed art thou, O Lord our God, King of the Universe, who createst fragrant oil . . ." is how one begins. She taught these things to her Child as all good mothers do.

Another time He told them: "The Kingdom of Heaven is like leaven, that a woman has taken and buried away in three measures of meal, enough to leaven the whole batch" (Matt. 13:33, Knox). He was telling those who possessed the Kingdom of Heaven to be like yeast in a dough and penetrate and lift the whole world with their life and their truth. Every day He saw His mother put leaven in her dough. Do not say He need not necessarily have asked her why she did this. Of course He did, as any mother who has baked bread with her children watching will know.

Again He was telling them how God loved and sought for the souls who were lost to Him. "Or if some woman has ten silver pieces by her, and has lost one of them, does she not light a lamp, and sweep the house, and search carefully until she finds it? And when she does find it, she calls her friends and her neighbors together; Rejoice with me, she says, I have found the silver piece which I lost. So it is, I tell you, with the angels of God; there is joy among them over one sinner that repents" (Luke, 15:8, Knox).

Here He seems to be remembering a particular occasion so vividly that the very words that were said come back to Him. Perhaps it was one of Mary's dowry coins — the ones she wore on her headdress — that was lost. Perhaps as a little lad He had brought her the broom and lifted their few pieces of furniture, helping her look for it.

The hidden childhood is revealed in the Gospels after all. The signs of it are in the words He spoke as a man. This is

---

Divinity, human attributes can be predicated of Him, e.g.: "God was born in Bethlehem," or "God learned from Mary." (See Wynne: *The Catholic Encyclopedia Dictionary*, 1929, p. 237). But it would be incorrect to affirm that God *as God* learns. (See the footnote on p. 154.) — *Publisher, 1995.*

law in the lives of humans. They learn from their parents and their family life; they become what these make them. Growing in wisdom and age and grace, God began to teach in the words and ways He had learned from His mother and His earthly father. He had already lived His teaching — as a child.

When He says to us: "Be perfect as my heavenly Father is perfect," and we gasp at the impossibility of *that,* He explains: "He who sees me sees also the Father." So it is not divinity we are asked to imitate, but His divine humanity, and that we can know by His example — and *be* by His indwelling. If we try with all our strength to live with Christ, as Mary and Joseph did, in our families, we will be holy families too.

> *O Lord Jesus Christ, you sanctified home life with untold virtues by being subject to Mary and Joseph. May they assist us to imitate the example of your holy family, so that we may share with them their eternal happiness: who lives and rules with God the Father. (Prayer from the Mass for the Feast of the Holy Family.)* [2]

[2] Maryknoll Missal (New York: P. J. Kenedy & Sons, 1957) p. 80.

PART II

1

ADVICE TO PARENTS FROM

St. Thomas More · Blessed Claude
de la Colombière* · Sister Josefa Menéndez

ON PREVENTING PRIDE AND VAINGLORY IN CHILDREN

St. Thomas More, the saint "who died laughing," was the best of fathers, a merry man of wit and learning, devoted to his family, tender and solicitous about the education of his children no less than about their knowledge of the things of God. His "dear little wife," Jane, did not live to see their four children grow up, and shortly after her death Sir Thomas married again to complete the Chelsea household and give a mother to Margaret, Elizabeth, Cecily and John.

The More home was no ordinary English household. In addition to his own children, Sir Thomas had under his roof his stepdaughter Alice Middleton and his wards Margaret Gigs and Anne Cresacre. Other young students lived with the Mores — William Roper, Sir Thomas's ward Giles Heron, his nephew William Rastell. For all these young people Sir Thomas maintained his "school," where "devotion to learning came second only to devotion to the Church."

When he wrote *Utopia* Sir Thomas had made much of the education of both sexes. Here in the pleasant house beside the Thames his ideas, visionary to most Londoners, were tried out and found workable. His daughters learned Latin,

*Now *Saint* Claude de la Colombière (canonized May 31, 1992).—*Publisher,* 1995.

Greek and Scripture; so did his son, nephew and wards (and later his eleven grandchildren also joined the "academy"). The head of the house taught them himself in the beginning; later he found tutors for them whom he carefully supervised and advised as to just what kind of things they should pour into his children's heads. He told them, for instance, "to warn my children to avoid the precipices of pride and haughtiness, and to walk in the pleasant meadows of modesty; not to be dazzled at the sight of gold; not to lament that they do not possess what they erroneously admire in others; not to think more of themselves for gaudy trappings, nor less for the want of them; neither to deform the beauty that nature has given them by neglect, nor to try to heighten it by artifice; to put virtue in the first place, learning in the second; and in their studies to esteem most whatever may teach them piety towards God, charity to all, and Christian humility in themselves."

Sir Thomas, whose experience in the law and at Court had taught him with what contempt the world holds such advice, went on to forestall objections:

"I fancy I hear you object that these precepts, though true, are beyond the capacity of my young children, since you will scarcely find a man, however old and advanced, who is not stirred sometimes with the desire of glory. But, dear Gunnell, the more do I see the difficulty of getting rid of this pest of pride, the more do I see the necessity of getting to work at it from childhood. For I find no other reason why this evil clings to our hearts so closely than because almost as soon as we are born, it is sown in the tender minds of children by their nurses, it is cultivated by their teachers, and brought to its full growth by their parents, no one teaching what is good, without at the same time awakening the expectation of praise as of the proper reward of virtue.

"That this plague of vainglory should be banished far from my children, I do desire you, dear Gunnell, and their mother and all their friends, would sing this song to them, and repeat it and knock it into their heads, that vainglory is a despicable thing, and that there is nothing more sublime than the humble modesty so often praised by Christ." [1]

The daily life of the More household — family *and* servants — revolved about the one great reality: man's end in God. At mealtime one of the girls would read a passage from Scripture, then the whole family would join in a discussion of its interpretation, followed by jesting and innocent merriment. Sometimes they must have had music in the evening for Sir Thomas loved singing and playing and had his wife instructed in the art of the lute and the virginals. Indeed it was a happy family where everything referred back to God. Perhaps it was his humility that made Sir Thomas so much "all things to all men." At any rate it was a virtue in which he counseled his children — to cultivate the humility that comes with seeing things as they really are — God's.

"How delectable is that dainty damsel to the devil, that taketh herself for fair, weening herself well-liked for her broad forehead, while the young man that beholdeth her marketh more her crooked nose! How proud be many men of these glistening stones, of which the very brightness, though he cost thee twenty pounds, shall never shine half so bright nor show thee half so much light, as shall a poor half-penny candle! How proud is many a man over his neighbor because the wool of his gown is finer! And yet as fine as it is, a poor sheep ware it on her back before it came upon his, and though it be his, is not so verily his as it was verily hers! All that ever we have, of God we have received; riches, royalty, lordship, beauty, strength, learning, wit, body, soul and all. And almost all these things hath He but lent us. For all these must we depart from, every whit again, except our soul alone. And yet that must we give God again also." [2]

[1] E. M. G. Routh, *St. Thomas More and His Friends* (London: Oxford University Press, 1934), p. 129.

[2] *Ibid.*, p. 130.

ON PARENTAL DUTY AND HOW PARENTS LET THEIR CHILDREN
RISK CHASTITY

Blessed Claude de la Colombière and St. Margaret Mary
Alacoque were the two souls God chose in the seventeenth
century to make His message of the Sacred Heart known to the
world. Claude was born in a very small town in the diocese of
Grenoble in 1641. Little is known of his childhood beyond the
fact that his family was well born, his parents devout, and his
upbringing very Catholic at a time when the churches were in
decay in France, the clergy reduced in numbers and many of
the faithful fallen away. After a brilliant career as a young
cleric, he was professed in the Society of Jesus following a retreat during which he was inspired to consecrate himself to the
Sacred Heart in a special way. Two months after profession, he
was made superior at the Jesuit house at Paray-le-Monial, a
rather unusual thing for a man only thirty-four.

Unknown to him at that time, there was also in Paray a
young nun to whom the Sacred Heart had been making remarkable revelations and who was in dire need of help. Under
obedience Sister Margaret Mary Alacoque had been confiding all
that occurred to a confessor who, while an upright man, understood little of the extraordinary things that were happening to
her and dismissed them as delusions. God sent Father de la
Colombière to preach at the Visitation convent and St. Margaret
Mary heard in her soul the words: "He it is I send you." Blessed
Claude heard her confession, recognized the hand of God in the
young nun's experiences, counseled her, and did much to spread
devotion to the Sacred Heart in the Church.

Not long after his appointment to Paray, he was transferred
to London as preacher to the Duchess of York, sister-in-law of
King Charles II. Mary Beatrice D'Este was a beautiful and devout Italian princess who at fifteen, sacrificed her desire for a
life in religion to marry James, heir to the English crown.
Chaste and lovely as she was, and as she remained, she nevertheless was living in a whirlpool of worldliness and it was not only

for her soul but for the souls of the others at the court that
Blessed Claude worked, prayed, preached, and bore in himself
the most severe deprivations.

After a little over two years in England, during which he converted many Protestants and brought many lapsed Catholics
back to the Church, Blessed Claude was accused of these "crimes,"
falsely implicated in the infamous Titus Oates plot, and thrown
into prison. Suffering from tuberculosis and hemorrhaging
heavily, he was finally released through the intervention of
Louis XIV and left England "at the height of the storm," arriving in Paris in January 1679. The harvest of martyrs in England that year "would result for the Jesuits alone in 'twenty-
three condemnations to death by torture and one hundred and
forty-seven deaths in the filth and squalor of the prisons.'"
Blessed Claude wrote: "It was very hard for me to leave. . . ."
Back in Paray-le-Monial, he lived three years, invalided, known
to all but a very few of his brothers in religion as merely a
brilliant, hard-working and now worn-out priest. He died on
the first Sunday of Lent, 1682, "carried off by a torrent of
blood." The morning after his death, St. Margaret Mary understood by a revelation that he was already in heaven and needed
no prayers.

It is from Blessed Claude's sermons and notes that the following passages are taken. The worldliness of the English and
French courts in the seventeenth century was little, if any,
different from worldliness in our own time. It would be hard to
find even among contemporary writers the case against parents
put more accurately, more bluntly, than in these words of
Blessed Claude de la Colombière. His words are brutally appropriate.

"Is it not surprising that Christian parents place before their
children only human motives to encourage them to do what is
asked of them, and that everything tends to nourish the love of
comfort and ambition: 'This man,' they tell them, 'who was of
low birth, has made himself important by his eloquence, and
has been promoted to the most illustrious offices, has acquired

great wealth, married a very rich wife, has built a superb mansion. He has made himself feared, he is in the limelight of renown. . . .' They never think of giving them for models any but those who have made their way in the world. They never speak to them about those who are reigning in heaven."

He goes on: "What are you doing at home if you do not busy yourselves in the upbringing of your children? It is the only thing you have to do. It is in this that God wishes you to serve Him. It is for this that He has established Christian marriage. It is of this that He will demand an account of you. You have amassed property for them. Is this what God expects of you? 'Come now,' He will say to you on the day of judgment, 'give me an account of that soul that I have confided to you. What has become of it? That was your field, the vineyard which the Lord had given you to cultivate;' To what degree of holiness have you led them? With what principles have you inspired them? Are they good? Do they fear God? Are they instructed in our mysteries? Some will have no answer to make, for they will not know what to make of these questions." [3]

He directs a passionate tirade at the conduct of Christians during the time of *carnival**— the equivalent of our "holidays" at Christmas time. It was the custom in London to masquerade for many of these parties; with a few variations the spirit still reigns.

"What! dear ladies, spend five or six hours of your time in dressing and painting your faces only to go into a group to lay snares against the chastity of men and to serve as a torch for the demon to enkindle everywhere the fires of lust; to remain whole nights exposed to the eyes and coaxing of young fools and a whole regiment of the city's rakes; to use all that is most dangerous in art and nature to attract their looks and vanquish their spirit, to disguise your person, your sex, so as to be ashamed of nothing . . . to join excess of food and drink to the excesses of lust and wantonness; not to be satisfied with

---

[3] Georges Guitton, S.J., *Prefect Friend* (St. Louis: B. Herder, 1955), pp. 65, 66.

* The "Carnival" season consists of the days preceding Ash Wednesday, culminating in Mardi Gras ("Fat Tuesday"). Carnival is a time of revelry and often of sin.—*Publisher*, 1995.

talk that blackens the name of the neighbor, but to go so far as to speak words that scandalize him; in a word, to add to the vices of women all the vices and disorders of men. Can these in truth be the amusements of Christians?"

He does not ignore nor is he fooled by the excuses parents make to authorize such "fun." "Our children have to find a way to get established," they told him then. "We want our children to be popular," is what they say now. He asks, is this the way they would do it?

"Unhappy mothers, mothers less than human . . . have you desired them only to corrupt them? Have you brought them into the world only to damn them? 'Who would think of them?' you ask. God, in any case, will think of them, if men do not. But is it possible that the designs which God may have on your family can be achieved only by such abominable means? . . . I do not blame you for wishing to make your daughter happy in this life. But you are indeed to be pitied, if you think that you must endanger her salvation, and your own, your eternity and hers, for so empty, so absurd a happiness, a happiness which must last but a moment. . . .

"O but this vain and coquettish girl will pay dearly by a long and cruel servitude for the faults which she is now committing and which she makes others commit! She thinks that by dint of dressing, of exhibiting herself, or parading her beauty, of appearing to be agreeable, being sweet-tempered, she will the sooner find a home. I am of the opposite opinion. These are the means, if I am not mistaken, to find ready lovers — but a husband, only very late and perhaps never. . . . It is certain that this is not the way to find a good one.

"This man who allows himself to be dazzled by this or that beauty, and who without examining her character, her education, her personal morals, wishes to marry her absolutely, and often against the advice of his friends, this man does not reflect that this beauty is not immortal, that nevertheless, he is binding himself until death. Let us suppose that her beauty lasts for ten years; you will perhaps have forty or fifty to live with her. So that if she hasn't something in her mind, or her soul, to hold you after the loss of her looks, you will have to suffer for the space of thirty or forty years. It will be like keeping a corpse in your home."

He goes on: "Do you want to know what it is really to love purity? Represent to yourself a woman in love with her own charms and infatuated with her own beauty. . . . Not only does she see with self-complacence that nature on this point has distinguished her from the common run of women, but she bestows cares beyond our power of expression for the preservation of the graces she has received. What does she not do to protect this complexion, now from sunburn, now from extremes of cold? What does she not do to maintain it, to keep it in its bloom, to make it if possible immortal? . . . One hair out of place, a little more pallor than usual, a little less luster and plumpness, a pimple, a swelling, throws her into despair.

"It is the same almost with a person who is truly chaste. It is not enough for her to avoid guilt and the last stages of disorder. She would never forgive herself for a word or a look that was even slightly free. The least voluntary thoughts, the most transient, cause her horror. In this matter everything seems essential to her. This fashionable gossip, these scandalous stories which are today the ordinary subjects of conversation, are enough to drive her from such gatherings, and if she had no other subject to talk about, her mind would find delight in solitude.

"Oh how far removed is she from the vanity of those whose headdress and attire seem to be made only to light the fires of impurity!" [4]

ON HOW OUR WORK IS LOVE, AND HOW WE CAN WORK WITH
CHRIST TO SAVE SOULS WITH OUR LOVE

The childhood of Josefa Menéndez was strikingly like the childhood of the Little Flower. She was born in Madrid in 1890, of an upright and pious father and a devout and conscientious

4 *Ibid.,* pp. 255, 256, 257.

mother. The family was reasonably well off. Josefa was the oldest girl, with three sisters and two brothers, both of whom died in infancy. At five she was confirmed, at seven she made her first confession and at eleven she made her First Communion. The family confessor, a Father Rubio, watched over her spiritual life, giving her training suited to her age, teaching her how to meditate and to pray, and cultivating in her a love for spiritual reading. Like little Thérèse Martin she was her father's pet, the likeness between the two extending even to the pet names used by their respective indulgent fathers. As Thérèse was called "my little Queen" by hers, Josefa was called "my little Empress" by hers. Indeed, the likeness between the two families was quite astonishing.

Every Sunday the Menéndez took their children to High Mass, as did the Martins, and the father gave his little ones a few coppers apiece to give as alms to the poor, a practice he cultivated very carefully in them, as did M. Martin in his daughters. Sunday afternoons when the weather was fair they too went for walks together, and when it was not fair they stayed at home and enjoyed each other's company, ending the day with family rosary. Like little Thérèse, Josefa longed to serve God from a very early age and after her First Communion, made in writing an offering of her virginity. Father Rubio thought this a bit rash for one so young and advised she tear up the paper and limit herself merely to the promise to be good, but she stubbornly clung to her resolve and kept the paper till she died — *and* the resolve.

She was taught at home by her father for a number of years until her family decided she should attend a school to learn the art of fine sewing. Home again at thirteen, she became a pupil at the free school conducted by the Society of the Sacred Heart and there, daily in the presence of the Blessed Sacrament, the young heart grew in love. At this time one of the great treats for the little Menéndez girls was a visit to the Carmel where their aunt was stationed. There they were treated like princesses and indulged by the chaplain who gave them the freedom of his quarters. There they also found a copy of the Carmelite rule and returning home played at being Carmelites, at chanting an office and performing penances, just as the Little Flower and her cousin Marie played at being hermits. Like Thérèse, Josefa was quite serious about the whole thing.

In order to garnish her accomplishments as a dressmaker with an equally good training in millinery, her parents now had her apprenticed in a millinery establishment and the hours spent in the workroom with girls far more worldly than herself often tried Josefa to the point of tears. The talk was sometimes far from edifying, and the dangers to purity of heart frightened her. Daily Communion was her protection. Sundays they often spent with a gracious lady, the daughter of their landlord, and Josefa's talents for little dramas, games and entertainments contributed to many delightful afternoons. She also shared with the older woman her love for the poor and the sick, noticing that the lady not only distributed alms generously but considered no task too humble for her to undertake for the love of God. This greatly attracted Josefa, as it will any child given the opportunity to observe it, and when the woman asked her if she would like to visit the poorest and most wretched of her clients, an old woman half-eaten with leprosy, Josefa was delighted. Their visits were made in secret so the heroism of such service should not be exhibited. Then Josefa made the mistake of asking one of her younger sisters if she would like to share this joy of a visit with old Trinidad; the child did, and was so horrified afterward that her manner betrayed it at home. Their father discovered what Josefa had been doing and forebade her to go again. One finds in this still another likeness to the Little Flower. Had little Thérèse kept her "cure" a secret from the Sisters at Carmel, she too might have enjoyed a different effect, she wrote. All of which recalls St. Syncletica and her wise sayings about keeping such treasures hidden; once exposed to view, she says, they will be stolen away.

Suffering entered the Menéndez' life with the death of one of the little sisters, then the death of a grandmother, followed by the collapse of both the father and mother, one with typhoid, the other with pneumonia. The doctor's bills and the expenses of sickness ate away all their savings and the family soon arrived at a state of complete poverty. Begging the doctor to leave her parents at home, Josefa put her entire trust in God, took over the managing of the household, and the family began a novena to the foundress of the Society of the Sacred Heart, Madeline Sophie Barat. At the end of the days of prayer, the mother called them about her bed. Everything would be all right, she assured them. Mother Barat had been at her bedside and promised her recovery. And recover she did.

Now Josefa was forced to sew to support her family. Her talent as a dressmaker was so outstanding that, after paying for the sewing machine by making thousands of Sacred Heart badges for the Sisters to distribute to soldiers, she soon had a clientele large enough to require the help of six girls in a workroom. Life had become almost "normal" again when her father died, followed by the departure of her younger sister for the convent. When the other sister also entered the convent, poor Josefa was left at home with her mother who had no desire to part from this third and last daughter. But Father Rubio thought it time she entered somewhere, so although she had had her heart set on the Society of the Sacred Heart, at his suggestion she applied to and was received by the Order of Mary Reparatrix. Shortly before the day of her clothing, Josefa's disconsolate mother appeared and, appealing to her with tears and lamentations, persuaded her to return home. Poor Josefa.

Once again she supported herself and her mother with her sewing. Another attempt to enter the convent, this time the Society of the Sacred Heart, ended in the same way. Her mother's consent was given, the day of entry arrived and, alas, another flood of tears from her mother and another surrender to them by Josefa. Two years passed and Josefa applied again, but this time the superiors said no; her repeated hesitations were hardly a good sign of vocation. Josefa had reached an impasse; there seemed nothing for her to do, nowhere for her to go. She begged

Our Lord either to permit her to be one of His religious or to let her die; to live in the world any longer was unbearable. Understanding suddenly that nothing should seem unbearable to her for love of whom He had borne so much, she begged Him to pity her weakness and began again the unending imploring that she be allowed to enter the convent of the Sacred Heart. The circumstance of her acceptance at long last into the Society was the reopening of the religious houses in France and the requisitioning of vocations by the Sacred Heart convent at Poitiers, the foundress' original novitiate.

This time Josefa left not only her mother and her sisters but her homeland, her very tongue. Long before, day-dreaming with her sister over their desire to be religious, she had said that when she gave herself to God, she wanted to give everything, even to going far from Spain. Her sister could not agree and Josefa answered her objection by saying that "nothing was too good to give to God."

But the devil tracks down such souls; he does not let the giving be easy. The first months of Josefa's postulancy, beyond a few peaceful weeks, saw the beginning of diabolical torments which would not end until her death. Following terrible attacks of homesickness and loneliness, she was set upon by invisible fists, wildly beaten, saw hideous faces around her in chapel, heard choruses of yells, was struck furiously and forced to leave. Only when the mother assistant would make a little sign of the Cross on her forehead, or when she reached the haven of her cell, determined to tell her everything, would the devil cease. She was almost ready to take the habit when, exhausted by these attacks, she at last told Our Lord she could not stay. She was in chapel one evening and said five times to Him: "I am going home . . ." but she could not go on. Suddenly she was "wrapped in a sweet slumber" and awoke to find herself in the wound of the Sacred Heart. There in the radiance that surrounded her she saw the sins of the entire world, and she was filled with the desire to unite herself to Him and offer her life to comfort His wounded heart. This was the beginning of her unique relationship with the Sacred Heart of Christ, the object of which was to communicate to the world that message of His mercy and love. "The world does not know the mercy of My Heart," He told her. "I intend to enlighten them through you. . . . I want you to be the apostle of my love and mercy." [5]

From His message to Sister Josefa we have selected excerpts that are extremely appealing to children as well as to parents, and are most helpful in forming in them an understanding of their part in the work of the Mystical Body. Here is something about work and love.

One evening Sister Josefa was on her way to the third floor of the convent to close some windows, and as she walked along she whispered to Jesus of her love. Suddenly as she reached the corridor on the top floor she saw Him coming to meet her from the other end. He was surrounded by light so radiant that it lit the dark passage. He hurried to her and asked: "Where do you come from?"

"I have been closing the windows, Lord."

"And where are you going?"

"I am going to finish doing so, my Jesus."

"That is not the way to answer, Josefa."

She did not understand what He meant, so He went on: "I come from love, and I go to love. Whether you go up or down, you are ever in My heart, for it is an abyss of love. I am with you." [6]

This story will help us teach our children how everything they do can be an act of love. Going about their work is a matter of going from love to love, from loving God at the kitchen sink where they help with the dishes, to loving God at the ironing board where they press their blouse for school; from loving God while mowing the lawn to loving God while cleaning the cellar. Only this knowledge of the worth of our duties can make some of them bearable, and this can make them not only bearable, but lovable.

[5] Sister Josefa Menéndez, *The Way of Divine Love* (Westminster, Md.: Newman Press, 1949), p. xviii. Also TAN, 1973, 1981 (pocket ed.).
[6] *Ibid.*, p. 52.

He told her: "Many souls think that love consists in saying: *My God I love Thee.* No, love is sweet, and acts because it loves, and all that it does is done out of love. I want you to love me in that way, in work, in rest, in prayer and consolation as in distress and humiliation, constantly giving me proofs of your love by acts; that is true love. If souls understood this they would advance in perfection rapidly, and how greatly they would console My heart." [7]

We may even give Him our sleep as an act of love — and thus be loving Him for the full twenty-four hours of every day!

One year on Spy Wednesday, she asked Jesus in her prayer what exactly He meant by "saving souls." He came and looked at her with great affection and said: "There are some Christian souls and even very pious ones that are held back from perfection by some attachment. But when another offers Me her actions united to My infinite merits, she obtains grace for them to free themselves and make a fresh start.

"Many others live in indifference and even in sin, but when helped in the same way, recover grace, and will eventually be saved.

"Others again, and these are very numerous, are obstinate in wrongdoing and blinded by error. They would be damned if some faithful soul did not make supplication for them, thus obtaining grace to touch their hearts, but their weakness is so great that they run the risk of relapse into their sinful life; these I take away into the next world without delay, and that is how I save them."

She asked Him how she could save a great many.

"Unite all you do to My actions, whether you work or whether you rest. Unite your breathing to the beating of My heart. How many souls you would be able to save that way!" [8]

Since she longed to make amends for the sins committed against His love, one day at the laundry she asked Our Lord

---

[7] *Ibid.*, p. 60.
[8] *Ibid.*, p. 93.

to "save as many souls as there were handkerchiefs to count. I offered my whole day for this object, uniting my sufferings to His heart and His merits." Towards nightfall she went into the chapel where the Blessed Sacrament was exposed. Our Lord appeared to her, coming very close, and in the wound in His heart she saw a long line of souls prostrate in adoration. "I understood that all these were the souls I had begged of Him that morning. . . ." [9]

He gave her these important counsels which she carefully wrote in her note book. They are important for everyone to know, but especially for parents striving to guide the spiritual formation of children:

"Never go to rest at night with the slightest shadow obscuring your soul. This I recommend to you with great insistence. When you commit a fault, repair it at once. I wish your soul to be as pure as crystal.

"Do not let your falls, however many, trouble you. It is trouble and worry that keep a soul from God. Beg pardon, and I say again, tell your Mother at once. . . ." (He is speaking of her Mother in religion.)

How careful we should be to see that the spats of the day are settled, the injured apologized to, the injuring forgiven.

"I want you to be very little and very humble and always gay. Yes, I want you to live in joy, while endeavoring all the time to be something of an executioner to self. Often choose what costs you, but without loss of joy and gladness, for by serving Me in peace and happiness you will give the most glory to My Heart." [10]

And there is this from Josefa to Our Lord, which might very well have been phrased for us who have families and households:

"I begged Him to accept all the little acts done here, the sufferings of the house, and above all the very real desire we all

[9] *Ibid.*, p. 90.
[10] *Ibid.*, p. 126.

have to comfort and please Him. I asked Him to purify and transform these very little things, and give them some value in His sight.

"He replied: 'I do not look at the act itself, I look at the intention. The smallest act, if done out of love, acquires such merit that it gives Me immense consolation . . . I want only love. I ask for nothing else.' " [11]

[11] *Ibid.*, p. 215.

2

THREE SAINTS WITH THREE STORIES
EACH THAT CHILDREN LOVE TO
HEAR AND TELL

St. Catherine of Siena · St. Philip Neri ·
St. Perpetua and St. Felicitas

On loving your neighbor and seeing christ in everyone
On giving to the poor and how our treasure is
in heaven
On how god is everywhere

St. Catherine of Siena is a saint most children know very
little about; in fact she is rarely thought of as one of the "children's saints." But truthfully she is theirs in a special way because
her story has all the enchantment of a fairy tale and she is the
kind of heroine children wish would come true — and she did!

She promised herself to her Prince when she was but a young
girl, endured suffering for His sake at the hands of her mother,
father, sisters and brothers, worked as a slave and sat in the
corner if not in the cinders, loved virginity, was vindicated in
the end and her unworthy suitors forever put to rout. She lived
in the silence of her cell preparing herself for her Beloved as
princesses do in their arbors, their gardens, their towers. She
went forth after her nuptials as a queen with her bounty, giving
alms to the poor, succor to the sick, clothing, feeding, teaching,
blessing, and each night she returned and held converse with her

King whose wedding band adorned her finger and whose jeweled raiment and rare repasts she enjoyed in the silence of the night. Offering her life for Him, she bore on her person the wounds of His suffering to buy back sinners, to win repentance for the condemned and virtue for the lukewarm. And then she died and went to heaven and lived happily ever after.

All this happened to Catherine, the twenty-fifth child of the Benincasas. One day, when she was only six, she was returning home with her brother when suddenly she saw in the sky over Siena a vision of Christ. Spellbound, this small girl with the cheery face and the amber-colored curls stared at the figure in the sky and He gazed back at her with such love that her heart was lost forever. Smiling, He reached out His hand and made the sign of the Cross, blessing her; then, shockingly, her brother pulled at her hand and cried sharply to her to come — and the vision faded. She cried out bitterly: "Oh! If you had seen what I saw, you would never have done that!" And that was how it began.

In her early teens, she realized that to convince her family that she would not marry was impossible, so she cut off her lovely hair. Her mother raged, wept, stormed in vain. Catherine would not and could not be made to adorn herself suitably in order to attract eligible young men. No appeal to reason or loyalty could change her mind. Her mother took to persecution and, dismissing the maid, set Catherine to serving the tremendous household. She took away Catherine's room, her very privacy, making her share a room with a younger brother, yet far from discouraging Catherine these trials were fruitful, for the Holy Spirit Himself taught her to bear them.

Since she had no privacy, He taught her how to build a cell within her own soul that no one could force her to leave. Since she was tormented endlessly by her family, He taught her to imagine her father was Our Lord Jesus Christ, her mother the Blessed Virgin Mary, her brothers and sisters the apostles and disciples, and thus she was able to serve them with such patience that they were at a loss to explain it. (We can ask St. Catherine to help our children as they struggle to see Christ in one another.)

When at last her family was convinced that this strange daughter did indeed have a unique vocation, she was allowed to live in complete seclusion, eating almost nothing and spending all but an hour or two a day in prayer and penance. Daily she received visits from Our Lord in her little room and in this way He taught her divine wisdom. Several years passed and one day He asked her to go out into the world to undertake her apostolate there. Frightened of her weakness and of the power of the devil to ensnare her, she begged to remain in solitude but He answered,

"I wish you to use the love of neighbor to unite you more closely to Me. You know that my commandment of love is two-fold: love of Me and love of neighbor. In this double command-ment are contained the law and the prophets. I wish you to fulfill these two precepts so that you will not walk with one foot but with two; that you will have two wings to fly to heaven." [1]

How delightful to hear how God has put these things to His saints. It is *so* hard to love others as well as we love ourselves. But to try to reach Jesus without this love for His *others,* He says, is like trying to reach heaven by walking there on one foot, while with love of neighbor we will truly fly to Him. It helps a child who has great difficulty loving someone, even if only with an act of his will, to see the issue set forth in the warmth of Christ's own illustration to this lovely saint.

Like our children, St. Catherine also imitated the saints, and she herself had an adventure much like St. Martin of Tours with his beggar by which she learned how our treasures are stored in heaven. On day she came out of the Dominican church in Siena to find a poor man begging alms "for the love of God." As she had nothing with her of much worth, she asked him to return to her home where she could help him. "If you have any-thing to give me, give it directly, I beg you, for it is impossible for me to wait," he said. But she had nothing except a little silver

[1] Martin S. Gillet, O.P., *The Mission of St. Catherine* (St. Louis: B. Herder, 1955), p. 164.

cross for saying *Pater Nosters* which was tied on a knotted string. She broke the cord and gave the man the cross which he joyfully received. That night as she prayed Christ appeared holding in His hand the little cross studded with precious stones. "Daughter, dost thou recognize this cross?" "Perfectly well," answered Catherine, "but it was not so handsome when it belonged to me." "Yesterday," said Our Lord, "thy heart gave it to me as an offering of love; *these precious stones represent thy love.* And I promise thee on the day of judgment in the presence of the angels and of men, I will return it to thee as it is now, so that it may be shown to thy glory." [2] How really and truly *is* Christ in the poor. What a glorious thing it will be to see Him present the jeweled cross to St. Catherine on the day of judgment. Will we find some of our possessions stored there as well, jeweled and resplendent in the sight of angels and men?

There are so many beautiful stories from the life of this saint that Blessed Raymond of Capua, her confessor and biographer, said if he were to attempt to put them all down one lifetime would not be enough. Added to these are the pages of her *Dialogue* in which are recorded her conversations with Our Lord and the wisdom He imparted to her during her ecstasies.* From the latter comes an explanation of how God is everywhere, so important to children as they begin to grow in consciousness of Him and His immensity.

"Where is God?" they ask. "Everywhere," we reply. Oh. "Is He in the fireplace?" "Well — yes, you can say He is in the fireplace, I suppose; because He is everywhere." But it disturbs us to hear one child inform another: "*God* is in the *fireplace.*" This will not do. It is not *enough.* We try again.

"God is not *just* in the fireplace, dear. He is everywhere. There is no place where God is not." This is a very big thought, leaving the littlest ones far behind, but the bigger children hear us out. "Well," says one after a few moments of intense thinking, "if there is no place where God is not, is He in hell?"

[2] Blessed Raymond of Capua, *Life of St. Catherine of Siena* (Dublin: Duffy & Co., 1853), p. 68.

* Actually, the *Dialogue* records St. Catherine's conversations with God the Father. — *Publisher,* 1995.

Oh dear. One must say yes, in a way He is because whatever exists is present to Him, but we cannot bear having them repeat in horrified tones: *"God is in hell!"* It is *very* difficult explaining how God is everywhere.

St. Catherine of Siena comes to our rescue. She has said it beautifully, simply, conclusively. We can never mistake again how God is everywhere. She was not pondering at the time *that* He is everywhere, but how unworthy she was that He should be in *her* at Holy Communion. As the priest held up the Host and she was saying, "Lord, I am not worthy that Thou shouldst enter under my roof . . ." she heard His voice answering her: "But *I, I am* worthy of entering thee." And it semed to her that as the fish which is in the sea is full of the sea, so her soul was in God and God in her soul.

Is this not the way God is everywhere? Are we not swimming in God as the fish swims in the sea? And are we not full of God as the fishes are full of the sea? And is not the sea everywhere full of the sea? So God is everywhere. There is no place where God is not. Very little children can grasp this in their little child's way. One we know who is five years old was heard to say on the way to Holy Mass, "This car is moving in God, and those mountains are in God, and that squirrel and the trees, and us — we are all moving in God." And so we were.

ST. PHILIP'S SUGGESTION FOR PEOPLE WHO HAVE NOTHING
TO DO
HOW HE LEARNED PATIENCE
HOW HE DID NOT TRUST HIMSELF

As a little boy St. Philip Neri was called *Pippo buono* — good little Philip — because he *was* good and merry and gentle, and he grew up to be a very cheerful saint. When he was in his teens, his father sent him to live with an uncle who had an estate and needed an heir, but something happened to Philip and he lost all interest in worldly estates and cared only that he was an heir of heaven, so he went off to Rome to discover what God wanted of him. There he prayed and studied and prayed some more, and after a time he began to frequent the public squares, the shops, the schools, sometimes even the banks of Rome, striking up acquaintances, engaging people in conversation, warming their hearts with his friendship. In reality it was the beginning of his special apostolate: the re-evangelizing of Rome. In his customary greeting parents will find the answer to the melancholy moan of many a plaintive child, "There's *nothing* to *do!*" St. Philip used to say, "Well, my brothers, when shall we begin to do good?" (And it is exactly the thing for the melancholy: "Do some *good.*")

By the time he became a priest, he was so advanced in the love of God that he could not say Mass without weeping or being caught up in an ecstasy and spending far more time at it than any sensible person thought fit. Two of the sacristans especially found him offensive and did all in their power to annoy him. Knowing he had a particular aversion to soiled vestments, they chose for him the oldest and most soiled they could find. They would pretend they thought he was not going to say Mass and lock the sacristy door before he arrived. Noticing that he ate only one meal a day, in the sacristy after Mass, and that it consisted only of a couple of rolls and a tiny flask of wine, they were scornful and took it for a parade of austerity. How they tried him! It is good to know it *did* try him.

One morning at Mass he gazed at the Crucifix and said: "O good Jesus! why is it that Thou dost not hear me? See how long a time I have besought Thee to give me patience! Why is it that Thou hast not heard me, and why is my soul disquieted with thoughts of anger and impatience?" The answer came in his soul: "Dost thou not ask patience of Me, Philip? Behold I will give it thee speedily on this condition: that, if thy heart desire it, thou earn it through these temptations of thine." That is how virtue is earned — by fighting its contrary.

More and more followers flocked to him until he finally formed a group called the Oratorians, the beginning of the foundation of his society. It is from the accounts of his relationship as father and confessor to his spiritual sons and penitents that the most endearing stories of St. Philip come. He had a particular — some thought it merely peculiar — genius for matching particular mortifications and penances to particular souls. Since pride is especially vulnerable before a sense of one's foolishness, St. Philip devised mortifications without end for attacking pride in souls of promise who could bear his heavy-handed humor. Giambattista Salviati, the brother of a cardinal, cousin of Catherine de Medici, the Queen of France, and grand-nephew of a pope, was one of the saint's favorite victims. His grandeur did not outshine his obedience, however, and he was seen sweeping the porch in his elegant satin finery and carrying Philip's little dog through the streets in his arms. Father Pietro Consolini was another special victim singled out by Philip for purification and his pride suffered mortal blows each time he was bade to appear abroad with purple taffeta and gold lace around his hat. An especially pious young man asked permission to wear a hair shirt and Philip granted his request with this stipulation: he wear it on the outside. He was known around Rome as "Berto of the hair-shirt."

But if he was demanding of obedience and humility from his sons in religion and his penitents in the confessional, he was ten times as demanding with himself. He went to incredible lengths to prevent people from having a good opinion of him, and it can be truly said that he had no good opinion of himself. He used to say, "Let me get through today, and I shall not fear tomorrow." He used to whisper to Our Lord every day at Mass, "Lord, beware of me today — lest I should betray Thee!"

ABOUT PERPETUA'S LITTLE BROTHER IN PURGATORY
ABOUT HER MODESTY AS A MARTYR IN THE ARENA
ABOUT HER DARLING FRIEND ST. FELICITAS

The story of Sts. Perpetua and Felicitas is beautifully told by Perpetua in her diary. Here she recorded everything that happened to them until the day they died and, fortunately for us, a friend finished the story where she was forced to leave it. It has been loved and reverenced by the faithful for centuries. Perpetua was twenty-two, well born, married and the mother of a tiny son still at her breast. Felicitas, an expectant mother, was a slave. They were among five catechumens whose arrest and imprisonment was meant as a warning to the other Christians in Carthage in the year 203. Tormented by her father who was a pagan and wanted her to apostatize, terrified by the darkness and stifling heat of the dungeon where they were imprisoned, Perpetua's greatest suffering nevertheless was for her baby who was with her. Baptism, however, drove away her fears and with the coming of the Holy Spirit she was at peace and the prison became to her as a palace; in visions she learned the manner of their martyrdom and caught glimpses of what awaits souls in the life after death. Among these was a vision of Purgatory where she saw her little brother Dinocratus suffering.

Dinocratus had died when he was only seven, painfully ulcerated about the face. Perpetua saw him "coming out of a dark place where there were many others," dirtily clad, pale, with the wound still on his face, and he was very hot and thirsty. Near him was a fountain but its brim was higher than he could reach and, though he stood on tiptoe, he could not drink. By this vision she knew he needed her prayers, and she prayed for him night and day. On the day the Christians were put in stocks, she had another vision and saw Dinocratus freed. This time he was clean and finely clothed, on his face was a clean scar and beside him a low fountain reaching only to his waist. On the edge of the fountain was a golden cup ever full of water, and Dinocratus drank. "And when he had drunk he came away — pleased to play, as children will."

What a wonderful story for children who ask questions about Purgatory, especially since Dinocratus was such a small boy and probably had committed only venial sins. It shows one ought to try *very* hard not to commit even those.

In the meantime, Felicitas was worried for fear her baby would not be born in time for her to die for Christ with her companions. There was a law which forebade throwing even a Christian woman to the wild beasts if she was with child. Three days before they were to go to the arena they prayed God would permit the birth of her child, and as soon as their prayers were done, her labor began. She gave birth to a little girl who was afterward adopted by her sister.

At last the scene of their martyrdom and in it Perpetua teaches a most beautiful lesson in modesty and a proper pride in one's appearance. Told to put on the garments of pagan priestesses, the two refused and so were stripped naked, covered with nets, and sent to face assault by a maddened cow said to have been used in insult to their womanhood and their maternity. Strangely enough the audience — screaming for blood though it was — yet was touched by the sight of these two so young and so valiant, and the people shuddered. Perpetua and Felicitas were called back and clothed in loose robes.

Now Perpetua was thrown, her garment rent and her thigh gored. Regaining her feet, she gathered her tunic over her thigh so in suffering she would not appear immodest, and looking about found her fallen hair ornament and repinned her hair lest one soon to be a martyr seem to grieve in her glory. Looking for Felicitas, she gave assistance to her and standing together they awaited another attack. But the mob cried, "Enough," and the two were led off to the headsman's block. Catching sight of her brother, Perpetua cried out: "Stand fast in the faith and love one another; and do not let our sufferings be a stumbling block to you." Felicitas was struck down first then Perpetua — but only after the nervous swordsman had struck her once and failed to sever her head. The second time she guided his sword with her own hands.

So brave, and so full of love; perhaps if she were dying now she would exhort us to be brave and full of love in slightly different words. Perhaps she would cry out, "Stand fast in the faith and love one another; and do not let our color be a stumbling block to you."

For Perpetua was white and Felicitas was black.*

---

* We have been unable to find this asserted in any source; perhaps it is a deduction from the fact that St. Felicitas was a slave in Carthage (in North Africa). — *Publisher,* 1995.

3

TWENTY STORIES OF SAINTS

To Help Parents Impress Particular Virtues

OBEDIENCE

The story of St. Francis and the cabbages

OBEDIENCE is something to be learned by all Christians and loved for itself alone for Christ's sake, who was "obedient unto death on the Cross." It is the key to humility. While there is need for us to teach our children to "use their heads," to "reason things out," there is also need to teach them that where obedience to an authority under God is concerned, in all things excepting sin there is no act more meritorious than obedience even when we question the wisdom of the commands we are given. We never lose when we are obedient for the love of God. The "duly constituted authorities" in a child's life are his parents first, after them his teachers, the police officers protecting him, his bus driver, Scout leader, and so forth, and of course in a special way his bishop, his pastor and the other priests of his parish.

Almost everyone knows the story of St. Francis of Assisi, christened Francis Bernadone, the son of a wealthy merchant who expected his boy to win honor and glory for the family name in the wars, then settle down to a life of pleasure and riches as partner in the family business. But Francis fell in love with God and left all things to become a beggar for Christ.

There are many stories about St. Francis; among our favorites is a legend from the friary at Monte Casale. Here every year the brethren plant a cabbage in the garden and let it flower to remind them of the time the saint bade two young brothers plant some cabbage plants upside down. One did, but the other knew better and planted his right side up. St. Francis dismissed the second brother, for, he said, it had been a test of obedience, not of planting cabbages.

PERSEVERANCE

A story from the Desert Fathers to help one stay with
what grows wearisome

WHO does not say to himself now and then, "What is the use of this! I am only doing what I have already done a thousand times and anyone could do it. It is a waste of time!"

One of the hermits of old who dwelt in the desert had a cell situated all of seven miles from the water, and it was necessary for him to walk the distance to the river and back each time he replenished his supply. Growing tired of this journey, he said to himself: "What need is there for me to endure this toil? I shall come and live near the water." As he said this, he caught sight of someone who followed behind him, counting his footsteps. He asked, "Who art thou?" and the one behind said, "I am the angel of the Lord, and I am sent to count thy footprints and give thee thy reward." And the monk, when he heard this, set his cell still farther from the water! [1]

CRITICISM

St. Simeon Stylites helps children accept the differences
in men as well as their sameness

CHILDREN and adults easily misjudge one another. A child who is quiet and introspective may seem to the noisy, outgoing ones

[1] *The Desert Fathers,* trans. Helen Waddell (New York: Henry Holt, 1936), pp. 121–2.

to be a snob. Another who has unusual hobbies might be thought deliberately aloof. One who is strong and healthy may suspect there is a lack of manliness in those who are not. Certain saints help us to see that God does give "different" vocations and we must be respectful of them, never scornful. St. Simeon Stylites certainly gave God a strange form of service, yet he is no less a saint. Although we are not to imitate him in his *ways* we *are* supposed to be like him in *love.*

Simeon was the son of a Syrian shepherd and kept his father's flocks. When he was thirteen, in about the year 402, he was deeply moved by a sermon on the Beatitudes and he asked a holy man their meaning. The old man told him that they taught that prayer, watching, fasting, weeping, humiliation and the patient suffering of persecution were the roads to true happiness and he explained that a life of solitude enabled a man best to practice these virtues. Simeon then begged God to lead him on the way of perfection and, seeing in a dream what his future life would be, he went to a monastery to live. After two years of austerity and holiness he went to another monastery. Here he practiced such terrible mortifications, among them the wearing of a rope of twisted palm fibres which embedded itself in his flesh and had to be cut free, that the abbot dismissed him as a warning to the others lest they try like singularities. Then Simeon took himself to a hermitage at the foot of a mountain and fasted the forty days of Lent in memory of the forty days' fast of Our Lord. At the end of this time, he was found senseless on the ground. Reviving, he took a bit of water and received Holy Communion. Thereafter he observed every Lent in this way, standing during the first weeks, sitting during the following, and finally, too weak to sit, he lay down for the final weeks. Thus he lived for three years, after which he moved to the top of the mountain, built himself an enclosure without roof or shelter, and chained himself to it. However, when he was told that a firm will supported by grace should be enough to keep him there — if there he must be — Simeon had a smith sever the chain.

As his reputation for wisdom and holiness grew, people flocked to see him, bringing their sick for his blessing, their problems for his solving. He cured and helped many but he regretted the loss of his solitude so he built himself a pillar about nine feet high and lived on it in prayer and silence for four years, eating little. On a second pillar about eighteen feet high he lived for three years and on a third pillar about thirty-three feet high he spent the last twenty years of his life. It is because the Greek word for pillar is *stylos* that St. Simeon is called Stylites.

It was to be expected that this singularity of St. Simeon's would be criticized as extravagance. To try his humility and discover if his performances were rooted in self-will, the bishops and abbots of the vicinity ordered him to come down. Immediately he prepared to descend. Seeing his obedience, they sent word that they were convinced his strange way of life *was* his vocation from God and they permitted him to follow it.

His pillar was never larger than six feet in diameter which made it difficult to lie flat, but Simeon would not allow a seat. He stooped, knelt and bowed in prayer. One visitor saw him bow profoundly twelve hundred and forty-four times. He wore animal skins for his clothing.

St. Simeon's way — right for him but certainly not for us — led him to the heroic practice of the virtues described in the Beatitudes, and he grew to such an awareness of God's love and majesty, in such an abhorrence for sin, that he sincerely believed himself to be the worst of men. He preached from his pillar with such sweetness and love that even barbarians and pagans were converted. He died on his pillar at the age of sixty-nine, a "different" saint but one who gave great glory to God.

SELFISHNESS

A story about St. Macarius the Younger for people who take the largest piece

ST. MACARIUS the Younger of Alexandria lived about the fourth century and was one of the Desert Fathers. Surprisingly enough, when he discovered his vocation to be a hermit, he was a confectioner — which proves that no matter where you may be, or what you may be doing, if you truly want to do God's will He will make it clear one day. St. Macarius lived in a tiny hermitage as a member of a desert community called the Cells, so called because everyone lived in a cell. Each hermit built his own cell and, when a new member came to join them, each offered the newcomer his cell, willingly building himself another. They lived in silence and out of sight of one another except on Saturdays and Sundays when they gathered together to celebrate Mass and receive the Holy Eucharist. They made baskets and mats and in this quiet way contemplated God and loved one another.

One time St. Macarius was given a bunch of fresh grapes. He thanked the donor of the gift, and when the latter had gone carried the grapes to a neighboring monk who was ill. That monk thanked St. Macarius and when *he* was gone, carried the grapes to a neighbor who, as soon as *that* monk was gone, carried the grapes to his neighbor, and this continued. Late that same evening St. Macarius saw a monk coming to his hut bearing him his bunch of grapes, and "gave thanks that he had seen in the brethren such abstinence and such loving-kindness."

PRAYER

A story from the Lives of the Brethren of the Order
of Preachers to help children say prayers with devotion

OFTEN children grow discouraged over the constant saying of prayers because they have no sense of being *heard*. Here is a tale to help them consider the other end of this conversation with God and His saints.

At the time the Dominican Order was established, it began immediately to be assailed by the devil. The brethren in Bologna and the brethren in Paris were grievously assaulted until it was ruled in desperation that nightly after Compline they would have recourse to their holy Mother Mary, and sing the *Salve Regina* in procession in her honor.

At once the phantoms were put to flight by her who is to the devil as terrible as an army in battle array, and many tales of wonders seen were told in various houses by holy persons. One woman of Marseilles was caught up in ecstasy one evening during the singing of the *Salve* and saw "four things deserving of being remembered and prized."

"First of all, as the brethren sang the words, *our life, our sweetness, and our hope,* she saw the Blessed Virgin graciously return their salutation. As the anthem was continued, at the words, *Turn then, O gracious advocate,* she observed her fall on her knees before her Son and make intercession for them. At the phrase, *thine eyes of mercy towards us,* she looked at them with a most gracious and happy smile; and lastly, as they sang, *After this our exile, show unto us the blessed fruit of thy womb, Jesus. O clement, O holy, O sweet Virgin Mary,* she saw her clasp her Son as a Child and hold Him out to each in turn." [2]

So — this is how Our Lady looks when we pray to her with love!

WAITING FOR PRAYERS TO BE ANSWERED

A story about St. Vincent de Paul
to show that God does answer prayers

VINCENT DE PAUL was a peasant boy who tended his father's sheep and pigs outside the village where he lived in southern France. Afoot in the good seasons, on stilts in the bad, every day he went with his charges through the boggy pastures at the mercy of sun and wind and weather. A lawyer friend recommended to his father that such an intelligent lad would be better off in school, so he was sent to Dax where he studied grammar and Latin and decided God wanted him to be a priest. Seven

---

[2] *Lives of the Brethren of the Order of Preachers,* trans. Placid Conway, O.P. (London: Blackfriars, 1955), p. 37.

years he studied, supporting himself at first on the price of a fine pair of his father's oxen then later by fees paid him at a little school he opened for boys, and finally he was ordained at the age of twenty in the year 1600.

Several years later he inherited a little money from a kind benefactress, only to discover that one of the old lady's debtors had run off with it. As Vincent was in need of funds he followed the man to Marseilles, caught up with him and regained his money, and then decided to return home the shorter distance by water across the Gulf of Lyons. His ship was barely out of sight of the coast when it was captured by Barbary pirates and carried off to Tunis. In a letter written to the friend who helped him through school, he describes these adventures and sufferings and tells something especially interesting about his encounter with a Moslem woman and her interest in Christianity.

"A renegade from Nice in Savoy . . . bought me and carried me off to his *temat* (property) . . . in the mountains where the country is very hot and parched. One of his three wives . . . a Turk by birth, was instrumental through the boundless mercy of God, in drawing her husband out of his apostasy back into the Church and delivering me from my slavery. She was very curious to know about our way of life and came to see us every day in the fields where I was digging and finally ordered me to sing the praises of my God. The memory of the children of Israel and their *Quomodo cantabimus in terra aliena* ('How shall we sing in a strange land') caused me with tears in my eyes to begin *Super flumina Babylonis* ('By the waters of Babylon') and then I sang the *Salve Regina* and several other pieces, in which she took so much pleasure that it was wonderful to behold. She did not fail to tell her husband that same evening that he had done wrong in giving up his religion, that to her mind it was extremely good, and all because of the account I had given her of our God and His praises which I had sung in her presence. She had, she said, felt such divine pleasure in all this that she did not believe that the paradise of her fathers which she had constantly hoped for could be so glorious or so full of joy as the pleasure she had taken while I praised my God. Her conclusion was that there was a marvelous element in this occurrence.

"This woman . . . was, by her account, the cause of her husband's telling me on the next day that he was merely waiting for a convenient opportunity for us all to escape to France and that he hoped in a short time to effect this to the praise of God."

And this the man did, not only returning to France, but, after public penance and reconciliation with the Church, accompanying Vincent to Rome where he entered a monastery.

In this same letter Vincent wrote. "God always preserved in me a hope of being set free through the earnest prayer which I made to Him and to the Blessed Virgin Mary through whose intercession alone, I firmly believe, I was delivered. . . ." [3]

There he was, young and a slave, digging in the hot fields of that strange land, praying to the Blessed Virgin Mary and wondering, no doubt, why it had happened and when his prayers would be answered. Little did he know when he was captured that God had an errand for him to do, an apostate to restore to the Faith, and a Moslem woman's heart to touch with the story of Christ. God chose Vincent to do these things before ever he discovered his great vocation as lover and protector of His poor. Everyone's life with Christ is an adventure. Prayer makes it come out right.

HEAR NO EVIL

A story about Father John Gerard, S.J.
and the clanking chains

IN THE *Autobiography of a Hunted Priest*, Father John Gerard, an English Jesuit, tells the story of his life in the disguise of a country gentleman during the years when Catholics and

---

[3] Jean Calvet, *St. Vincent de Paul*, trans. Lancelot Sheppard (New York: David McKay, 1948), p. 24.

their priests were outlawed by the English. Appearing openly and in high fashion, playing at cards, hunting, making himself a charming guest and companion, he secretly said Mass for Catholic families, instructed converts, gave retreats and from time to time hid in hiding-holes to escape arrest by the *pursuivants* — priest-hunters. Finally he was caught and imprisoned in a place called "the Counter in the Poultry," a set of four houses used by the Crown for a prison.

The jailer had been told to put him in close confinement but to treat him well as he was a gentleman, but this made no impression on the jailer. He put him instead in a tiny garret with a doorway so small he had to crawl through on his hands and knees, a ceiling so low he could stand only by the bed, and the window always open so that on rainy days and nights the bed, his only piece of furniture, was always soaked. The stench from the prison privies was ever-present, but the priest was at peace and wrote, "By God's blessing, I enjoyed that peace of soul which the world does not and cannot give."

Nearby, out of sight, were other prisoners, *not* gentlemen, and it was because of them that during the three-month stay in the Counter in the Poultry, Father Gerard polished the chains on his legs.

"When I first had them on, they were rusty, but I had made them bright and shining by wearing them every day and moving about in them. My cell was narrow and I could have walked across in three paces if my legs had been free. I used to shuffle from side to side with short steps. In this way, I got some exercise. Also, and this mattered more, when the prisoners below started singing lewd songs and Geneva psalms, I was able to drown out their noise with the less unpleasant sound of my clanking chains."[4]

There is always something we can do to keep our sense of hearing from being an avenue of sin for us — even if it is just walking away.

[4] John Gerard, S.J., *The Autobiography of a Hunted Priest,* trans. Philip Caraman, S.J. (New York: Pellegrini & Cudahy, 1952), p. 77.

IMPURE THOUGHTS

About St. Camillus de Lellis and what he used to say to his spiritual sons

ST. CAMILLUS DE LELLIS was a giant of a man, six feet, six inches tall and big in every way. Named after his mother, he was born to her, heralded by a dream, when she was almost sixty years old. In her dream, Camilla saw her baby, "his breast signed with the cross, and followed by a troop of children similarly signed." During Mass on the 25th of May in the jubilee year of 1550, she began to go into labor and, hastening home, was persuaded by a friend to lie in the stable that her son might be born there as was the Infant Saviour. This she did, and at the moment of the Elevation at the High Mass, Camillus was born. His father was so delighted that he leaped about the house like a wild man, and in answer to the protests of the mother he asked how she could object to his dancing for joy, "seeing we have such a big son that we could send him to school this very day!"

As he grew older he became increasingly difficult to manage and finally his disposition was quite beyond control. He ran away from school whenever he felt like it, took to playing cards, was the despair of his mother and, after her death, of his tutor as well. At seventeen he went off to the wars with his father; they both fell sick, his father died and left Camillus an orphan and destitute with only his sword, his dagger and his honorable name for his inheritance — together with his extravagant tastes and his mad passion for gambling. Hobbling home from the wars, humiliated and in pain from horrible sores on his legs, he was overcome by remorse for his sins and vowed to become a Franciscan. This was something he would try to do twice, in vain, for his vocation was not Franciscan, nor was his disposition, intolerable to his companions in the world, one to add to the harmony of a religious community. Repenting, falling back into his quarrelsome, gambling ways, repenting again, he was finally "converted," as he called it, on the feast of the Purification, 1575. Then began the long life of service to God's sick, the gathering together of men who would serve them with him, the forming of a religious congregation called the Ministers of the Sick for this work. He was the spiritual father of many priests and brothers and the spiritual son of St. Philip Neri, his confessor and dear friend.

Well might such a man know how best to put the devil and his temptation to rout. He never forgot, it is said, the advice given him by a Capuchin friar during the days when he struggled so to overcome himself, and all his life he counseled others with the same words. While temptations against chastity seem not to have been St. Camillus' greatest difficulty, his words apply stunningly to such temptations and boys especially will find them to their liking. They are fighting words, from a giant of a saint. In our idiom St. Camillus says, "When the devil tempts you in your thoughts, spit in his eye!"

DARE TO BE DIFFERENT

A story about St. Galla of Rome

ST. GALLA was the daughter of a noble Roman who was unjustly slain in the year 525, leaving behind him three daughters. Young and wealthy and, one cannot help hoping, beautiful, she married and within a year she was widowed. She determined to become a bride of Christ and persevered over much opposition — not the least of which came from her physicians — and joined a community of women who resided hard by the basilica of St. Peter. There for many years she lived a life dedicated to God and His poor and needy. Finally she fell ill with cancer; then one night she saw St. Peter standing before her between two candlesticks and she asked him if her sins were forgiven her. St. Peter nodded and said, "Come, follow me." But Galla asked if her dear friend Benedicta might come too. Yes, she might, said St. Peter, after thirty days — and that is precisely what happened. St. Galla and another holy woman departed this life for heaven three days later, and Benedicta thirty days after them. As for the physicians and their dire threats — nothing came of that nonsense. She never did grow the beard.

Not only girls who want to be nuns, but girls who just want to be *good* have to ignore a marvelous lot of nonsense from those who "follow the pack." Life will pass you by, they say, and you won't have any fun if you don't do as we do! About as fast as St. Galla grew her beard, it will!

HUMBLE CONFESSION

A story about Father Damien the leper

ONE of Father Damien's greatest sufferings after he left for Molokai was his inability to go to confession. Two months after his arrival on the island, the Honolulu Board of Health ruled that no one on Molokai would be allowed to return, even temporarily. This was a cruel blow to a man of such delicate conscience as Father Damien, accustomed to receiving the grace of the sacrament of Penance weekly. Since he was forbidden to leave, it seemed someone must come to him.

In September, a steamer stopped outside the shore settlement of Kalaupapa with the usual load of provisions, patients banished from the mainland, and this time with Father Damien's provincial, Father Modeste, who knew the young priest was longing to see him. As he prepared to land, Father Modeste was confronted by the captain. "I have formal orders to stop you," he announced. There was nothing left but for Damien to come out to the ship. He did, in a small boat rowed by two of his leper friends, and prepared to board. "Stay back! Stay back!" shouted the captain. "I've been strictly forbidden to let you see anyone!" Father Damien stood in the little boat, so near and yet so far. Quickly he made up his mind. "Very well, I will go to confession here." And with his provincial leaning over the railing on the deck, the priest confessed his sins and received absolution.

It is said no one on board knew French. Nevertheless, one cannot help feel that in this case the walls, the very skies, had ears. It was truly heroic: a man making the choice between human respect and sacramental grace. There is no comparison. Penance is the torrent that will cleanse us. Let no pride nor human respect prevent our making humble confessions.

TEMPER TROUBLE

A story to tell about one of the Desert Fathers

A CERTAIN brother living in one of the desert communities was restless and irritable and frequently lost his temper. Despairing of ever correcting his anger where he was, he removed himself to a hermitage in a cave and there lived as a solitary, certain that without the interruptions and distractions of monastery life he would be unmoved by anger. One day he drew some water for himself, set the water jug on the ground, and it tipped over. He drew the jug full again, set it on the ground, and a second time it tipped over. He drew the jug full a third time and a third time it tipped over and then, in a fit of terrible anger, he hurled it to the ground. It broke into a thousand pieces. Suddenly he came to himself and saw how he had been tricked by the spirit of anger. And he said: "Behold, here I am alone, and nevertheless he hath conquered me. I shall return to the community, for in all places there is need for struggle, patience and above all for the help of God." [5] And he arose and went back to his monastery.

So we must admit, if we are to make headway with our tempers or whatever our faults, that the devil, when he sees we have them, will try to stir them up. For a time we may leave the people or things that might move us to anger, but there is no cure for a bad temper but hard work on ourselves!

[5] Waddell, *op. cit.*, pp. 122–3.

HUMILITY AND DETACHMENT

*Some good advice from St. Syncletica who might
be called one of the Desert Mothers*

MANY times children are so exhilarated by their success at overcoming some fault (at least temporarily) or performing some act of virtue that they can hardly wait to tell it. Yet the fruitfulness of such acts depends in part on resisting any pride that may rise up out of success and concealing (except perhaps from a parent or confessor who is helping the child conquer himself) its triumphs. If the soul is to profit from its triumphs, it must remember it succeeds only because God has given it the grace to succeed. Its only independent accomplishments are its sins. In the life of St. Syncletica there are many wise things about humility and the secret possession of one's virtues.

St. Syncletica was a Macedonian, born at Alexandria in Egypt. Her family was wealthy and this, together with her beauty, brought many young men to her as suitors. But she had given her heart to Christ so she fled to the desert to escape the lure of life in the world. Many women came to her for counsel and it is evidently from her discourses to them that her wise quotations derive. About humility and the need to keep triumphs secret between ourselves and God, she said this,

"A treasure that is known is quickly spent: and even so any virtue that is commented on and made a public show of is destroyed. Even as wax is melted before the face of fire, so is the soul enfeebled by praise, and loses the toughness of its virtues." [6]

Asked if it were a perfect good to have nothing, she said this about detachment and poverty of spirit (which, if one cannot live the kind of life where one can have nothing, is necessary if possessions are not to be a danger) in a way which shows how the work of women — wives, mothers, grandmothers — can lead them to profound meditation: "It is a great good for

[6] *Ibid.,* p. 130.

those who are able (to bear it). For those who can endure it endure suffering in the flesh, but they have quiet of soul. Even as stout garments trodden underfoot and turned over in the washing are made clean and white, so is a strong soul made steadfast by voluntary poverty." [7] When so many families live in at least a state of frugality, which while not entirely voluntary is nevertheless accepted by them because it is God's will, it is helpful to see how great a *good* such a state can be and to be reminded to praise Him for it. It is especially necessary to point this out to children, who will otherwise accept the standards set by the world which complains that enough is *not* enough — one must want *more*.

PAIN AND SUFFERING

A story about St. Patrick and the Prince

DOES someone in your house have to have a penicillin shot, or boosters for all those things you get booster shots for? Or is there one who is chronically ill and has frequent pain, perhaps every day? Here is a story to help the fearful grow stout of heart and the stout-hearted to endure even when they grow weary of *offering up*.

It is told of the time when St. Patrick baptized Aengus, prince of Munster, at Cashel. As you know, St. Patrick was a bishop and in addition to mitres and copes and rings, bishops always appear for ceremonies bearing their staves, or crosiers. Apparently St. Patrick's crosier was sharply spiked. On the day he was baptizing Aengus, he reached that part of the ceremony where he needed the use of both hands, so he stuck his crosier firmly into the ground — or so he thought. Unknowingly he had stuck it through Aengus' foot! The prince said not a word. The baptism continued and only when the final words and the pouring on of water was done and the birth of the new Christian was completed, did St. Patrick discover what he had done. He was

[7] *Ibid.,* p. 117.

horrified! Full of concern and pity for the suffering prince, he asked why he had not cried out. Aengus replied simply. "But is this not part of the ceremony? I thought it was, and since Christ whose feet were pierced by nails shed His blood for me, I am glad to suffer pain at Baptism to be like Him."

Oh glory — what a wonderful thing to do with shots and all our suffering! In pain and suffering we can be like Him!

HOW GOD PROVIDES

About St. Paul the Hermit and St. Anthony of the Desert

EVERY family has some experience with need, either the need for food or care or clothes, sometimes for fathering or mothering, and always the need for spiritual favors. When Our Lord taught that God the Father cares more for us than He does for the birds of the air and the lilies of the field (and mind you, He *loves* these), He did not mean God would always provide what *we* think we need, but what He *knows* we need; and He was chiding us not to worry. We will be provided for, sometimes with a special grace or a trial so we will grow strong or a hardship to purify us, besides the clothes, food, shelter, warmth and other things that we can see we need. Hundreds of saint stories tell how God has provided for those in need. One of them, showing how careful He is to provide what is exactly right and no more (how often this happens!) is about St. Paul the Hermit and St. Anthony of the Desert.

St. Anthony had dwelt in the desert for many years and there came to his mind the thought, tempting him to vanity, that no better monk than he had his dwelling in the desert. That night God sent him a dream in which he saw St. Paul the Hermit, deep in the desert, older than he and far better. The next morning he straightway started out to find him, even though he was an old man of ninety and Paul an even older one of one hundred and thirteen. The journey was a long and arduous one during which he saw and received directions from, it is said, a centaur and a satyr — creatures even St. Jerome reported as having been seen in those days.

Two days he journeyed in the scorching heat and on the third day he saw a she-wolf creep into a cave at the foot of a mountain. Dark and fearsome as it was, Anthony went in and reaching the closed door of Paul's abode cried out to him to open it which he did and invited Anthony to enter, revealing "a spacious courtyard open to the sky, roofed by the wide-spreading branches of an ancient palm, and with a spring of clear shining water hasting from it." The two hermits greeted each other with embraces and sat down to talk about the world and whether idolatry still reigned there. As they talked, a raven settled on the branch of the tree, then "softly flying down, deposited a whole loaf before their wondering eyes." "Behold," said St. Paul, when the bird had withdrawn, "God hath sent us our dinner, God the merciful, God the compassionate. It is now sixty years since I have had each day a half loaf of bread; but at thy coming, God hath doubled His soldiers' rations." [8]

HOW THE DEVIL TEMPTS US

As told by the Devil to St. Dominic

CHILDREN are always interested in the devil, as indeed we all should be, but often the effect of tales about how he tried the saints is to imply he is not interested in such ordinary souls as we. This is one of his *best* tricks, of course, for he is interested in all souls and nothing pleases him quite so much as to discover they think he is *not*. This leaves him quite free to trip them up by the simplest devices.

Once St. Dominic was making the rounds of the convent "like a watchful sentinel," when he met the devil prowling about like a beast of prey. Commanding him to be still, the saint asked him, "Why are you prowling about in this fashion?" The devil answered that it was to great profit that he prowled so. And what

[8] *Ibid.,* p. 48.

profit did he gain, asked St. Dominic, in the dormitory (in our case, the bedroom)? "Oh, I keep them from enjoying their rest," said the devil, "and tempt them not to get up in time for their prayers. And if this does not work, I frighten them with terrible dreams." They walked along to the choir, the place where the monks said their prayers together (in our case, wherever the family says its prayers together). "And what do you gain here?" asked St. Dominic. "Oh, much! I make them come late for prayers and leave before they are done and I busy their minds with distractions so they cannot meditate." Then St. Dominic led him to the refectory (or in our case the dining room and wherever else we eat our meals) and, asking the devil what he did there, the saint got his reply: "Who is there who does not eat more than he should and make a glutton of himself, or less than he should and commit disobedience?" Then taking the devil to the parlor (or wherever we would take our recreation) the saint was about to ask the devil what he gained there when the devil chuckled in high glee. "Oh-ho-ho! This is truly my spot! This is the place for improper laughter and dangerous and foolish pastimes and idle gossip!" But when they came to the chapter house (which in our lives would be wherever we examine our consciences and make our confessions) he shrieked and tried to make off. "I loathe this spot!" he screeched, "for I lose here whatever I may have gained elsewhere, since here they are told of their faults, correct one another in charity, do penance, and are absolved of their sins." [9]

So — he is always about! It is good to know so we can be on guard.

ST. ISAAC JOGUES

A story to remember when one is tempted to sin with his hands

ISAAC JOGUES was one of the French Jesuits who came from France in the seventeenth century to bring the gift of Baptism and the Faith to the Indians in the New World. It would be

---

[9] Conway, *op. cit.,* p. 52.

hard to find in all the lives of the saints a story more filled with danger, terror and blazing love than that of these Jesuits. Men of refinement from gracious homes and loving families, who entered religion and lived surrounded by the love and the regard of their brother priests, they left all for a life of utter deprivation that was harder than their wildest imaginings. The people they had come to serve were truly savage. Suspicious, crafty, cruel, unclean, coarse, impure, accustomed to the most primitive ways, these children of the One God*worshipped many gods and offered them many things in sacrifice, including the flesh of their enemies which these Indians often ate. To such people the Jesuits adapted themselves, gave themselves. Nothing in the lives of the early martyrs of the Church surpasses these modern martyrs. Their story is a *must* for every boy and girl, mother and father. It is a tale of how men are supposed to love — as their Master loves — to the last drop of blood and the last shred of flesh.

The plague of the French settlements on the St. Lawrence and of the Jesuits working among the Hurons was the Iroquois, the five nations of Indians below the St. Lawrence occupying what is now part of New York State. Among these tribes the Mohawks were the most fierce and their avowed determination to wipe the Hurons from the face of the earth kept them constantly on the warpath, harrassing both their enemy and their enemy's French friends.

On the morning of August 2, 1642, a party including Father Isaac Jogues, René Goupil, William Couture, several Christian Hurons and others, forty in all, were ambushed and captured. The Mohawks did them unspeakable violence. It is hard to imagine that ever in the history of mankind have there been blood baths worse than these. The torture march took them mile after mile, sometimes on foot, sometimes cramped in canoes, bleeding, infected, feverish, set upon wildly at the nightly encampments and dragged about by the hair, the beard, pinched, plucked, probed, pierced for the delight it afforded their captors. Entering encampments and villages, they were forced to run

---

*Strictly speaking, of course, a person becomes a child of God by Baptism, not by birth.—*Publisher,* 1995.

the gauntlet, climb the torture platforms, endure the same outrages repeated for the amusement it afforded the villagers. At night they were tied to the ground, their hands and feet staked, and left for whatever torments the women and children devised. It amused the Indians to sprinkle hot coals on the prisoners' bodies and wait to see if the captives would betray their pain. Years of hardening in the forests, enduring the fierce Canadian winters, living with the minimum of shelter, clothing and accommodation had seasoned and tried the fortitude of the Indians. Love of God accounted for the fortitude of the priests. They knew the worst lay ahead of them with their arrival at the village of their captors where they would again be tortured and at last, perhaps, mercifully meet death.

The day came. Hideously "embraced" by the villagers who met them at the bank of the river, they were marched across a ford and herded into a field. The Mohawks solemnly offered thanksgiving to the sun and to the war demons who had delivered the French and the Hurons into their hands to be roasted and eaten. Next the prisoners were forced to run the gauntlet: William Couture the catechist was first, then the Christian Hurons, followed by René Goupil, more Hurons, and last of all the prize, the hated blackrobe *Ondessonk* — Isaac Jogues. The assaults were unbelievable. Jogues reached the end of the gauntlet to find his comrades "a bleeding pile of bodies. . . . Worst of all was Goupil. His face and head were smeared over with blood, so that there was left no white except that of his eyes. His features were smashed and swollen. . . . So pitiable was his condition, that he would have inspired compassion in cruelty itself. I found him all the more beautiful as he had more in common with Him who, bearing a face most worthy of the admiration and delight of angels, appeared to us, in the midst of His anguish, like unto a leper."

Next they were made to ascend the platform. Again they were beaten, cut, the skin of their fingers slit; then an old man, a sorcerer, ascended the platform dragging after him an Algonquin squaw named Joan who was known to be a Christian. He drove the others off and gnashed the fingers of *Ondessonk* in his teeth. "I hate this one most of all," he cried, and he ordered the Algonquin woman to cut off the left thumb. She shrank away, horrified. She loved the Blackrobes and their God, but the old man and the braves hedged her about, threatening to kill her if she delayed. Finally she took the knife and shaking with fright and terror horribly hacked off his thumb. He endured it silently. He saw his thumb lying at his feet where the woman had dropped it.

"Picking up the severed thumb with my right hand, I offered it to You, my living and my true God, for I remembered the Holy Sacrifices which I had offered to You upon the altars of your Church through seven years. I accepted this torture, O my God, as a loving vengeance for want of love and respect that I had shown in touching Your Holy Body . . ." [10]

ABOUT NOT HOLDING A GRUDGE

From the story of St. John Gualbert

ST. JOHN GUALBERT was the son of a noble Florentine, who had only one other and older son, Hugh. When Hugh was murdered by a man supposed to be his friend, John swore vengeance and, in spite of the warnings and sorrow of his father, he set out to destroy him. Well might his father sorrow more over John than over his murdered son, for the motive of revenge is not excusable even in the punishment of a murderer. Still less is it acceptable before God to try to right one injury with another or one murder with another. By chance one day John met his enemy in a very narrow passage and, having the advantage, drew his sword to run him through. The enemy, knowing he had no chance to save himself, fell to his knees, crossed his hands over his breast (let us hope he made a good act of contrition) and awaited the death blow. John advanced in a

[10] Francis X. Talbot, S.J., *Saint Among Savages* (New York: Harper, 1935), p. 206.

fury — halted and remembered Christ had *prayed* for *His* murderers as He hung on the cross. He put up his sword, gave his enemy his hand and, drawing him to his feet, embraced him. They parted in peace.

As he went down the road, filled with contrition for the terrible deed he had intended to do, he came to the monastery of San Miniato, entered it, and kneeling before the Crucifix he poured out his heart in contrition. As he prayed, the Crucifix miraculously bowed its head as though to bless John's victory over revenge and John was filled with the desire to serve only Christ. He went to the abbot to ask permission to wear the habit, and, when the abbot hesitated for several days for fear of the displeasure of John's father, John hacked off his hair and put on a borrowed habit. This convinced Father Abbot that the young penitent was a serious prospect and he received him into the community.

HOW SANCTITY DOES NOT COME EASILY

About the Struggle of St. Benedict of San Fradello*
to carry his cross

St. Benedict of San Fradello, born in 1526 on the Island of Sicily, was the son of slaves whose owner thought so highly of them that he promised them to free this child even before Benedict was born. One day, in the year he was twenty-one, he was working beside some others when they took to tormenting him on the score of his enslaved parents and his low estate in life. Benedict answered with such gentleness and humility that a passerby stopped to listen. This man happened to be a Sicilian nobleman named Lanzi who had left his wealth and rank to retire with a few companions to live a life of prayer. "You make fun of this man now," he said, "but one day you will hear more of him," and he asked Benedict if he would like to join their community. This Benedict did and was so loved for his gentle ways, his holiness, that when Brother Jerome Lanzi died the

---

* Also known by the inaccurate nickname, "St. Benedict the Moor." — *Publisher,* 1995.

monks asked him to be their superior. He accepted with regret
— only for the sake of obedience.

When the Holy See decreed that the hermits must join an
established order or disband, Benedict became a Franciscan and
was soon employed, to his great content, as a cook. His career as
a cook did not last long, however. Soon he was made guardian
of the monastery and was given the task of converting it into a
house of recollection for the friars. When he was not busy about
his work as superior, he busied himself with what he considered
much more to his measure: helping in the kitchen, washing
dishes, carrying wood and water, sweeping floors, digging in
the garden and begging. He was not fit to be superior, he would
say: he could not read or write. But his brothers repeated that
the first requirements were wisdom and holiness and these he
had.

Benedict performed many miracles although he disclaimed
credit for any since, he said, they were Our Lady's doing. He
multiplied bread for the poor — giving all the bread in the
house away with the result that there was as much left as he had
given away. One day he noticed the brothers in the kitchen had
thoughtlessly thrown the fragments of leftover bread in the dish
water with the plates. He admonished them to save these pieces
of bread for the poor, saying, "This food is the blood of those who
have given it to us for the love of God." Silently the brothers
returned to their work, glancing at one another in amusement
at the notions of this scrupulous Father Guardian. Benedict
picked out of the dish water one of the brushes they used to
scrub the plates and said to them, "Look, my children!" To
their horror they saw him squeeze from the brush a stream of
what looked like blood — and they knelt and asked his forgive-
ness. Benedict used to say that in the matter of food, the best
form of mortification was not to deprive oneself of it, but
to desist after eating a little, adding that it was right to partake
of food given in alms as a token of gratitude and to give pleasure
to the donors.

Relieved at last of all but the simplest duties, he was sent back to his kitchen and here, he thought, he would happily be alone. But not any more. His fame had spread far and wide and the love of the people as well as the friars brought souls to him for all sorts of help. The poor came for alms, the sick for healing, the sorrowful to be consoled, the learned to imbibe his wisdom; even the Archbishop came to ask his advice in administrative matters. He healed, advised, prayed for, prayed with and served. He drove out evil spirits. He was to become one of the patrons of those afflicted with hernia, sciatica, catarrh and headache, because of the innumerable times he had cured these maladies. He was to become one of the patrons of farmers because of the many times he had saved the fields and gardens and vineyards from the ravages of insects and adverse weather. Perhaps he is also one of the patrons of families who must bear scandal and disgrace, for he had a brother Mark who murdered a man and was sentenced to death. Asked to appear before the viceroy so he might plead for mercy for his brother, Benedict startled the man by saying he had no right, nor did he want to influence the official to a miscarriage of justice. The viceroy was so impressed by this that he granted a full pardon to the brother all the same, saying that Benedict's penances would atone for the crime, and his example and prayers would help Mark mend his ways.

All of which, we must admit, must sound as though sanctity came very easily to Benedict of San Fradello. It did not. Love for Our Lord in the Blessed Sacrament accounted for it all. He suffered terribly from the insults and abuse of people who considered themselves his superior because of his lowly birth, the slavery of his parents, the condition of life God had chosen for him. On one occasion he was seen to struggle to control his temper during so violent a temptation to anger that his eyes became bloodshot, he was seized with trembling, and the blood burst from his nose. Why should he be attacked so, who was so good, so kind, so holy, so beloved by men? We neglected to say he was a Negro.*

*He is the patron of Blacks in the United States.—*Publisher,* 1995.

ST. MADELEINE SOPHIE BARAT

A story about Love

MADELEINE LOUISE SOPHIE BARAT became a child of God on the feast of St. Lucy (whose name means *light*) on the 13th of December, 1779. Her godfather was her older brother Louis, nine years old. She had been prematurely born when her mother was frightened by a fire and, when asked as a little girl of five (because they loved to hear her answer) what it was that brought her into the world, she invariably answered: "Fire."

It was fitting. She was to spend her life spreading the fire of Christ's love, and it was her brother Louis, later a priest, who trained this little girl so she grew up to be a saint. Her story is long and beautiful but we will tell only the least bit of it here, something from the beginning which was a sign of the end. It is a lovely story for children to hear after all the other stories are told, because it says in the simplest way what we are supposed to be about. St. Madeleine Sophie tells it in her own words.

"When I was a child, I once had a lamb that was very fond of me; when I called it, it came at once even leaving its food. One day it was lying quite still at my feet when my brother came into the room. He stood for a short time looking at it and then said: 'Look, Sophie, at your lamb and see what it is doing. It is loving.' " [11]

That is what we are supposed to be doing: loving.

AND NOW A WORD TO US ALL

From Blessed Oliver Plunkett, followed by a fitting conclusion from a Desert Father

BLESSED OLIVER PLUNKETT, the martyr, is a "symbol of Irish resistance to the political and religious persecutions of England."

[11] *Life of Blessed Madeleine Sophie Barat* (Roehampton: Convent of the Sacred Heart, 1911), p. 13.

*Now *Saint* Oliver Plunkett (canonized 1975).—*Publisher,* 1995.

He was arrested in Ireland, held for trial and absurdly accused of attempting to bring 20,000 French soldiers into the country and levying a tax on his clergy (he was a bishop) to support 70,000 men! For two days no witnesses appeared to testify against him and, when on the third day one did show up (drunk), it was apparent that a conviction of Bishop Plunkett was not to be had in Ireland so he was removed to England. The first time his trial came up the grand jury found no true charge against him, but he was not released. Eventually nine false witnesses were procured to testify and he was found guilty of high treason. He was sentenced to be hanged, disembowelled and quartered. "It is good," he declared, "for me at this time to give an example to the Irish people, since I have already given them so much good advice." [12] And he died for God and the Church on July 1, 1681. His feast is celebrated on July 11.

Now that we have given our children so much good advice on how to live the Christian life, let us not fail them in good example.

And here is the last story in this book. It is for all those who want to be saints but aren't, for those who try and fall, and get up and try again, who fall again and get up again, and try again — until it seems, discouragingly enough, that this will go on forever! Once again the story is from the Desert Fathers.

The abbot Moses asked the abbot Silvanus, saying, "Can a man every day make a beginning of the good life?" The abbot Silvanus answered him, "If he be diligent, he can every day and every hour begin the good life anew." [13]

All ye holy saints in paradise, help us begin anew!

[12] Omer Englebert, *The Lives of the Saints* (New York: David McKay, 1951), p. 268.
[13] Waddell, *op. cit., p.* 149.

BIBLIOGRAPHY

Balthasar, Hans Urs van. *Thérèse of Lisieux.* New York: Sheed & Ward, 1954.

Beevers, John. *Storm of Glory.* New York: Sheed & Ward, 1950.

Blanton, Margaret Gray. *Bernadette of Lourdes.* New York: Longmans, Green & Co., 1939.

Buehrle, Marie Cecilia. *Saint Maria Goretti.* Milwaukee: Bruce Publishing Co., 1950.

Calvet, Jean. *St. Vincent de Paul.* Translated by Lancelot C. Sheppard. New York: David McKay, 1951.

Caraman, S. J., Philip (ed.) *Saints and Ourselves.* New York: P. J. Kenedy & Sons, 1953.

Collected Letters of St. Thérèse of Lisieux, The. Translated by F. J. Sheed. New York: Sheed & Ward, 1949.

Commentary on the New Testament, A. The Confraternity of Christian Doctrine. New York: William J. Sadlier, 1942.

Daniel-Rops. *Jesus and His Times.* New York: E. P. Dutton, 1956.

Daniel-Rops. *Sacred History.* New York: Longmans, Green & Co., 1949.

Danielou, Jean. *Advent.* New York: Sheed & Ward, 1950.

Desert Fathers, The. Translated by Helen Waddell. New York: Henry Holt & Co., 1936.

Dialogue of St. Catherine of Siena. Translated by Algar Thorold. Westminster, Md.: Newman Press, 1943.

Englebert, Omer. *Lives of the Saints.* Translated by Christopher and Anne Fremantle. New York: David McKay, 1953.

Estrade, J. B. *My Witness Bernadette.* Springfield, Illinois: Templegate, 1951.

Farrow, John. *Damien the Leper.* New York: Sheed & Ward, 1937.

Filas, S.J., Francis L. *Joseph and Jesus.* Milwaukee: Bruce Publishing Co., 1952.

Filas, S.J., Francis L. *Joseph Most Just.* Milwaukee: Bruce Publishing Co., 1956.

Gerard, S.J., John. *The Autobiography of a Hunted Priest.* Translated by Philip Caraman, S.J. New York: Pellegrini & Cudahy, 1952.

Gheon, Henri. *The Secrets of the Saints.* Translated by F. J. Sheed. New York: Sheed & Ward, 1944.

Gillet, O.P., Martin S. *The Mission of St. Catherine.* Translated by Sister M. Thomas Lopez. St. Louis: B. Herder, 1955.

Grollenberg, O.P., L. H. *An Atlas of the Bible.* New York: Thomas Nelson & Sons, 1956.

Guitton, S.J., Georges. *Perfect Friend.* Translated by William J. Young, S.J. St. Louis: B. Herder, 1956.

Habig, O.F.M., Marion A. "Race and Grace: St. Benedict of San Fradello." Franciscan Herald Press.

Heaton, E. W. *Everyday Life in Old Testament Times.* New York: Scribner's, 1956.

Higgins, Daniel. *The Challenge.* Paterson, N.J.: Salesiana Publishing Co.

The Holy Bible

John Bosco, St. *The Life of St. Dominic Savio.* Paterson, N.J.: Salesiana Publishing Co., 1955.

Jourdain, SS.CC., Vital. *The Heart of Father Damien.* Translated by Francis Larkin, SS.CC. and Charles Davenport. Milwaukee: Bruce Publishing Co., 1955.

Lives of the Brethren of the Order of Preachers, The. Translated by Placid Conway, O.P. London: Blackfriars, 1955.

MacConastair, C.P., Alfred. "Convict Number 3142," *The Sign* (January, 1951).

MacConastair, C.P., Alfred. *Lily of the Marshes.* New York: Macmillan, 1951.

Martindale, S.J., C.C. *The Life of St. Camillus de Lellis.* New York: Sheed & Ward, 1946.

Maynard, Theodore. *Mystic in Motley: The Life of St. Philip Neri.* Milwaukee: Bruce Publishing Co., 1946.

Menéndez, Sister Josefa. *The Way of Divine Love.* Westminster, Md.: Newman Press, 1951.

Nolan, A. M. *A History of Ireland.* Chicago: J. S. Hyland & Co., 1913.

Orchard, Bernard, O.S.B., Edmund F. Sutcliffe, S.J., R. C. Fuller, Ralph Russell, O.S.B. (eds.). *A Catholic Commentary on Holy Scripture.* New York: Thomas Nelson & Sons, 1953.

Petitot, O.P., Henri. *The True Story of St. Bernadette.* Translated by a Benedictine of Stanbrook Abbey. Westminster, Md.: Newman Press, 1950.

Raymond of Capua, Blessed. *The Life of St. Catherine of Siena.* Dublin: Duffy, 1853.

Reynolds, E. E. *St. Thomas More.* New York: P. J. Kenedy & Sons, 1954.

Ricciotti, Guiseppe. *The Life of Christ.* Milwaukee: Bruce Publishing Co., 1952.

Robot, Etienne. *Two Portraits of St. Thérèse of Lisieux.* Chicago: Henry Regnery, 1955.

Rondet, S.J., Henri. *Saint Joseph.* Translated and edited by Donald Attwater. New York: P. J. Kenedy & Sons, 1956.

Routh, E. M. G. *Sir Thomas More and His Friends.* London: Oxford University Press, 1934.

Saint-Pierre, Michel de. *Bernadette and Lourdes.* Translated by Edward Fitzgerald. New York: Farrar, Straus & Young, 1954.

Salesians of St. John Bosco, The. "An Ounce of Prevention." Paterson, N.J.: Salesiana Publishing Co.

Sandhurst, B. G. *We Saw Her.* New York: Longmans, Green & Co., 1953.

Sattler, C.S.S.R., Henry. *Parents, Children and the Facts of Life.* New York: Image Books, 1956.

Sheed, F. J. (ed.). *Saints Are Not Sad.* New York: Sheed & Ward, 1949.

Shewring, W. H. *The Passion of Perpetua and Felicity.* London: Sheed & Ward, 1931.

Steinmueller, John E. *A Gospel Harmony.* New York: William J. Sadlier.

Talbot, S.J., Francis X. *Saint Among Savages: The Life of Isaac Jogues.* New York: Harper & Bros., 1935.

Thérèse of Lisieux, St. *Autobiography.* New York: P. J. Kenedy & Sons, 1927.

Thurston, Herbert, S.J., and Donald Attwater (eds.). *Butler's Lives of the Saints.* New York: P. J. Kenedy & Sons, 1956.

Vawter, C.M., Bruce. *A Path Through Genesis.* New York: Sheed & Ward, 1956.

Von Matt, Leonard and Walter Hauser. *St. Francis of Assisi.* Translated by Sebastian Bullough. Chicago: Henry Regnery, 1956.

William, Franz M. *Mary, the Mother of Jesus.* St. Louis: B. Herder & Co.

Yeo, Margaret. *These Three Hearts.* Milwaukee: Bruce Publishing Co., 1940.

If you have enjoyed this book, consider making your next selection from among the following . . .

St. Philomena—The Wonder-Worker. *O'Sullivan* 6.00
The Facts About Luther. *Msgr. Patrick O'Hare* 13.50
Little Catechism of the Curé of Ars. *St. John Vianney* 5.50
The Curé of Ars—Patron Saint of Parish Priests. *Fr. B. O'Brien* 4.50
Saint Teresa of Ávila. *William Thomas Walsh* 18.00
Isabella of Spain: The Last Crusader. *William Thomas Walsh* 20.00
Characters of the Inquisition. *William Thomas Walsh* 12.50
Blood-Drenched Altars—Cath. Comment. on Hist. Mexico. *Kelley* 18.00
The Four Last Things—Death, Judgment, Hell, Heaven. *Fr. von Cochem* 5.00
Confession of a Roman Catholic. *Paul Whitcomb* 1.25
The Catholic Church Has the Answer. *Paul Whitcomb* 1.25
The Sinner's Guide. *Ven. Louis of Granada* 12.00
True Devotion to Mary. *St. Louis De Montfort* 7.00
Life of St. Anthony Mary Claret. *Fanchón Royer* 12.50
Autobiography of St. Anthony Mary Claret 12.00
I Wait for You. *Sr. Josefa Menendez* 75
Words of Love. *Menendez, Betrone, Mary of the Trinity* 5.00
Little Lives of the Great Saints. *John O'Kane Murray* 16.50
Prayer—The Key to Salvation. *Fr. Michael Müller* 7.00
Sermons on Prayer. *St. Francis de Sales* 3.50
Sermons on Our Lady. *St. Francis de Sales* 9.00
Passion of Jesus and Its Hidden Meaning. *Fr. Groenings, S.J.* 12.50
The Victories of the Martyrs. *St. Alphonsus Liguori* 8.50
Canons and Decrees of the Council of Trent. *Transl. Schroeder* 12.50
Sermons of St. Alphonsus Liguori for Every Sunday 16.50
A Catechism of Modernism. *Fr. J. B. Lemius* 4.00
Alexandrina—The Agony and the Glory. *Johnston* 4.00
Life of Blessed Margaret of Castello. *Fr. William Bonniwell* 6.00
The Ways of Mental Prayer. *Dom Vitalis Lehodey* 11.00
Fr. Paul of Moll. *van Speybrouck* 9.00
St. Francis of Paola. *Simi and Segreti* 7.00
Communion Under Both Kinds. *Michael Davies* 1.50
Abortion: Yes or No? *Dr. John L. Grady, M.D.* 1.50
The Story of the Church. *Johnson, Hannan, Dominica* 16.50
Religious Liberty. *Michael Davies* 1.50
Hell Quizzes. *Radio Replies Press* 1.00
Indulgence Quizzes. *Radio Replies Press* 1.00
Purgatory Quizzes. *Radio Replies Press* 1.00
Virgin and Statue Worship Quizzes. *Radio Replies Press* 1.00
The Holy Eucharist. *St. Alphonsus* 8.50
Meditation Prayer on Mary Immaculate. *Padre Pio* 1.25
Little Book of the Work of Infinite Love. *de la Touche* 2.00
Textual Concordance of The Holy Scriptures. *Williams* 35.00
Douay-Rheims Bible. *Leatherbound* 35.00
The Way of Divine Love. *Sister Josefa Menendez* 17.50
The Way of Divine Love. (pocket, unabr.). *Menendez* 8.50
Mystical City of God—Abridged. *Ven. Mary of Agreda* 18.50

Prices guaranteed through June 30, 1996.

Miraculous Images of Our Lady. *Cruz* 20.00
Raised from the Dead. *Fr. Hebert* 15.00
Love and Service of God, Infinite Love. *Mother Louise Margaret*. 10.00
Life and Work of Mother Louise Margaret. *Fr. O'Connell* 10.00
Autobiography of St. Margaret Mary 4.00
Thoughts and Sayings of St. Margaret Mary 3.00
The Voice of the Saints. *Comp. by Francis Johnston* 5.00
The 12 Steps to Holiness and Salvation. *St. Alphonsus* 7.00
The Rosary and the Crisis of Faith. *Cirrincione & Nelson* 1.25
Sin and Its Consequences. *Cardinal Manning* 5.00
Fourfold Sovereignty of God. *Cardinal Manning* 5.00
Dialogue of St. Catherine of Siena. *Transl. Algar Thorold* 9.00
Catholic Answer to Jehovah's Witnesses. *D'Angelo* 8.00
Twelve Promises of the Sacred Heart. (100 cards) 5.00
Life of St. Aloysius Gonzaga. *Fr. Meschler* 10.00
The Love of Mary. *D. Roberto* 7.00
Begone Satan. *Fr. Vogl* 2.00
The Prophets and Our Times. *Fr. R. G. Culleton* 11.00
St. Therese, The Little Flower. *John Beevers* 4.50
St. Joseph of Copertino. *Fr. Angelo Pastrovicchi* 4.50
Mary, The Second Eve. *Cardinal Newman* 2.50
Devotion to Infant Jesus of Prague. *Booklet* .... .75
Reign of Christ the King in Public & Private Life. *Davies* 1.25
The Wonder of Guadalupe. *Francis Johnston* 6.00
Apologetics. *Msgr. Paul Glenn* 9.00
Baltimore Catechism No. 1 .... 3.00
Baltimore Catechism No. 2 .... 4.00
Baltimore Catechism No. 3 .... 7.00
An Explanation of the Baltimore Catechism. *Fr. Kinkead* 13.00
Bethlehem. *Fr. Faber* 16.50
Bible History. *Schuster* 10.00
Blessed Eucharist. *Fr. Mueller* 9.00
Catholic Catechism. *Fr. Faerber* 5.00
The Devil. *Fr. Delaporte* 5.00
Dogmatic Theology for the Laity. *Fr. Premm* 18.00
Evidence of Satan in the Modern World. *Cristiani* 8.50
Fifteen Promises of Mary. (100 cards) 5.00
Life of Anne Catherine Emmerich. 2 vols. *Schmoeger* 37.50
Life of the Blessed Virgin Mary. *Emmerich* 15.00
Manual of Practical Devotion to St. Joseph. *Patrignani* 13.50
Prayer to St. Michael. (100 leaflets) 5.00
Prayerbook of Favorite Litanies. *Fr. Hebert* 9.00
Preparation for Death. (Abridged). *St. Alphonsus* 7.00
Purgatory Explained. *Schouppe* 13.50
Purgatory Explained. (pocket, unabr.). *Schouppe* 7.50
Fundamentals of Catholic Dogma. *Ludwig Ott* 20.00
Spiritual Conferences. *Tauler* 12.00
Trustful Surrender to Divine Providence. *Bl. Claude* 4.00
Wife, Mother and Mystic. *Bessieres* 7.00
The Agony of Jesus. *Padre Pio* 1.50

Prices guaranteed through June 30, 1996.

Is It a Saint's Name? *Fr. William Dunne* 1.50
St. Pius V—His Life, Times, Miracles. *Anderson* 4.00
Who Is Teresa Neumann? *Fr. Charles Carty* 2.00
Martyrs of the Coliseum. *Fr. O'Reilly* 16.50
Way of the Cross. *St. Alphonsus Liguori* .... .75
Way of the Cross. *Franciscan version* .... .75
How Christ Said the First Mass. *Fr. Meagher* 16.50
Too Busy for God? Think Again! *D'Angelo* 4.00
St. Bernadette Soubirous. *Trochu* 16.50
Passion and Death of Jesus Christ. *Liguori* 8.50
Treatise on the Love of God. 2 Vols. *St. Francis de Sales* 16.50
Confession Quizzes. *Radio Replies Press* 1.00
St. Philip Neri. *Fr. V. J. Matthews* 4.50
St. Louise de Marillac. *Sr. Vincent Regnault* 4.50
The Old World and America. *Rev. Philip Furlong* 16.50
Prophecy for Today. *Edward Connor* 4.50
The Book of Infinite Love. *Mother de la Touche* 4.50
Chats with Converts. *Fr. M. D. Forrest* 9.00
The Church Teaches. *Church Documents* 15.00
Conversation with Christ. *Peter T. Rohrbach* 8.00
Purgatory and Heaven. *J. P. Arendzen* 3.50
Liberalism Is a Sin. *Sarda y Salvany* 6.00
Spiritual Legacy of Sr. Mary of the Trinity. *van den Broek* 9.00
The Creator and the Creature. *Fr. Frederick Faber* 13.50
Radio Replies. 3 Vols. *Frs. Rumble and Carty* 36.00
Convert's Catechism of Catholic Doctrine. *Fr. Geiermann* 3.00
Incarnation, Birth, Infancy of Jesus Christ. *St. Alphonsus* 8.50
Light and Peace. *Fr. R. P. Quadrupani* 5.00
Dogmatic Canons & Decrees of Trent, Vat. I. *Documents* 8.00
The Evolution Hoax Exposed. *A. N. Field* 6.00
The Primitive Church. *Fr. D. I. Lanslots* 8.50
Ven. Jacinta Marto of Fatima. *Cirrincione* 1.50
The Priest, the Man of God. *St. Joseph Cafasso* 12.00
Blessed Sacrament. *Fr. Frederick Faber* 16.50
Christ Denied. *Fr. Paul Wickens* 2.00
New Regulations on Indulgences. *Fr. Winfrid Herbst* 2.50
A Tour of the Summa. *Msgr. Paul Glenn* 18.00
Spiritual Conferences. *Fr. Frederick Faber* 13.50
Latin Grammar. *Scanlon and Scanlon* 13.50
A Brief Life of Christ. *Fr. Rumble* 2.00
Marriage Quizzes. *Radio Replies Press* 1.00
True Church Quizzes. *Radio Replies Press* 1.00
St. Lydwine of Schiedam. *J. K. Huysmans* 7.00
Mary, Mother of the Church. *Church Documents* 3.00
The Sacred Heart and the Priesthood. *de la Touche* 7.00
Revelations of St. Bridget. *St. Bridget of Sweden* 2.50
Magnificent Prayers. *St. Bridget of Sweden* 1.50
The Happiness of Heaven. *Fr. J. Boudreau* 7.00
St. Catherine Labouré of the Miraculous Medal. *Dirvin* 12.50
The Glories of Mary. (pocket, unabr.). *St. Alphonsus Liguori* 9.00

Prices guaranteed through June 30, 1996.

All About the Angels. *Fr. Paul O'Sullivan* 5.00
AA—1025: Memoirs of an Anti-Apostle. *Marie Carré* 4.00
All for Jesus. *Fr. Frederick Faber* 13.50
Growth in Holiness. *Fr. Frederick Faber* 15.00
Behind the Lodge Door. *Paul Fisher* 15.00
Chief Truths of the Faith. (Book I). *Fr. John Laux* 8.00
Mass and the Sacraments. (Book II). *Fr. John Laux* 8.00
Catholic Morality. (Book III). *Fr. John Laux* 8.00
Catholic Apologetics. (Book IV). *Fr. John Laux* 8.00
Introduction to the Bible. *Fr. John Laux* 13.00
Church History. *Fr. John Laux* 20.00
Devotion for the Dying. *Mother Mary Potter* 8.00
Devotion to the Sacred Heart. *Fr. Jean Croiset* 13.50
An Easy Way to Become a Saint. *Fr. Paul O'Sullivan* 5.00
The Golden Arrow. *Sr. Mary of St. Peter* 10.00
The Holy Man of Tours. *Dorothy Scallan* 10.00
Hell—Plus How to Avoid Hell. *Fr. Schouppe/Nelson* 10.00
History of Protestant Ref. in England & Ireland. *Cobbett* 15.00
Holy Will of God. *Fr. Leo Pyzalski* 6.00
How Christ Changed the World. *Msgr. Luigi Civardi* 6.00
How to Be Happy, How to Be Holy. *Fr. Paul O'Sullivan* 7.00
Imitation of Christ. *Thomas à Kempis. (Challoner transl.)* 9.00
Life & Message of Sr. Mary of the Trinity. *Rev. Dubois* 8.50
Life Everlasting. *Fr. Garrigou-Lagrange, O.P.* 12.50
Life of Mary as Seen by the Mystics. *Compiled by Raphael Brown* . 12.50
Life of St. Dominic. *Mother Augusta Drane* 10.00
Life of St. Francis of Assisi. *St. Bonaventure* 8.00
Life of St. Ignatius Loyola. *Fr. Genelli* 15.00
Life of St. Margaret Mary Alacoque. *Rt. Rev. Emile Bougaud* 12.00
Mexican Martyrdom. *Fr. Wilfrid Parsons* 8.50
Children of Fatima. *Windeatt*. (Age 10 & up) 6.00
Cure of Ars. *Windeatt*. (Age 10 & up) 9.00
The Little Flower. *Windeatt*. (Age 10 & up) 7.00
Patron of First Communicants. (Bl. Imelda). *Windeatt*. (Age 10 & up) 4.00
Miraculous Medal. *Windeatt*. (Age 10 & up) 5.00
St. Louis De Montfort. *Windeatt*. (Age 10 & up) 9.00
St. Thomas Aquinas. *Windeatt*. (Age 10 & up) 5.00
St. Catherine of Siena. *Windeatt*. (Age 10 & up) 4.00
St. Rose of Lima. *Windeatt*. (Age 10 & up) 7.00
St. Hyacinth of Poland. *Windeatt*. (Age 10 & up) 8.00
St. Martin de Porres. *Windeatt*. (Age 10 & up) 6.00
Pauline Jaricot. *Windeatt*. (Age 10 & up) 10.00
Modern Saints—Their Lives and Faces, Book II. *Ann Ball* 20.00
Prayers and Heavenly Promises. *Compiled by Joan Carroll Cruz* .. 4.00
Preparation for Death. (Unabr., pocket). *St. Alphonsus* 8.50
Rebuilding a Lost Faith. *John Stoddard* 12.00
The Spiritual Combat. *Dom Lorenzo Scupoli* 7.50
Retreat Companion for Priests. *Fr. Francis Havey* 6.00
Spiritual Doctrine of St. Cath. of Genoa. *Maribotti/St. Cath.* 9.00
The Soul of the Apostolate. *Dom Chautard* 9.00

Prices guaranteed through June 30, 1996.

Brief Catechism for Adults. *Cogan* 9.00
The Cath. Religion—Illus./Expl. for Child, Adult, Convert. *Burbach.* 9.00
Eucharistic Miracles. *Joan Carroll Cruz* 13.00
The Incorruptibles. *Joan Carroll Cruz* 12.00
Pope St. Pius X. *F. A. Forbes* 6.00
St. Alphonsus Liguori. *Frs. Miller and Aubin* 15.00
Self-Abandonment to Divine Providence. *Fr. de Caussade, S.J.* . . . 16.50
The Song of Songs—A Mystical Exposition. *Fr. Arintero, O.P.* . . . 18.00
Prophecy for Today. *Edward Connor* 4.50
Saint Michael and the Angels. *Approved Sources* 5.50
Dolorous Passion of Our Lord. *Anne C. Emmerich* 15.00
Modern Saints—Their Lives & Faces. *Ann Ball* 18.00
Our Lady of Fatima's Peace Plan from Heaven. *Booklet* .... .75
Divine Favors Granted to St. Joseph. *Père Binet* 4.00
St. Joseph Cafasso—Priest of the Gallows. *St. John Bosco* 3.00
Catechism of the Council of Trent. *McHugh/Callan* 20.00
The Foot of the Cross. *Fr. Faber* 15.00
The Rosary in Action. *John Johnson* 8.00
Padre Pio—The Stigmatist. *Fr. Charles Carty* 13.50
Why Squander Illness? *Frs. Rumble & Carty* 2.00
The Sacred Heart and the Priesthood. *de la Touche* 7.00
Fatima—The Great Sign. *Francis Johnston* 7.00
Heliotropium—Conformity of Human Will to Divine. *Drexelius* . . . 11.00
Charity for the Suffering Souls. *Fr. John Nageleisen* 15.00
Devotion to the Sacred Heart of Jesus. *Verheylezoon* 13.00
Who Is Padre Pio? *Radio Replies Press* 1.50
Child's Bible History. *Knecht* 4.00
The Stigmata and Modern Science. *Fr. Charles Carty* 1.25
The Life of Christ. 4 Vols. H.B. *Anne C. Emmerich* 55.00
St. Anthony—The Wonder Worker of Padua. *Stoddard* 4.00
The Precious Blood. *Fr. Faber* 11.00
The Holy Shroud & Four Visions. *Fr. O'Connell* 2.00
Clean Love in Courtship. *Fr. Lawrence Lovasik* 2.50
The Prophecies of St. Malachy. *Peter Bander* 5.00
St. Martin de Porres. *Giuliana Cavallini* 11.00
The Secret of the Rosary. *St. Louis De Montfort* 3.00
The History of Antichrist. *Rev. P. Huchede* 3.00
The Douay-Rheims New Testament. *Paperbound* 13.00
St. Catherine of Siena. *Alice Curtayne* 12.00
Where We Got the Bible. *Fr. Henry Graham* 5.00
Hidden Treasure—Holy Mass. *St. Leonard* 4.00
Imitation of the Sacred Heart of Jesus. *Fr. Arnoudt* 13.50
The Life & Glories of St. Joseph. *Edward Thompson* 13.50
Père Lamy. *Biver* 10.00
Humility of Heart. *Fr. Cajetan da Bergamo* 7.00
The Curé D'Ars. *Abbé Francis Trochu* 20.00
Love, Peace and Joy. (St. Gertrude). *Prévot* 5.00
The Three Ways of the Spiritual Life. *Garrigou-Lagrange, O.P.* 4.00

At your Bookdealer or direct from the Publisher.

Prices guaranteed through June 30, 1996.